T0314072

MOBILIZING FOR DEVELOPMENT

MOBILIZING FOR DEVELOPMENT

The Modernization of Rural East Asia

Kristen E. Looney

CORNELL UNIVERSITY PRESS   ITHACA AND LONDON

Cornell University Press gratefully acknowledges receipt of a grant from the Dean's Office of the Edmund A. Walsh School of Foreign Service and the Department of Government, both at Georgetown University, which aided in the publication of this book.

First published 2020 by Cornell University Press

Library of Congress Cataloging-in-Publication Data

Names: Looney, Kristen E., 1978– author.
Title: Mobilizing for development : the modernization of rural
    East Asia / Kristen E. Looney.
Description: Ithaca [New York] : Cornell University Press, 2020. |
    Includes bibliographical references and index.
Identifiers: LCCN 2019029562 (print) | LCCN 2019029563 (ebook) |
    ISBN 9781501748844 (hardcover) | ISBN 9781501748851 (epub) |
    ISBN 9781501748868 (pdf)
Subjects: LCSH: Rural development—East Asia. | Rural development—Taiwan—
    History—20th century. | Rural development—Government policy—Taiwan. |
    Rural development—Korea (South)—History—20th century. | Rural
    development—Government policy—Korea (South) | Rural development—
    China—History—20th century. | Rural development—Government
    policy—China.
Classification: LCC HC460.5 .L665 2020 (print) | LCC HC460.5 (ebook) |
    DDC 338.95009173/4—dc23
LC record available at https://lccn.loc.gov/2019029562
LC ebook record available at https://lccn.loc.gov/2019029563

For Alan and Talia

Contents

Tables

Figures (Appendix)

Acknowledgments

There are many people who made this book possible. First, I want to thank my advisers from the Harvard University Department of Government. Words cannot express how fortunate I feel to have studied Chinese politics with Elizabeth Perry and Roderick MacFarquhar. I never would have undertaken a comparative, multicountry study without Liz's initial encouragement and steadfast support. She helped me at every stage, generously offering her time, knowledge, and insights about the profession. She also opened several doors for me in China, where I was able to see firsthand just how much she has done to advance the field and assist both young and established scholars there. Rod was a similarly fantastic mentor. He taught me almost everything I know about the Maoist period and elite politics. But more than that, he pushed me to read as much as possible in Chinese and to seriously engage with the work of Chinese scholars. Sadly, he passed away as I was completing the final edits for this book. I can only hope it would have made him proud. Timothy Colton introduced me to the classic works in comparative politics and inspired me to think about China from a broader perspective. Even so, he once half-jokingly remarked that a three-country study would take me forever—a prediction that has felt pretty accurate over the years but is thankfully no longer true. Katharine Moon of Wellesley College, besides helping me to understand Korea better, has been a constant source of support since my undergraduate years when I started down this path.

I would additionally like to thank Robert Bates, Peter Hall, Nancy Hearst, Sebastian Heilmann, Nahomi Ichino, Iain Johnston, Kyung-ok Joo, Mi-hyun Kim, Steven Levitsky, Sang-suk Oh, Anthony Saich, and Andrew Walder for providing excellent instruction and advice during my graduate studies. I am also indebted to my former teachers from Wellesley who first kindled my interest in Chinese studies, including Dai Chen, Karl Gerth, Pat Giersch, Ann Huss, William Joseph, Ruby Lam, Sherry Mou, and Weina Zhao. Bill and Sherry especially influenced me to become a lifelong student of China and East Asia. Yawei Liu at the Carter Center also taught me a great deal about China during an internship there.

At various stages of this project—from half-baked ideas to early drafts, conference papers, and revised chapters—I benefited from comments by Joel Andreas, Jennifer Bachner, Harley Balzer, Richard Doner, Benjamin Goodrich, Kyle Jaros, Diana Kapiszewski, Christine Kim, James Kai-sing Kung, Didi Kuo, Wendy Leutert, Janet Lewis, Claire Schwartz Litwin, Elena Llaudet, Daniel Mattingly,

Andrew Mertha, Sara Newland, Abraham Newman, Jean Oi, Benjamin Read, Maria Repnikova, Christopher Rhodes, Meg Rithmire, Jordan Sand, Sarah Shehabuddin, Graeme Smith, Dorothy Solinger, Rachel Stern, Patricia Thornton, James Vreeland, Jeremy Wallace, Xiaojun Yan, David Zweig, and the members of the George Washington University Comparative Politics Workshop. I am grateful to Rick, Andy, Ben, and Meg in particular for traveling to DC in order to participate in my book workshop, which was supported by the Georgetown University Department of Government. I must also thank my Georgetown colleagues Victor Cha, David Edelstein, Eileen Fenrich, Michael Green, Diana Kim, Charles King, Robert Lyons, Kathleen McNamara, Daniel Nexon, Irfan Nooruddin, Carole Sargent, Yuhki Tajima, Charles Udomsaph, and Ding Ye, among many others, for the extra time and support I needed to see this project through to completion. Several Georgetown students provided valuable research assistance: Jayme Amann, Brian Bumpas, Sungmin Cho, Thomas Christiansen, Minjung Kang, Jonathon Marek, Andrea Moneton, Stefan Rajiyah, Ying Sun, and Mengjia Wan. Sungmin, most of all, went above and beyond to help me understand the contemporary Korean-language scholarship on the New Village Movement. I would furthermore like to express my sincere thanks to Roger Haydon, Mary Kate Murphy, and their colleagues at Cornell University Press, as well as Glenn Novak, Kate Mertes, and two anonymous reviewers whose comments significantly improved the manuscript.

A number of institutions and granting agencies facilitated my research in Asia, including the Center for Asia-Pacific Area Studies at Academia Sinica in Taipei; the Inter-University Program for Chinese Language Studies at Tsinghua University in Beijing; the Rural Development Institute at the Chinese Academy of Social Sciences in Beijing; the Korean Language Institute and the Department of Political Science at Yonsei University in Seoul; the Blakemore Foundation; the Chiang Ching-kuo Foundation for International Scholarly Exchange; the Edmund A. Walsh School of Foreign Service at Georgetown University; the Foreign Language and Areas Studies Fellowships Program; and the Fulbright-Hays Doctoral Dissertation Research Abroad Fellowship Program. Research for this book was also conducted at the Asian Reading Room of the Library of Congress in Washington, DC; the C. V. Starr East Asian Library at Columbia University in New York; and the University Services Center for China Studies at the Chinese University of Hong Kong.

I owe a debt of gratitude to many people at each of these institutions but want to give a special thanks to those who welcomed and hosted me as a visiting researcher: Professors Hsin-huang Michael Hsiao and Cheng-yi Lin at Academia Sinica; Professor Chung-in Moon at Yonsei; and Professors Yu Jianrong, Li Renqing, and Lu Lei at the Chinese Academy of Social Sciences. In Korea, I received help and guidance from Do-hyun Han, Seung-mi Han, Joon-kyung Kim, Junmin Kim, Seung-hyun Kim, Lucy Sojung Lee, Peter Joon-sung Park, Hyeon-suk Shin, Min-young Shin, and Wonwoo Yi. In China, I was greatly helped by Li Chang-ping, Li Shuishan, Qian Qian, Song Junling, Tan Yifei, Weng Ming, Xiao Yalin, Zhao Shukai, Zhou Yi, Zou Yongxiong, and especially Ren Jianghua. I owe my positive fieldwork experience in Jiangxi to Ouyang Qiaowen, Wen Xiaomin, Yang Jingwei, Zeng Xinfang, and many others affiliated with the Ganzhou Rural Work Department and the county governments of Anyuan, Longnan, Ruijin, Shicheng, and Xingguo. Additional trips to Dazhai (thanks to Yu Jianrong), Huaxi (thanks to Zhou Yi), and Qing County, Hebei, further enriched my understanding of the Chinese countryside. I am also deeply appreciative of my friendships with Dai Shuping, Guo Yingtao, Li Shumei, Li Yi, Liu Xiaoxia, Su Dan, Su Jianjing, Yi Benyao, and Zhang Guoliang. They have supported me in immeasurable ways over the years, especially Shuping.

My friends and family have also shared their love and unwavering confidence in my ability to finish this book. I cannot possibly thank all of them, although I would like to recognize Heather Brent, Karen Colin, Joshua Friess, Jana Kiser, April Kuehnhoff, Laura Murray, Katharine Poundstone, Johnnetta Russell, Amber Samuel, Paulraj Samuel, Yael Sherman, Andrew Silverman, Cena Maxfield Smith, Van Smith, Philip Tinari, Mabel Tso, Marisa Van Saanen, Peggy Wang, Mary Ellen Wiggins, and Misti Yang for helping me to keep things in perspective. Meg Rithmire was my friend long before she became my colleague and has been there every step of the way. My incredible parents, Craig and Katherine Looney, have supported all of my choices, and my sisters, Meghan Rubiano and Shannon Looney, have always been there to lend an ear. Along with my grandparents, Jack and Jimmie Looney and Alonzo and Patricia Poll, and my in-laws, Aaron and Cathy Rappeport, they have been my biggest cheerleaders. My husband, Alan Rappeport, has been part of this book from the beginning. I will forever be grateful to him and our little ones, Talia and Buster, for reminding me of what is important.

Abbreviations

ARDP	Accelerated Rural Development Program (Taiwan)
DRC	Development Research Center of the State Council (China)
FA	Farmers' Association (Taiwan)
FPC	Farmers' Professional Cooperative (China)
JCRR	Sino-American Joint Commission on Rural Reconstruction
NACF	National Agricultural Cooperative Federation (South Korea)
NRA	nominal rate of assistance to agriculture
ORD	Office of Rural Development (South Korea)
PAC	primary agricultural cooperative (South Korea)
P.L. 480	Public Law 480 Food for Peace Program
RRA	relative rate of assistance to agriculture
SAIC	State Administration for Industry and Commerce (China)
SAU	small agricultural unit (Taiwan)
SLTI	National Saemaul Leadership Training Institute (South Korea)
TVE	township and village enterprise (China)

Note on Transliteration

I have used the pinyin system of transliteration from Chinese to English, except for Taiwanese author names, which appear in Wade-Giles (pinyin equivalents are listed in the Works Cited).

Full citations for the Korean-language materials follow the McCune-Reischauer system, although author names are first listed by the Revised Romanization system. The English translations of those titles come from the original publications.

MOBILIZING FOR DEVELOPMENT

THE STATE AND RURAL DEVELOPMENT IN EAST ASIA

Global poverty continues to be a predominantly rural phenomenon despite increasing urbanization. The World Bank estimates that 78 percent of the world's poor, or nearly 800 million people, live in rural areas and depend on agriculture, forestry, and fishing for their livelihoods. Related to this point, the majority of people suffering from hunger are smallholder farmers in developing countries. In sub-Saharan Africa, agriculture still accounts for one-third of gross domestic product (GDP) and three-quarters of employment.[1] Fundamentally, rural development matters for poverty reduction, food security, and economic growth. And yet, governments routinely fail their rural citizens. The history of modernization is replete with stories of promised resources that never materialize and development projects that harm the environment and displace rural communities.

The barriers to rural development are largely political. In many developing countries, ruling elites pursue industrial development at the expense of the rural sector. They regard industry as critical for national security and economic competitiveness, and many believe that industry-led growth is sufficient to reduce poverty. This preference for industry, known as urban bias, translates into a policy environment that systematically discriminates against agriculture. For decades, developing countries have relied on price controls and overvalued exchange rates to lower the cost of food, wages, and industrial inputs. Although these policy tools distort farmers' incentives and threaten long-term agricultural productivity, they confer benefits on a diverse set of actors (government, industry, urban consumers, and large farmers) that together constitute a strong political coalition.[2] Empirical analysis shows that while exchange-rate distortions in the world's least-developed countries have decreased since the late 1980s, other measures like rural-urban differences in capital stocks, government expenditures, and public service outcomes point to worsening conditions for the rural poor.[3] The result of urban bias is growth without development—industrial growth and urban expansion occurring alongside rural stagnation and poverty.

Such policies are not, however, without political costs. In attempting to resolve one kind of dilemma, satisfying the urban-industrial coalition, modernizing states may create another in the form of high-stakes rural unrest. From protest marches to violent confrontations with police, farmers no longer resemble the "sack of potatoes" that Karl Marx saw as incapable of collective revolt.[4] Take India, for example. In 2014–2015, land acquisitions and rural distress led to a surge in clashes between farmers and government agencies, posing a challenge to the newly formed National Democratic Alliance government.[5] A few years before, in the wake of deadly conflict over industrial land grabs in West Bengal, rural citizens voted out the Communist Party, which had ruled the state for over three decades.[6] For anyone familiar with peasant movements in Mexico, Brazil, Ecuador, and beyond, these kinds of stories are nothing new and have only become more prevalent with globalization.[7] Land- and development-related conflicts have exploded across Africa as well, from Kenya to Sierra Leone and Sudan to Zimbabwe, fueling social tensions, political crises, and wars.[8]

Ironically, countries with higher levels of discrimination against agriculture are often controlled by regimes that came to power on the back of rural discontent. Following China's example, twentieth-century communist and nationalist movements in Asia, Africa, and Latin America staked their legitimacy on delivering not just workers but peasants from oppression. Practically, they needed to expand their base to succeed in an agrarian context, yet once in power, they pursued modernization policies that sacrificed the countryside. The skewed allocation of resources was justified on economic as well as political grounds, since the potential for large-scale urban unrest was considered a bigger threat than localized rural protests. Previous research has shown that, in the long run, urban bias is risky, insofar as it induces migration to cities, puts a strain on urban resources, and increases the likelihood of urban collective action against the regime.[9] Still, in other more direct ways, it can undermine ruling elites' hold on the countryside. Protests that first appear to be localized can spread, opening up space for opposition parties or rival forces to establish a presence. Even in closed authoritarian systems, mounting rural unrest can disrupt development plans and imperil the state's capacity to govern.

In contrast with most developing countries, East Asia emerged in the post–World War II period as a region that seemed to defy the logic of urban bias, achieving both urban-industrial growth and rural-agricultural development. Breakneck industrialization, characterized by double-digit growth rates, produced incredible prosperity. In less than two decades, between 1955 and 1970, Japan's GDP per capita rose from around US$3,000 to over $10,000, propelling the country from lower-middle-income to high-income status using the World Bank's classification. Taiwan and South Korea experienced a similar change, with GDP per capita climbing from less than $1,500 in 1955 to over $10,000 in 1988 and 1991, respectively, moving from the low-income to high-income categories.[10]

Because of the effective implementation of rural land reform, the distribution of wealth in each of these countries was remarkably egalitarian. The Gini coefficient was about .33 in Japan (1969) and South Korea (1970) and only .28 in Taiwan (1978), indicating lower levels of inequality than in most of the world, including many Western European countries (the OECD average in 1967–1972 was .36).[11] Public investment in irrigation and the spread of green revolution technologies, such as high-yield varieties of rice and chemical fertilizers, enabled agriculture to play a key role in the region's postwar recovery and industrial take-off. In the 1950s–1960s, agriculture grew about 3.2 percent annually (a conservative estimate), compared to the global average of 2.7 percent.[12] Despite problems with the reliability of data for that period, the overall trends are clear: along with industrialization, the rural economy grew, household incomes improved, poverty rates dropped, and life expectancy increased. Fast-forward to the 1980s, and China would likewise boast such achievements following the spread of economic reforms.

Nevertheless, it is also true that East Asian governments exploited agriculture, eroding the prospects for long-term development and giving rise to significant rural-urban disparities. They imposed hidden taxes on rice and fertilizer, relied on cheap food imports to depress domestic prices, and directed the lion's share of productive resources to the urban-industrial sector. The nominal and relative rates of assistance for agriculture (the NRA and RRA), which measure how domestic farm prices stack up against international market prices and nonfarm product prices, were negative in Taiwan and South Korea until about 1970, and in China until about 2000, implying that the main concern before then was to extract a rural surplus for industrialization.[13] Of course, in the early stages of development, most governments aim to transfer resources from agriculture to industry, a strategy known as the developmental squeeze on agriculture.[14] Only at the later stages are resources more likely to flow in reverse, when the problem of agricultural adjustment, or rural decline, generates sufficient political pressure to trigger a change in policy, and when the rural sector is small enough that the cost of redistribution becomes more acceptable. Even then, the transition from taxing to subsidizing agriculture is far from automatic. It happened faster in East Asia than in early industrializers, but in other parts of the developing world, reforms to agricultural price, trade, and investment policies remain gradual and uneven.[15] The evolution of rural policy thus demands explanation. At the same time, it should be noted that price adjustments and the like do not capture very much about how rural transformation unfolded in the region.

The Argument in Brief

This book examines how and why East Asia achieved rural development, and it advances a theory to explain variation among East Asian countries. While the analysis has obvious relevance to the study of the region's political economy, it was motivated by broader concerns about the role of institutions and the state in development. Since the late 1970s, scholars have stressed the effects of institutional design on economic performance. The rise of new institutional economics marked a departure from neoclassical theory, which tended to ignore institutions or regard them as constant over time.[16] Related to this shift was a movement in the social sciences to "bring the state back in," that is, to recognize the state as a distinct political actor, with varying degrees of autonomy and capacity but still separate from interest groups or class structures.[17] Conceptual and measurement issues aside, few would disagree that East Asia has strong institutions and that industrialization was, by and large, a state-led process. The region's success ignited debates about the merits of state intervention in the economy and a rethinking of state-market relations. Following the publication of several influential studies, it became widely accepted that regime type matters greatly for development outcomes and that the "East Asian miracle" could be attributed to the emergence of so-called developmental states.[18]

A major goal of this study is to expand and challenge the developmental state literature, which despite its contribution to explaining industrialization in East Asia, generally ignores the role of the state in rural development, fails to account for variation in the region, and excludes China from the comparative analysis. Addressing these gaps is important—the developmental state not only remains the dominant framework for understanding East Asia's political economy, but has also informed contemporary debates about alternative (post-neoliberal) development models in the wake of the 2008 global financial crisis.[19] Additionally, this study advances the political economy of development literature by moving beyond the traditional focus on land tenure and agricultural prices to specify the conditions under which rural institutions and state campaigns can promote development. It furthermore demonstrates that rural transformation in East Asia was not a byproduct of industrialization, but the result of aggressive interventions by strong and activist (if not exactly developmental) states.

Through a structured comparison of Taiwan, South Korea, and China, I show that different types of development outcomes—improvements in agricultural production, rural living standards, and the village environment—were realized to different degrees, at different times, and in different ways. The general argument can be summarized as follows: during the first few decades of industrialization, certain institutions facilitated growth in agricultural production. These included smallholder agriculture, a technocratic bureaucracy, and (except for China) encompassing farmers' organizations. Although there was some variation among these countries (deriving from the impact of Japanese colonialism, US assistance, and in China's case the legacy of socialism), they had similar institutions and exhibited the same broad patterns of rural development. Still, uneven progress along different dimensions of development occurred as a result of urban bias. Changes in incomes and infrastructure, for example, did not keep pace with agricultural production because of policies that exploited the rural sector. Eventually, fast-paced industrialization led to a deterioration of rural conditions, which raised concerns of unrest and pressures to adopt pro-rural policies. The reversal of urban bias was not, however, about the state retreating from the countryside so that market forces could then function without distortion. Instead, it was marked by the commencement of sweeping modernization campaigns, producing mixed results both within the rural sector and across national contexts.

I define campaigns as policies that aim to transform the countryside through the intensive use of bureaucratic and popular mobilization. During campaigns, governments may employ such tactics as sending official work teams to the villages, ratcheting up propaganda, setting core tasks, designating model sites, training local activists, and rewarding the most fervent participants with prizes, media attention, and other benefits designed to foster competitive emulation. Common in authoritarian and communist states, though by no means limited to them, state-led campaigns for development run the gamut from land reforms and green revolutions, to cooperative movements and collectivization schemes, to mass literacy, health, and sanitation drives. Many of them failed, sometimes tragically, and for that reason they have largely been overlooked by scholars of development or mentioned only to underscore the dangers of social engineering.[20] Nevertheless, within East Asia, campaigns are often described as powerful tools for state-society cooperation and rural transformation, a view completely at odds with Western ideas about the illiberal and destructive tendencies of campaigns.

In fact, throughout the region, political leaders believed that campaigns were a necessary solution to the "rural problem," an effective means of addressing the tensions caused by the relative decline of agriculture. While it is uncontroversial to see this kind of politics in China, given its long history of state-sponsored campaigns, it is somewhat surprising to find it in the wider region. Technocratic governance and careful economic planning are key features of the developmental state model. Yet shifting the focus from industrial policy to rural policy reveals a different type of politics. To borrow Max Weber's terminology, campaigns are a manifestation of charismatic authority, and institutions are rooted in bureaucratic or legal authority.[21] These modes of politics are distinct but not mutually exclusive: the same technocrats who follow administrative routines can also be revolutionaries who serve as a conduit for campaigns. Whereas previous studies have dismissed the region's campaigns as misguided deviations from a more successful, technocratic approach to development, I contend that they had a major impact on the countryside, especially in terms of changing the village environment (infrastructure, sanitation, housing), and that divergent development outcomes may be explained by the interaction of campaigns and institutions. Looking at this dynamic, rather than institutions alone, provides a more complete understanding of how rural development occurred in East Asia.

To clarify, by interaction I mean, first, that institutions and campaigns matter for different types of outcomes—complex goals like the promotion of scientific agriculture versus technically simpler goals like basic construction projects—so attention to both variables is crucial for understanding rural development as a whole. Second, the quality of rural institutions, namely local governments and farmers' organizations, and their relationship with the central government, affects campaign outcomes. Specifically, I argue that campaigns are more likely to succeed when the overarching goal is development rather than extraction, when the center can control local authorities, and when the campaign is carried out in partnership with rural citizens. I further hypothesize that farmers' organizations are better for development when they exhibit the right balance of linkage and autonomy vis-à-vis the state and the village community. Effective farmers' organizations can provide an institutionalized way of transferring resources in and out of the rural sector, resulting in stronger extension services and longer-term productivity gains. They can also strengthen the government's commitment to rural development and, in the context of a campaign, push back against negligent or overzealous officials.

The next chapter presents a more formal discussion of the theory and causal mechanisms that connect institutions, campaigns, and rural development. Here I would like to emphasize it was not just the use of campaigns but the timing of them that was unusual: they occurred at the later stages of industrialization when, supposedly, the benefits of growth had begun to trickle down to the countryside, and after these regimes had settled into a postrevolutionary phase of governance.

This book upends the assumptions about these stages, and, in doing so, offers an entirely new perspective on East Asia's economic and political development.

Empirical Context

I focus on the 1950s–1970s for Taiwan and South Korea and the 1980s–2000s for China because these decades were the most important for industrialization and rural development. Though rarely thought of as agricultural anymore, these countries initially had large and growing rural populations. In early 1950s Taiwan, more than 4 million people, comprising over 50 percent of the total population, lived in the countryside; and in South Korea, upward of 13 million people, or more than 60 percent of the total population, were considered rural. The rural population in each country peaked around 1967 and then started to decline, but the rural share of the total population remained above 30 percent until roughly 1980. At the start of China's reform period in 1978, about 790 million people, or 82 percent of the total population, lived in the countryside. The rural population peaked in the early 1990s and then began to drop, although the share of the rural population stayed above 50 percent until 2011. Even with record levels of rural-to-urban migration and structural changes in the rural economy, agriculture continues to account for about one-third of total employment in China.[22]

Even though China is a much larger country and is controlled by a communist government, it shares some things in common with Taiwan and South Korea, including a technocratic bureaucracy that prioritizes growth and a development ideology that supports significant state intervention in the market. It furthermore sees itself as part of the East Asian model, which, with regard to rural development, is rooted in the existence of a strong state and a smallholder farm economy. This circumstance provides the basis for state-led development, whether through governmental (and quasi-governmental) institutions or through rural modernization campaigns. I do not mean to suggest that China is a developmental state. As other scholars have shown, it loosely fits the model at best.[23] But the resemblances in rural policy are striking, in part because East Asian countries looked to one another's experience with land reform, rural cooperatives, the green revolution, and so forth. Certainly, with any comparative project, there are variables that cannot be controlled, yet having two cases that are similar (Taiwan and Korea) allows for a more effective evaluation of alternative explanations such as colonial heritage. At the same time, including a third case that is quite different (China) allows for the incorporation of some of those differences into theory development. For example, I assert that the strength of central controls, a key factor in campaign success, is determined by a country's size and administrative structure.

I do not include Japan as a primary case because its industrialization started in the nineteenth century, following the Meiji Restoration of 1868; and given that many breakthroughs in agriculture actually date back to the Tokugawa era (1603–1868), a thorough treatment would require an extended longitudinal analysis, complicating the comparison. Still, it cannot be ignored. As an imperial power, Japan had an enormous influence on economic development in the region, both directly, through colonial expansion, and indirectly, by providing a model for other modernizing regimes. I discuss these issues throughout the book and, in the next chapter, present Japan as an illustrative case to demonstrate the plausibility of the argument.[24]

To be clear, all these countries have relatively successful records of rural development from a global comparative perspective, but there is also substantial variation among them. I characterize Taiwan as the most successful case, South Korea as an intermediate case, and China as the least successful of the three. To give just one point of reference, in the decade after Taiwan's land reform, agriculture grew 4.8 percent annually (1953–1962), while for most of that same period in Korea, the average growth rate was only 2.4 percent (1954–1960). In the early 1980s, Chinese agriculture experienced a one-off boost from decollectivization—as with land reform in the other cases, it produced 10 percent growth for a few years—but then slowed to 3.9 percent for the next two decades (1984–2006). This performance was similar to Korea's under Park Chung-hee (1960s–1970s), though it was still not as strong as Taiwan's under Chiang Kai-shek (1950s–1960s).[25] While numerous statistics are used to describe the cases (production, incomes, consumption, infrastructure, the rural-urban gap, and other indicators of urban bias), some of the differences among them are difficult to quantify, especially those related to the village environment. I have therefore used a mix of quantitative and qualitative measures, such as the extent of housing renovation and the degree of uniformity across villages (with more being less favorable), to assess the cases and the effects of various policies.

To briefly summarize each case, Taiwanese agriculture played a textbook role in the early stages of development, meeting the domestic demand for food, contributing to the majority of exports, and supplying capital and labor for industrialization. Robust agricultural growth was supported by exponential gains in staple crops, livestock, fruits, and vegetables, which provided the foundation for a competitive food-processing industry. Because of extractive policies, however, rural incomes and infrastructure developed slower than one might expect given the boost from land reform, agriculture's strong performance, and the growth of the economy as a whole. Later, after years of lobbying by the national Farmers' Association (FA or FAs), rural policy was overhauled and significant gains were

TABLE 1. The Cases

COUNTRY	TIME PERIOD	RURAL DEVELOPMENT RECORD (AGRICULTURAL PRODUCTION, LIVING STANDARDS, VILLAGE ENVIRONMENT)
Taiwan	1950s–1970s	Most successful
South Korea	1950s–1970s	Less successful
China	1980s–2000s	Least successful

made in these other areas too. Through an examination of the FAs and related institutions, my research confirms that Taiwan represents a "farmers' association approach" to development.[26] But it also moves beyond this idea, revealing that, in addition to subsidies and the usual farm protection measures, the government's response to rural decline was to launch a mass mobilization campaign. In the 1970s, the Community Development Campaign transformed the village environment, bringing paved roads, clean water, and trash collection services to poor and isolated communities. Of the three cases, Taiwan best exemplifies the conditions under which farmers' organizations and campaigns are likely to promote development. Specifically, I find that the FAs' power derived from seemingly contradictory attributes, namely linkage with the state and autonomy from it, and that campaigns can succeed when local leaders are subject to bureaucratic checks from above and participatory pressures from below.

In contrast, South Korean agriculture underperformed for most of the 1950s–1960s. The government devoted nearly all of the country's economic resources to the industrial and military sectors, and it made little effort to stimulate farm production, choosing instead to rely heavily on food aid from the United States. Besides surplus labor, Korean agriculture contributed minimally to industrialization and was not much of a concern for policymakers until the 1970s. But after two close presidential elections, during which rural voters lent their support to opposition candidates, and the abrupt cancellation of US food aid, the government did an about-face and started investing seriously in rural development. Of central importance was the New Village Movement, a modernization campaign that started in the countryside and eventually engulfed the cities as well. The results were more mixed than in Taiwan. While the quality of rural infrastructure and housing dramatically improved, plans to develop rural industry and promote a new high-yield variety of rice ended in failure. The Korean case illustrates the strengths and weaknesses of campaigns. It shows how, compared to market forces, campaigns can deliver greater change to more places in a shorter period of time. Yet, the campaign also set unrealistic goals and created a highly politicized environment. Local officials faced extreme top-down pressure to deliver results, which limited the space for popular feedback. For example, the National Agricultural Cooperative Federation (NACF) used heavy-handed tactics to steer the rice production drive, such as destroying the seedbeds of traditional varieties, and was generally unresponsive to concerns about the financial and ecological risks of rapidly diffusing the new variety. I argue that the NACF functioned as an appendage of the state and was not accountable to farmer members. It exhibited linkage with the state (and to some extent with villagers) but not autonomy, and in the context of the campaign, its statist character was exaggerated.

China's rural modernization is a story of huge successes and huge failures. During the 1980s, marketization, along with decentralization and decollectivization, resulted in unprecedented growth and poverty reduction. And at least for the years 1978–1984, agriculture played a more pivotal role in the economy than industry. After that period, government investment and growth rates in agriculture started to decline. The rise of township and village enterprises allowed some rural communities to prosper, but in many localities, industrialization drained the countryside of resources, as local governments imposed heavy taxes on farmers and cut spending on rural public goods. By the late 1990s, China's agricultural adjustment problem had become apparent in the escalation of rural protests and other kinds of "mass incidents." The government took decisive action in the 2000s by abolishing agricultural taxes and passing legislation that elevated the status of rural work. Under the banner of Building a New Socialist Countryside, numerous programs were rolled out to encourage agricultural production, raise rural living standards, and upgrade village infrastructure. Over time, however, housing became the primary target of local efforts, and despite an initial emphasis on moderate change in this area, the policy evolved into a top-down campaign to demolish and reconstruct villages. Rural resource extraction continued in the form of land grabs, the rural-urban gap grew wider, and problems with the quality of goods and services surfaced. The Chinese case underscores how easily campaigns can spiral of control. The decentralized nature of the country's political system enabled local officials to neglect some goals while taking others to extremes. Bureaucratic checks on their authority were weak, and popular constraints were even weaker. The Farmers' Professional Cooperatives (FPCs) were shell organizations possessing neither linkage nor autonomy, and rural associational life in general was lacking. In most places, villagers were entirely left out of the policy process. It is unfortunate and somewhat paradoxical, considering China's revolutionary history, that villagers would be least involved in this campaign. Of course, this is not to say that the days of Maoist populism were better, only that campaigns without mass participation carry their own dangers.

TABLE 2. The Argument

	RURAL MODERNIZATION CAMPAIGNS				FARMERS' ORGANIZATIONS		
	NAME	DEVELOP-MENTAL GOALS	CENTRAL CONTROL	RURAL PARTICI-PATION	NAME	LINKAGE	AUTONOMY
Taiwan	Community Development Campaign	+	+	+	Taiwan Farmers' Association (FA or FAs)	+	+
South Korea	New Village Movement	+	+	+	National Agricultural Cooperative Federation (NACF)	+	—
China	Building a New Socialist Countryside	+	+	—	Farmers' Professional Cooperatives (FPCs)	—	—

+ Present, strong   + Present, weak   — Mostly absent

Sources and Methods

This book is based primarily on archival and documentary sources, as well as fieldwork conducted in Taiwan, South Korea, and China during 2009–2010 and 2013–2014. Most of the materials on Taiwan were collected at Academia Sinica in Taipei and the Library of Congress in Washington, DC. In addition to government and party documents, I found the memos, reports, surveys, and letters of the Sino-American Joint Commission on Rural Reconstruction (JCRR) to be particularly helpful for understanding the evolution of rural policy in Taiwan.[27] I also benefited from a wealth of primary and secondary sources published by Taiwanese scholars. These materials offered a more nuanced picture of how certain policies and institutions affected Taiwanese society. For instance, through reading the oral histories of local FA leaders and the speeches of national legislators, I was able to gain insight into the FAs' social embeddedness and their growing political power. Another useful source was a collection of reports and manuals produced by the Republic of China Community Development Research and Training Center. These documents allowed me to see how, in the context of 1970s Taiwan, Leninist campaign tactics were fused with international notions of community-based development.

The materials on Korea were obtained from the Yonsei University Library, the Korea Development Institute, and the Korea Saemaul Undong (New Village

Movement) Center. Because of my limited proficiency in Korean, I relied mostly on English-language publications. I consulted numerous secondary sources concerning Korea's economic and political development, as well as studies focused on the New Village Movement. I read the translated speeches and memoirs of political elites and a whole range of things that can only be described as propaganda about the campaign: books, pictorials, pamphlets, national conference proceedings, and the "success stories" of Saemaul leaders who led their villages to prosperity. The abundance of such materials has to do with the fact that, since the 1970s, the Korean government has upheld the campaign as a model for developing countries. Though clearly biased, these sources shed light on the sheer intensity of the campaign—the enormous scale of collective mobilization and the physical transformation of the countryside. I tried to balance this information with the perspectives of Korean scholars, some of whom I met in person, and others whose work I was able to access with the help and translation skills of a research assistant. Their assessments, while certainly more varied, confirm that the campaign was not just an exercise in social control, as many critics have asserted, but that it had a very tangible impact on rural life.

The majority of sources on China were collected from the National Library in Beijing, where I examined nearly all the available materials on rural development and the New Socialist Countryside published in the 2000s and early 2010s (my analysis of earlier decades is based mainly on secondary sources). These included scholarly books, government and legal documents, surveys and field reports, statistical yearbooks, the memoirs of economic planners, and retrospectives on rural policy. It is worth noting that China's interest in learning from the experiences of its neighbors was evident from many of these sources, as was a recognition of campaigns as being integral to the region's rural development. Also, perhaps because there was such a large volume of material, I actually found Chinese sources to be less propagandistic and more diverse than was the case for Taiwan and Korea.

While the Taiwanese and Korean cases are historical, I was able to observe the New Socialist Countryside as it unfolded in China. In 2010, I was affiliated with the Rural Development Institute of the Chinese Academy of Social Sciences, which was an early advocate for rural reform and "China's first real think tank."[28] Through this connection, I was able to carry out research in Ganzhou city, Jiangxi, a landlocked province in the southeast. Ganzhou is a large, predominantly rural prefecture comprising eighteen counties and over nine million residents. Under the leadership of a charismatic party secretary, it launched a local New Socialist Countryside initiative in 2004, one year before the policy was adopted nationally, and it became known for villagers' active involvement in policy implementation. Ganzhou was an ideal site for in-depth fieldwork. It allowed me to understand the origins of the campaign and to assess villagers' potential to influence policy under seemingly favorable conditions. The officials I encountered were generally confident about their work and let me select field sites and conduct many interviews unsupervised. Altogether, during the summer months of 2010 and 2013, I interviewed more than one hundred people (officials, villagers, and FPC leaders) and visited close to forty villages spread across five counties. The interviews were semi-structured and normally lasted for about an hour. Whenever possible, I tried to interview villagers in their homes without too many other people present, and luckily, I could usually find a student or returned migrant worker to translate between the local dialect and Mandarin. The interviews provided an invaluable source of data for contextualizing and expanding the insights gained from documentary research.

This project falls within the tradition of comparative historical analysis, which emphasizes identifying causal sequences and patterns to explain a finite set of cases.[29] Specifically, my approach combines cross-case and within-case analysis to make inferences about East Asian rural development. The developmental state literature, taken as a whole, is a good example of iterated hypothesis testing: a theoretical framework was first developed with reference to Japan and then applied to other cases in the region, which all seemed to confirm the original model. This study is different in that the aim is not so much hypothesis testing as hypothesis elaboration—using an initial causal hypothesis for the development and testing of new theoretical propositions.[30] Diverse forms of evidence are used to evaluate common explanations for the region's success and to support my claims about the relative success or failure of individual cases. My goal is to advance a new way of thinking about the political economy of East Asia and to encourage more studies of rural development in general, a topic that has largely been neglected in political science research.

1

THE ROLE OF RURAL INSTITUTIONS AND STATE CAMPAIGNS IN DEVELOPMENT

Most accounts of rural development in East Asia privilege the role of land reform and the emergence of developmental states. While this narrative is not incorrect, it is woefully incomplete. A thorough examination of rural sector change in the region reveals the transformative effects of rural modernization campaigns, which I define as policies demanding high levels of bureaucratic and popular mobilization to overhaul traditional ways of life in the countryside. East Asian governments' use of campaigns runs counter to standard portrayals of the developmental state as wholly technocratic and demonstrates that rural development was not the inevitable result of industrialization. Rather, it was an intentional policy goal accomplished with techniques that aligned more with Maoism or Leninism than with market principles or careful economic management.

This chapter begins by assessing common explanations for East Asian rural development in the post–World War II period. First, I consider the argument that Japan and its former colonies, Taiwan and Korea, had favorable initial conditions. Although the rural sector in each country was badly damaged by war, it quickly recovered because of prewar technological, infrastructural, and institutional development. Second, communist movements at home and abroad, as well as the United States' strong presence in the region, provided an impetus for land reforms that contributed to agricultural production, social equality, and political stability. Third, all these factors—Japan, the US, and the spread of communism—led to the emergence of developmental states. Even though these states prioritized industrial development, the countryside also benefited from institutions that promoted rural development, including a technocratic bureau-cracy and encompassing farmers' organizations.

Next, I turn to the case of China and discuss some of the reasons for rural policy failures in the Mao era (1949–1976) and successes in the reform era (1978–present). Like these other countries, China completed a land reform pro-gram in the early 1950s and implemented several policies that improved rural living standards. However, land reform was quickly followed by collectivization, and many development achievements were wiped out by such factors as exces-sive extraction, poor institutions, and ideological extremism. Under reform, China moved away from socialist agriculture. Decollectivization, characterized by some as a "second land reform," led to unprecedented poverty reduction.[1] Agriculture and rural industry also benefited from the rise of a technocratic ruling elite. In this and other ways, China started to resemble a developmental state, and much of its economic success has been attributed to a kind of con-vergence with its East Asian neighbors. I suggest that while all these arguments (initial conditions, land reform, developmental states) have partial explanatory power, they do not fully account for variation across countries, over time, or along different dimensions of rural development (agricultural production, liv-ing standards, the village environment). They also fall short of explaining how these countries dealt with the problem of agricultural adjustment as the indus-trialization process deepened.

I then present the book's main arguments about the effects of institutions and campaigns on rural development. Rural modernization campaigns are different from the typical response to agricultural adjustment—namely, import restric-tions, subsidies, and other measures designed to raise farm incomes—and they furthermore have played a central role in East Asian rural development. This is an empirical claim, not a normative one. Campaigns only work under a narrow set of conditions that cannot be easily replicated, and within East Asia, they produced a mixed range of outcomes. I hypothesize that rural modernization campaigns are more likely to succeed when the goal is development rather than extraction, when the central government can control local officials, and when rural citizens can meaningfully participate in the policy process. After elaborating these points, I relate them to the main cases of Taiwan (most successful), South Korea (less successful), and China (least successful) by comparing their local governments and rural organizations, key institutions that affected campaign outcomes. I also develop two additional hypotheses about farmers' organizations and the quali-ties that make them more or less effective advocates for small farmers, both in terms of providing essential services and shaping rural policy. I contend that they exhibit varying degrees of linkage and autonomy in relation to the state and villagers, and that these features, in turn, explain long-term differences in government responsiveness and agricultural production, an area where campaigns have enjoyed limited success.

The last part of the chapter revisits the case of Japan and concludes with a few points about why existing theories of state-led development need to be reexamined. Japan provides the earliest example of a campaign approach to development in the region. From the 1900s through the 1960s, there were in fact several campaigns launched by the state in order to protect and develop the countryside—the Local Improvement Movement, the Rural Revitalization Campaign, the New Village Campaign, and the New Life Campaign. Not all these campaigns were successful, but they illustrate the book's basic premise about the strategic use of campaigns in East Asia. They also provide preliminary support for the arguments about how campaigns and institutions interact to affect development outcomes. In that sense, the Japanese case serves the purpose of a "plausibility probe," defined by Harry Eckstein as a "stage of inquiry preliminary to testing," which aims to establish the potential validity of candidate theories.[2] Overall, the ideas developed in this chapter present a challenge to studies that portray state intervention in rural society as inherently predatory. They also suggest a need to reconsider some fundamental assumptions about how developmental states operate and the foundations of their success.

Existing Theory and Its Limitations

The Japan Factor

After World War II, agricultural production in East Asia quickly returned to, and then surpassed, prewar peak levels, as early as 1950 in Japan, 1951 in Taiwan, and 1954 in South Korea (following the Korean War). Even during the "economic miracle" period of 1955–1970 in Japan, when industrialization pushed gross national product growth into double digits, agriculture's performance remained strong, averaging 3 percent per year.[3] In Taiwan, agriculture experienced a fifteen-year stretch of accelerated growth, averaging 4.6 percent per year from 1952 to 1967. In the 1970s, it slowed down but maintained an impressive average growth rate of 3.2 percent.[4] South Korea exhibited a similar pattern, with agricultural production growing 3.5 percent per year from 1954 to 1973, and then decelerating slightly in the 1970s.[5]

Comparing East Asia with the rest of the world reveals just how exceptional this performance was. According to the Food and Agriculture Organization of the United Nations, the global average annual growth rate for agriculture during the 1952–1971 period was 2.7 percent, lower than all the averages just reported.[6] Looking only at crop yields (not total sector production), East Asia and the Pacific registered 2.7 percent annual growth for the 1961–1975 period, compared to 1 percent for Latin America and the Caribbean, 0.8 percent for the Middle East and North Africa, 1.7 percent for South Asia, and 1.3 percent for sub-Saharan Africa.[7]

To explain the success of Japan, Taiwan, and Korea, scholars have highlighted the favorable initial conditions these countries inherited. During Japan's Tokugawa era (1603–1868), significant progress was made in agriculture, such that by the time of the Meiji era (1868–1912), Japanese farmers had already adopted advanced techniques in irrigation, double cropping, fertilizer application, land reclamation, and seed improvement.[8] The Meiji government established numerous rural extension and cooperative institutions, but these were actually secondary to Japan's "cultivating landlords" in terms of promoting rural development.[9] Unlike many rural societies where absentee land ownership is common, Japanese landlords were small-scale operators based in their villages. According to Penelope Francks, they integrated rural areas into the larger economy by acting as "a conduit, bringing new agricultural techniques, commercial opportunities and ideas and education into nineteenth-century Japanese villages."[10] This grassroots technological development resulted in five decades of sustained agricultural growth (1870s–1910s) and spurred Japan's industrial take-off through the generation of government revenue and exports.[11]

In colonial Taiwan (1895–1945) and Korea (1910–1945), Japanese authorities developed modern systems of transport, finance, education, and administration. Taiwan, for example, had almost no roads, railways, or financial institutions before Japan arrived, and the proportion of primary-age children enrolled in school was less than 10 percent. By the 1940s, Japan had connected the northern and southern ports of Keelung and Kaohsiung by railway, built over twelve thousand kilometers of roads, opened more than four hundred banks and credit cooperatives, and increased primary school enrollment to over 70 percent.[12] In both Taiwan and Korea, cadastral surveys were used to clarify property rights, formalize landlord-tenant relations, and facilitate land taxation. These state-building efforts would have important long-term consequences for development. Writing about Korea, Atul Kohli observes that Japan's successful penetration of the agrarian periphery "stands out as a fairly unique display of state efficacy in the comparative history of colonialism." This legacy, he argues, helps to explain why later state-led industrialization efforts in South Korea and, by extension, Taiwan were so successful compared with India, Brazil, and Nigeria, where colonialism did not result in the creation of strong state institutions.[13]

On the question of how colonialism affected rural development specifically, previous research shows that its effects were mixed. Conditions were difficult for Taiwanese and Korean farmers because Japanese authorities exploited agriculture, but they also left behind modern technologies, infrastructure, and institutions. Under the policy of "Industrial Japan, Agricultural Taiwan," the colonial government engineered a shift from subsistence to export agriculture, transforming Taiwan into a major supplier of rice, sugar, and other products for Japan's domestic market.[14] In fact, Taiwan underwent a green revolution in the 1920s–1930s, four decades before the rest of Asia, owing to the adoption of chemical fertilizers, high-yield varieties of rice, and new cultivation practices. Irrigated farmland increased from 32 to 64 percent of total cultivated land, and an extensive network of farmers' organizations was built, employing about forty thousand people, with one extension worker for every thirty-two households. Through this system, the state distributed newly developed fertilizers and a variety known as ponlai rice, which led to 45 percent higher yields and a 5 percent growth rate for agriculture in the 1920s.[15]

Although not on the same scale as Taiwan, the colonial government in Korea built similar institutions and introduced advanced farming practices as part of its "Rice Production Increase Plan," leading to 3 percent growth in rice output for most of the 1920s–1930s.[16] Unfortunately for Korean farmers, consumption declined even as production increased, since one-third of the rice crop was exported.[17] The threat of starvation drove many Koreans to migrate to Japan and Manchuria.[18] Taiwanese farmers were slightly better off because the food-processing sector created local employment opportunities, allowing households to earn wages and engage in part-time farming.[19] And while farmers in both places were subject to exploitation, farmers in Taiwan probably suffered less because of the island's lower population density (which affected tenure security) and its different assigned role in the Japanese empire: Taiwan was designated as a base for agriculture and Korea as a base for industry.[20] In contrast with Taiwan, Japanese-built industries in Korea were concentrated in urban areas, and the agricultural sector was largely neglected until after the Japanese Rice Riots of 1918, a series of demonstrations against escalating rice prices that prompted the government to increase supplies coming from the peninsula.[21]

These different prewar levels of agricultural development and patterns of industrialization created divergent postwar economic trajectories, with Taiwan prioritizing agriculture and Korea prioritizing industry. Nevertheless, advancements made during the Japanese colonial period, both in the metropole and the periphery, were part of the reason for these countries' quick recovery and subsequent growth. The postwar governments of Taiwan and Korea were able to draw from existing institutional resources and rehabilitate, rather than build from scratch, the farmers' organizations and extension systems first set up by the Japanese.[22] Similarly, Japan's postwar government established its national farmers' association, Nokyo (also known as the Japan Agricultural Cooperatives Group, or JA), on the foundation of preexisting cooperatives. As during the colonial era, all these organizations would prove essential for rural policy implementation.

Still, initial conditions cannot explain much about other aspects of rural development besides the region's strong record of agricultural production. Nor can they explain why farmers' organizations were more than just instruments of resource extraction for the industrializing state. Later in the chapter, I theorize about when farmers' organizations are more likely to provide effective extension services and advocate successfully for the interests of small farmers.

The Land Reform Agenda

The United States, as an occupying power in postwar Japan and South Korea, and as a major supporter of the Kuomintang (KMT) regime in Taiwan, had considerable influence over the region's rural development. In 1951, President Harry Truman established the Inter-Agency Committee on Land Reform Problems to ensure that land reform was broadly incorporated into US foreign policy.[23] In the context of the Cold War, the goals of land reform were intertwined with national defense—tenant societies would be transformed into freeholder societies in order to stop the spread of communism.

Wolf Ladejinsky, known as the architect of Japanese land reform, was one of the first people in the United States to write extensively about land as a political resource.[24] He believed the Russian and Chinese communists had correctly recognized a political opportunity in addressing the grievances of tenants and landless farmers, and he called on the US government to "fight Communist ideology with an effective version of the American farm tradition."[25] Ladejinsky repeatedly emphasized how small family farms would promote democracy, or at least give farmers a stake in Asia's noncommunist regimes. Indeed, several prominent scholars have noted a strong link between land ownership and political stability. Samuel Huntington writes, "no social group is more conservative than a landholding peasantry and none is more revolutionary than a peasantry which owns too little land or pays too high a rental."[26] Similarly, Jeffery Paige found that of all agrarian systems, smallholder economies were the most stable.[27]

US-backed land reforms in Asia amounted to the largest noncommunist land reforms on record. They were also some of the most successfully executed and nonviolent examples of land redistribution ever attempted. The US military government in Japan carried out land reform between 1946 and 1950 with the help of local land commissions, which were elected bodies composed of landlords, owner-cultivators, and tenants. More than 2 million hectares (4.9 million acres) of farmland changed hands, a cap of 3 hectares (7.4 acres) was placed on the scale of ownership, with a higher allowance for Hokkaido, and the proportion of farm households classified as full owner-cultivators increased from 37 to 62 percent. Tenancy was not completely eliminated, but written contracts were introduced that capped rents at 25 percent of the value of the main crop.[28] Taiwan's land reform, which lasted from 1949 to 1953, occurred in three stages: rent reduction, the sale of public land formerly held by the colonial government, and the sale of private land through the "Land-to-the-Tiller" program. As in Japan, local land commissions assisted with policy implementation, limits were placed on the scale of ownership, and tenant rights were strengthened. Almost 50 percent of Taiwan's households obtained some land as a consequence of the reforms, and the share of full owner-cultivators increased from 36 to 55 percent, eventually reaching 82 percent by 1975.[29]

In South Korea, it appears that internal rather than external forces played a more decisive role in pushing the land reform agenda forward. The American military government announced a land reform package in 1945 but hesitated to implement it, and Syngman Rhee's government, established in 1948, dragged its feet for fear of alienating political supporters from the landed classes. It was not until after North Korean–backed "people's committees" started gaining ground in the South that serious steps were taken to carry out land reform. The perceived threat of communism was also a key factor in the Japanese and Taiwanese cases, but in South Korea that threat was very real. According to Gi-Wook Shin, tenancy disputes erupted into a major agrarian rebellion in 1946, involving 2.3 million participants across forty counties. In the midst of this chaos, the communists stepped in to seize the farmland that had been slated for redistribution in the stalled land reform bill, prompting many landlords to preemptively sell off their holdings.[30] Once the crisis produced a political consensus, land reform progressed quickly. During the Korean War, more than 1 million hectares (2.5 million acres) of farmland were transferred to tenants through government and private sales. By 1964, the proportion of full owner-cultivators had risen to 72 percent, up from 14 percent in 1945.[31]

To some extent, land reform was made possible by the formal systems of land classification and property rights that were developed during the colonial period. Another contributing factor was the increasingly weak position of landlords. As in Korea, Japan's landed classes found themselves confronted with a rising number of tenancy disputes, which in the 1930s coalesced into a nationwide tenant union movement. The war temporarily halted the movement, but it reemerged after 1945 and did not subside until land reform was completed.[32] In Taiwan's case, there were at least two reasons why landlords did not block the reforms. First, large absentee landlords disappeared in the early 1900s when Japan conferred property rights on smaller landlords, who in turn assisted the government with rural policy implementation.[33] Second, KMT leaders were outsiders with no ties to the landed classes, and most of Taiwan's local elites, who might have raised objections, were killed during the 2–28 Incident of 1947, a mass uprising against KMT rule that was brutally suppressed.[34] The United States' role was critical as well, in terms of providing administrative and financial support for the reforms.

Existing scholarship points to land reform as a key variable that accounts for East Asia's economic success. It stabilized the countryside politically, reduced the incidence of rural poverty, and compelled former landlords to transfer some of their wealth to the industrial sector. It also facilitated the emergence of strong developmental states by increasing state autonomy from traditional agrarian power holders.[35] Yet its impact on the agricultural sector appears to be mixed. Whereas some scholars show that land reform raised agricultural output and rural incomes, others have argued that these outcomes should not be attributed to land reform per se, and that its main effect was to further reduce farm size. To be sure, the reforms had a positive effect on farmers' incentives and short-term productivity, but the extreme parcelization of land limited the prospects for long-term growth and forced many households to find other, nonfarm sources of income. Perhaps land reform's most notable legacy was to freeze in place the position of small farmers, such that efforts to mechanize and scale up agriculture (from small to medium-size holdings) proved unusually difficult.[36]

Even Ladejinsky, one of land reform's most vocal proponents, recognized its limitations. Land reform, he notes, is but one component of a successful agrarian reform agenda, which must also include the provision of rural credit, irrigation systems, extension services, market access, and other public goods.[37] Another shortcoming is that land reform cannot solve the problem of urban bias. As Michael Lipton observes, "the case for equalization within the rural sector" through measures such as land reform "is weakened by the size of the urban-rural gap."[38] Moreover, research on East Asian land reform has found little evidence to support the idea of an inverse relationship between farm size and crop yields.[39] While some scholars maintain that small farms are more efficient, the reality is that landholdings were typically too small to support a family. That was certainly the situation in Taiwan, where 42 percent of farmers owned less than 0.6 hectares (1.48 acres) in 1960, and where, according to a famous 1964 survey, 43 percent of farm households reported no improvement or even a decline in living conditions since land reform.[40]

To summarize, the effects of land reform were primarily political and social rather than economic. In each case, land reform neutralized the threat of communism and reduced the level of inequality. It should be acknowledged that, despite the problems just mentioned, Taiwan's income distribution was among the most equal in the world: in the 1970s, the bottom 40 percent of the population received

20 percent of national income (versus only 12.5 percent of national income in the world's least developed countries).[41] Land reform thus created a more equitable and stable society. It was not, however, a sufficient condition for long-term growth or a solution to the growing rural-urban gap. For these reasons, it is necessary to move beyond land reform and examine other variables that might explain the region's development.

The East Asian Developmental State

By the early 1980s, the rapid industrialization of Japan, Taiwan, South Korea, Singapore, and Hong Kong had transformed East Asia into a global economic hub. The region's success inspired a large body of research on the developmental state, a regime-centered theory of industrialization pioneered by Chalmers Johnson in 1982. To briefly describe the model, developmental states tend to exhibit the following characteristics: strong state institutions, an elite technocratic bureaucracy, a state-centric development ideology, a commitment to export-led growth, and a state-corporatist relationship with the private sector (understood as the top-down organization and regulation of interest groups, whose dependence on the state works to minimize political opposition).[42] In spite of some criticisms of the theory, several decades later it remains the dominant framework for comparing East Asian countries in political science and has been applied more broadly to the case of China and other emerging economies.[43]

On the question of the developmental state's origins, a few factors were important. First, the region inherited strong state institutions from Japan's prewar modernization and colonization efforts. Second, the United States provided substantial economic assistance and preferential access to its domestic market, which made export-oriented industrialization possible. Third, national security concerns produced elite cohesion and a firm commitment to development as a means of stopping communism.[44] According to Richard Doner and colleagues, it was not autonomy from social forces but rather the threat of popular unrest that, combined with national security concerns and hard budget constraints, led to the creation of developmental institutions in some countries but not others.[45] Even though its origins are context-specific (and thus not easily replicated), the developmental state model presented a challenge to dependency theory and the practice of import substitution common throughout Latin America in the 1960s and 1970s.[46] The "East Asian model" became a buzzword for the World Bank and other international organizations, and it continues to be a point of reference for many developing countries.

Considering the size of the developmental state literature, it is surprising just how little attention has been paid to the issue of rural development. Most accounts assume that East Asia conformed to W. Arthur Lewis's dual-sector model in which agriculture's contribution to industrialization is limited to the supply of surplus labor. As Lewis explained in his seminal 1954 essay, for countries with large rural populations, the reallocation of labor from agriculture to industry—or what he calls the subsistence and capitalist sectors—fuels rapid growth because the deep pool of excess labor ensures that wages remain low. However, the eventual exhaustion of surplus labor, a milestone known as the "Lewis turning point," leads to rising wages, labor shortages, and slower growth, thereby necessitating economic rebalancing away from manufacturing and exports toward services and consumption. Most economists believe that Japan, Taiwan, and Korea reached this point in the 1960s–1970s and that China will reach it soon.[47] The model implies that agriculture is inherently backward and that the trickle-down effect of industrialization is what paves the way for rural development. While some scholars have challenged these ideas, the developmental state literature still tends to either ignore agriculture because of its minimal role in industrialization or to focus on land reform as the region's most successful rural policy.[48]

Although the developmental state's impact on rural development is under-theorized, a few themes can nevertheless be drawn from previous scholarship. Besides land reform and the release of surplus labor, which helped the industrializing state and rural society in different ways, the provision of rural public goods and services was more effective than in other developing regions. Take education, for example. Before World War II, Japan had already attained high levels of education as a result of the growth of Buddhist temple schools in the Tokugawa era, followed by the nationalization of primary schools in the Meiji era. By 1950, the average farmworker in Japan had seven years of schooling, and the average factory worker had ten.[49] In Taiwan and Korea, basic education expanded under colonialism, yet access to higher education was limited to the elite classes. This situation changed in the postwar period, with literacy rates in both countries climbing from less than 30 percent in 1945 to more than 80 percent by 1970, owing to significant public and private investment in education.[50] Regarding rural extension services, the presence of a technocratic elite and encompassing farmers' organizations facilitated the diffusion of new technologies to virtually all rural households. The organizations' parastatal status was similar to the corporatist arrangements found in the industrial sector. While technically separate from the state, they were responsible for entrusted activities like fertilizer sales and rice purchases. State modernizers used them to exploit agriculture (by manipulating prices) but also worked closely with them to stimulate production.[51]

It should be noted here that the effect of US assistance was different in Taiwan and South Korea. For starters, higher levels of food aid to Korea hurt the rural sector. Imports from the Public Law 480 (P.L. 480) "Food for Peace" program killed any incentive the Rhee government might have had to develop agriculture. Park Chung-hee's government, established in 1961, paid greater attention to agriculture but ultimately continued to rely on cheap food imports to depress domestic grain prices. Park terminated the program in the early 1970s, only after the US began requiring that food be purchased with foreign exchange instead of local currency.[52] Food aid had a similar effect on Taiwan but was not as detrimental, mainly because of another difference between the two countries: even though Taiwan received far less US economic and military assistance than Korea (roughly US$4 billion versus $13 billion), it was applied very efficiently and in a way that promoted rural development.[53] In particular, the Sino-American Joint Commission on Rural Reconstruction (JCRR) was remarkably successful at providing technical assistance and is widely considered to be an exemplary institution in the history of US aid missions. Established in 1948 as part of the US China Aid Act, the JCRR was to oversee China's postwar rural rehabilitation. As conditions for the KMT worsened on the mainland, the JCRR relocated to Taiwan in 1949. Over the course of its thirty-year history, the JCRR implemented thousands of rural development projects. It was also instrumental during land reform and helped to promote democratic governance within Taiwan's farmers' organizations.[54]

Despite these differences, Taiwan and South Korea shared similar institutional features with Japan: (1) a smallholder farm economy dominated by owner-cultivators with secure private property rights to land; (2) effective rural extension systems maintained by a technocratic bureaucracy and parastatal farmers' organizations; and (3) extensive state control over agriculture, especially with regard to the production of rice and staple foods.[55] This combination of institutions was powerful. It led to widely dispersed, long-term gains in production, enabled the back-and-forth transfer of resources between the industrial and agricultural sectors, and militated against rural policy decisions that were purely extractive. In contrast, many poor countries in the developing world have weak and unequal extension services, with crucial inputs being directed toward large farmers tasked with producing cheap food for the state.[56] Gains in production are more random than systematic, and the state lacks both the capacity to transfer resources between sectors and the will to support broad-based rural development.

These convergences suggest an East Asian model of rural development, which, in line with the conventional wisdom, derives from regime type and institutional design. However, a deeper analysis reveals that rural transformation was much more complex than land reform followed by the release of surplus labor for industrialization, and furthermore, that developmental states were not always good for development. In the empirical chapters, I show that urban bias was a fundamental characteristic of East Asian agricultural policy. Though not as severe as in some developing countries, the presence of discriminatory price, trade, and investment policies meant that farmers did not necessarily benefit from the gains in agricultural production; and relative to other social classes, farmers' living standards noticeably declined in the years after land reform. It was not until later in the industrialization process that East Asian governments stopped exploiting agriculture and significant gains were made in other areas besides production (incomes, infrastructure, and housing), although the degree of success was also different in different countries. More importantly, the way these states intervened, through rural modernization campaigns, was not only risky but also had more in common with Maoism than with the technocratic leanings of developmental states.

Rural Policy Transition in China

China's reform and opening policy, initiated by Deng Xiaoping's government in 1978, started with rural reform. Within just a few years, collective farms and the grain rationing system were dismantled; household farming and rural markets were introduced; semiprivate farmers' organizations were developed to help producers navigate the new economy; and state control in general was greatly diminished. The reforms amounted to a wholesale rejection of Mao Zedong's agricultural policies. Given the tragic failure of the Great Leap Forward (1958–1960), a campaign that resulted in tens of millions of famine deaths, and agriculture's lackluster performance in the years that followed, it is perhaps unsurprising that a leadership transition at the top would produce major policy changes.[57] After all, Deng Xiaoping was among those central officials who spearheaded the post-Leap readjustment policies of the early 1960s, which included the promotion of household farming, sideline production (e.g., handicrafts), and limited markets. These policies did not last long, as Mao worried they were undermining his vision for the countryside, but in some places the practice of family farming continued underground. It is partly for this reason that many people believe decollectivization was a bottom-up process, pushed forward by a peasantry who had already abandoned socialism.[58]

To be clear, the legacy of the Mao era was not entirely negative. The peasant revolution that brought the Chinese Communist Party (CCP) to power was to some extent rooted in the success of local experiments with redistributive tax and land reforms. In the early 1950s, land reform was completed on a national scale, and rural marketing towns damaged by war reemerged as important economic and cultural centers. These developments had a positive effect on rural production and living standards.[59] In the late Maoist period as well, investments in irrigation and electricity led to the spread of new technologies and higher crop yields.[60] And, of course, remarkable progress also occurred in the areas of literacy and public health.[61] However, it is equally true that certain policies were harmful to rural development. Through collectivization and the "unified purchase and marketing system," which required farmers to sell grain to the state at fixed prices, rural resources were extracted for industrialization. Grain procurement reached extreme levels during the Great Leap Forward and was a primary cause of the famine.[62] The people's communes, besides being large and difficult to manage, at different times rejected scientific agriculture and material incentives. Institutional dysfunction was especially pronounced during moments of ideological extremism, such as the Anti-Rightist Movements and the Learn from Dazhai in Agriculture Campaign.[63] In sum, the combination of excessive procurement, inadequate institutions, and ideological radicalism—not to mention the country's rapid population growth—severely undermined the prospects for sustained rural development.

Considering these circumstances, Deng's reform agenda was nothing short of extraordinary. Between 1978 and 1984, agriculture grew 10 percent annually, and the number of people living in absolute poverty dropped from 250 million to 128 million, or from 31 percent to 15 percent of the rural population.[64] Apart from the changes already mentioned, the rise of technocrats within the party affected every level of government, including the village.[65] It facilitated the spread of scientific practices in agriculture and the growth of township and village enterprises (TVEs). These small-scale firms would become the engine of Chinese industrialization. By the mid-1990s, TVEs employed over 135 million people, or one-third of the rural labor force, and were producing more than 50 percent of total industrial output and exports.[66]

Although China is not a perfect fit for the developmental state model—it is larger, more predatory, and transitioning from socialism—it does exhibit some key characteristics, including a technocratic bureaucracy, a commitment to state-led (and export-led) growth, and a corporatist relationship with the private sector. These attributes are often cited as contributing factors in China's economic rise.[67] And yet, the similarities with other developmental states should not be overstated.[68] With regard to rural institutions, China has a unique land tenure system of village collective ownership and household usage rights, and there is much debate about the effects of this system on rural households' economic security. Whereas proponents assert that it serves as a social safety net for rural labor (by guaranteeing a source of livelihood if alternative employment cannot be found), critics maintain that the lack of private ownership suppresses investment and enables government land grabs, which have escalated since the mid-1990s.[69]

Moreover, Chinese farmers' organizations are underdeveloped. They have a small membership base and limited access to the state's developmental resources. As a result, rural extension services have been relatively ineffective in China. Finally, narrowing the rural-urban divide has proven more difficult because of institutional hangovers from the Mao era restricting the circulation of land, labor, and capital.

This overview of policy change in China identifies some of the underlying causes of rural economic growth in the 1980s–1990s as well as some of the ongoing problems affecting the countryside. Still, as in the other cases, there are certain things that demand further explanation: How were various types of rural development outcomes achieved? What was the state's response to agricultural adjustment? Delving into these questions reveals that institutions do not tell the whole story about how rural development occurred in China or the rest of East Asia.

The Argument

This book sheds light on the interplay between rural institutions and state campaigns in development. I argue that while institutions were important for East Asia's postwar agricultural recovery and subsequent gains in production, campaigns were critical at the later stages of development for improving rural conditions overall, which had deteriorated as a result of industrialization and urban bias. I furthermore assert that the region's campaigns produced mixed outcomes depending on the political-institutional context in which they were implemented. Before laying out the theory, I want to address some basic questions about what campaigns are, why states use them, and their relationship with institutions.

The General Logic of State Campaigns

State campaigns are policies that demand high levels of mobilization to achieve dramatic change. They may have broad or specific goals, but in general they are transformative policies dressed up in revolutionary language. Mobilization, understood as any effort to activate and involve a population in the pursuit of certain goals, serves as the dominant mode of policy implementation. While the extent of popular mobilization varies based on campaign targets, bureaucratic mobilization is a central feature of all campaigns. Another hallmark is their Leninist-inspired tactics: defining core tasks, dispatching work teams, empowering local activists, identifying models, disseminating propaganda, and exerting of all kinds of pressure in order to break up standard work routines and overwhelm ingrained attitudes and behaviors.[70]

This type of politics has long captured the attention of scholars like Robert Tucker, who put forward the idea of movement regimes to describe communism in the Soviet Union, fascism in Europe, and nationalist revolutionary movements throughout the postcolonial world.[71] State-sponsored mobilization is also a defining characteristic of totalitarian regimes. As Juan Linz explains: "Citizen participation in and active mobilization for political and collective social tasks are encouraged, demanded, rewarded, and channeled through a single party and many monopolistic secondary groups. Passive obedience and apathy, retreat into the role of 'parochials' and 'subjects,' characteristic of many authoritarian regimes, are considered undesirable by the rulers."[72] Mobilized participation, though anathema to liberal democratic principles, is fundamental to understanding politics and policy implementation in much of the world.[73]

Campaigns are more likely to occur when political leaders determine there is an urgent need for change, typically in response to a challenge or crisis, and when the change envisioned is considered so extensive that it cannot be accomplished through normal means. In launching campaigns, the state draws on latent power resources, including traditions and cultures of mobilization rooted in the legacies of revolution, war, and militarism. Examining the historical origins of campaigns in China, scholars have noted the Soviet Union's influence and, more importantly, Mao's penchant for mass mobilization developed during the Jiangxi Soviet (1927–1934) and Yan'an (1935–1946) periods when the party had to rely on the peasantry for survival and guerrilla warfare. According to Tyrene White, campaigns were used under Mao to advance collectivist goals and instill "a revolutionary ethic deep within society."[74]

Through campaigns, the state can circumvent institutional constraints to change by reordering existing power structures or creating alternative ones. Depending on campaign objectives, these structures may include extra-institutional actors, such as social activists, grassroots organizations, and interest or pressure groups. Campaigns thus resemble social movements—and may in fact try to co-opt or draw strength from social movements—but are conceptually distinct because of the preeminent role of the state in their execution. Campaigns also resemble informal institutions in the sense of being grounded in particular norms, traditions, and cultures, rather than formal organizations and laws. Indeed, a few China scholars have argued that campaigns are institutions. In the Mao era, people grew accustomed to cycles of mobilization and demobilization, campaign activities were routinized, and even the timing of some campaigns became predictable.[75] However, I believe this line of reasoning stretches both concepts too far. Campaigns diverge from institutions in their uncertainty. They are about suspending politics as usual in order to overhaul existing conditions, which makes them powerful, but also more susceptible to unintended consequences. Institutions can affect campaign outcomes, and those outcomes sometimes include new institutional arrangements—for example, land reform (a campaign) resulting in smallholder farming (an institution). Yet ultimately, campaigns and institutions represent two different modes of politics.

There are many types and examples of campaigns. Again looking at the Chinese case, the CCP launched over one hundred national campaigns between 1950 and 1975, with hundreds more occurring at the local level.[76] Early scholarship classified them as economic (e.g., the Great Leap Forward), struggle (Elimination of Counter-Revolutionaries), or ideological (Learn from the People's Liberation Army), based on the nature of the problems they were intended to resolve.[77] While it appeared for a time that campaigns would disappear in the reform era, as Deng Xiaoping shifted the country's focus to economic development, they have nevertheless persisted. Campaigns have featured prominently in studies of the one-child policy, environmental policy, intellectual property enforcement, regional economic development, ideological work, patriotic education, crisis management, and the repression of social movements such as Falungong.[78] To give another example, Xi Jinping's anticorruption drive should leave no doubt that the party still believes in the positive utility of campaigns.[79] This book confirms the view that mobilization is an enduring part of Chinese politics, but it also proposes a new idea that campaigns are not just a legacy of Maoist rule. As explained below, situating China's rural policies within the broader region reveals they are part of a long tradition of rural modernization campaigns dating back to Meiji-era Japan.

The Phenomenon of Rural Modernization Campaigns

I define state-led rural modernization campaigns as policies that aim to transform the countryside through bureaucratic and popular mobilization. Besides land reform, examples include green revolutions, collectivization drives, and sanitation campaigns, among many others. Rural modernization campaigns can serve as a legitimation strategy, by shoring up support for the regime through propaganda and pork barrel politics. They can also serve as a development strategy, by overcoming resource shortages and institutional barriers to change.

Faced with the problem of agricultural adjustment, East Asian governments turned to campaigns instead of going through normal administrative channels because they viewed the rural situation with urgency. Campaigns were considered a viable solution, capable of producing quick results and minimizing resistance from actors invested in the status quo. In addition to building political loyalty, the objective was to achieve breakthroughs in rural economic and infrastructure development—to stimulate agricultural production, raise rural incomes, and improve access to quality roads, electricity, water, sanitation, and housing.

Although the transition from squeezing agriculture to subsidizing it has occurred in every industrialized country, it is not a natural outcome of development. Urban bias is a systemic problem that is very difficult to reverse because of the entrenched interests that support it. Even as the agricultural sector shrinks and the cost of protection goes down, governments are still more likely to stick with policies that favor the urban-industrial sector, that is unless the backlash from rural stakeholders is sufficiently great to trigger a response. In Taiwan, farmers' organizations, along with the political leaders and constituencies they produced, directly pressured the government to adopt protective policies for agriculture. In South Korea, Park Chung-hee changed course after being challenged in the 1967 and 1971 presidential elections by opposition candidates who used the issue of low rice prices to capture the rural vote. Political pressure was also a key factor in China, where escalating rural protests, combined with growing public discussion about an impending rural crisis, prompted the central government to revise its policies. The contentiousness of the agricultural adjustment issue in each case was magnified by the pace of structural economic change: it took a century or more for agriculture's share of GDP to fall from 40 to 7 percent in early industrializing countries, compared with three decades or less for late industrializers like Korea.[80] The empirical chapters provide a more detailed account of policy change, but what is notable here is that the state's reversal of urban bias in East Asia was not just about import restrictions, subsidies, and other farm protection measures (although these were adopted as well). Instead, it was about producing revolutionary change.

A few words of clarification about terminology and the negative connotations associated with campaigns are in order. The phrase "state-led rural modernization campaign" is not meant to imply the absence of markets or the presence of state-owned farms, as this kind of campaign can occur within the context of capitalism and private farming. Still, it suggests that the government is more important than the market in allocating resources to rural communities. In East Asia, there is a tendency to use the word "construction" (an action) in place of "development" (a process) and "modernization campaign" (a policy) in place of "modernization" (a process).[81] This discourse conveys a more activist role for the state than most Western development ideologies prescribe. Asian scholarship also tends to describe campaigns in a positive light, as policies that are capable of inspiring state-society cooperation and participatory development. While a few leftist intellectuals have sympathized with this view, the Western scholarship on campaigns is generally very negative. It describes campaigns as instruments of state domination that are prone to excesses—production failures, political persecution, social alienation, and violence. Mass participation is achieved through manipulation rather than genuine commitment, and campaign success, if it occurs at all, is coincidental at best. It typically dismisses campaigns as ill-conceived deviations from technocratic governance or focuses solely on explaining failures such as the Great Leap Forward.[82]

The fact is that most campaigns fall somewhere in between state domination at one extreme and participatory development at the other, and the impact of campaigns on development is usually mixed. Not all campaigns turned out like the Great Leap Forward. Gordon Bennett argues that, except for the Leap, Maoist economic campaigns helped spur development by involving the population to overcome managerial and resource bottlenecks: "in balance, they contribute more to economic growth than they take away."[83] Land reform, for example, was a campaign that produced mixed but mostly positive outcomes. Interestingly, apart from the communist cases, Western scholarship hardly acknowledges that land reform was a campaign. This is not to say that skepticism of campaigns is wrong or unfounded, only that overlooking them has produced a certain narrative about East Asian development that is not entirely accurate.

The Relationship between Campaigns and Institutions

As has already been suggested, I view campaigns and institutions as concepts that are interrelated but also distinct from one another. First, the uncertainty of campaigns stems from the mobilization of new actors and the creation of new incentives to support radical change. In this regard, institutions are quite different. Defined by Douglass North as the rules that shape or constrain human behavior, institutions "reduce uncertainty by providing a structure to everyday life."[84] They serve as the foundation for routine governance, and even though some institutions are rooted in conventions rather than laws, they influence actors' behavior in ways that are far more predictable than campaigns. Second, campaigns generally have a strong spiritual or moral content, and they use affective appeals to produce change. Institutions may be rooted in morality as well, but more often rely on cognitive or rational appeals to elicit compliance. Third, campaigns produce change quickly and are constantly evolving themselves. In contrast, institutions are slow moving and path dependent, meaning they are relatively stable because of the increasing returns that come from working within them.[85] Fourth, campaigns and institutions play different roles in development. As North and others have noted, institutions can lower transaction costs among diverse actors and generate incentives to engage in productive activities. Moreover, differences in institutional capacities—the strength, efficiency, and functions of institutions—may explain cross-national variation in governmental and economic performance.[86] Related to these insights, I would add that institutions are critically important for achieving technically complex, long-term goals, such as the promotion of scientific agriculture. Campaigns, on the other hand, are more likely to achieve outcomes that are technically simple and attainable in a shorter time frame, such as production surges and basic construction projects.

Campaigns, like social movements, can create, destroy, revitalize, or circumvent institutions. They are a powerful means of mobilizing resources for change and have been frequently used in Leninist systems as a check against bureaucratic ossification. The Cultural Revolution in China is perhaps an extreme example of how campaigns can be destructive and firmly anti-institutional, but in other cases campaigns and institutions have worked in tandem.[87] Mobilization and technocracy, ad hoc and organized approaches to governance and development—all these things can coexist, just as any complex system can exhibit different strands of political culture simultaneously.

Furthermore, the process of political development and institutionalization that occurs as a revolutionary regime matures does not necessarily mean that mobilizational politics will disappear. Examining the evolution of Leninist regimes in Europe, Kenneth Jowitt found that even with greater, more systematic social inclusion in political decision making, mobilization still served the purpose of expanding state control over society and addressing political challenges.[88] The same can be said for China. As Elizabeth Perry has observed, despite China's apparent entry into a more rational-bureaucratic, postrevolutionary phase of governance, campaigns have remained an instrument of rule in many realms. Compared to the Mao era, campaigns today have more pragmatic goals and involve less popular mobilization, but they continue to employ such mechanisms as cadre work teams and propaganda teams. She proposes the concept of a "managed campaign" to describe the blending of technocratic pragmatism with Maoist tactics, which underscores the point that different modes of politics can work together.[89]

Finally, it is important to understand that while institutions can function independently of campaigns, campaigns actually need institutions. Without organized channels for bureaucratic monitoring and popular participation, campaigns are likely to be ineffectual or, quite the opposite, to spiral out of control. If present, institutions can function as feedback mechanisms to correct misguided policy and rein in campaign excesses.

A Theory of Campaigns

This book makes the following argument about campaigns:

> *Rural modernization campaigns are more likely to work, that is produce policy compliance and positive outcomes, when the state's goal is rural development rather than extraction, when the central government can control local authorities, and when the campaign is carried out in partnership with rural citizens.*

GOALS

Campaigns often suffer from having unrealistic and vague goals, and the intention of the state—in this case, whether to develop the countryside as an end in itself or to extract resources for industrialization—is not always obvious. Because political elites are inclined to favor the urban-industrial sector, slogans about balanced or integrated development may obscure the state's real agenda. In addition to economic goals, rural modernization campaigns can also have political goals, such as bringing rural communities into closer contact with the state and turning peasants into loyal citizens.

One thing that sets the campaigns in this study apart is that their overriding objective was rural development. This was clear from official statements about the need to protect the countryside from further decline, the repudiation of policies that imposed direct or hidden taxes on agriculture, and an increase in the proportion of government expenditures allocated to the rural sector. Unlike the Great Leap Forward, which despite rhetoric to the contrary was a massive exercise in extraction, Taiwan's Community Development Campaign, South Korea's New Village Movement, and China's Building a New Socialist Countryside were fundamentally about the government and the cities making sacrifices for the countryside.

That being said, these campaigns were also affected by problems related to their content and goals: having too many goals, having an unclear hierarchy of goals, and setting goals that were technically too complex to be realized in the time frame demanded by the government. Without well-defined goals, gaps can easily arise between what the central government aims to accomplish and what local governments are doing in practice. Another downside of campaigns is that they create a highly politicized environment, which can result in false compliance on the one hand and excessive compliance on the other—the erection of Potemkin villages to deceive inspecting officials, or an all-out effort to exceed the central government's expectations through grandiose applications of the policy. Strong oversight and feedback mechanisms are therefore necessary for campaign success.[90]

CENTRAL CONTROL

Although bureaucratic monitoring intensifies during campaigns, cheating and corruption may be exacerbated by the political pressures facing local authorities charged with implementation. These behaviors are less likely, however, if there is a coherent link or alignment between central objectives and local realities. In the absence of a unifying purpose, to which officials at all levels assign similar importance, central-local government coherence depends largely on structural conditions. The size and organization of the state, and how power is distributed within it, can determine the efficacy of bureaucratic oversight mechanisms. These include performance evaluations, education and training programs, administrative and fiscal regulations, and the placement of local officials with demonstrated loyalty to the center in positions of authority. The amplified use of these otherwise ordinary policy tools is precisely what gives East Asian states their strong mobilization capacity.

Yet, while central controls may reduce the risk of shirking, there is still the challenge of obtaining reliable feedback about the quality of campaign implementation, especially in systems where state power is more dispersed. One way that campaigns try to get around this problem is by encouraging mass participation, or to put it another way, by bringing the intended beneficiaries of the policy into an implementing coalition. In contrast to the idea that decentralization is inherently good for development (and other outcomes), the implication is that too much local government autonomy can be detrimental during campaigns and, relatedly, that checks from above and below are important for curbing potential excesses.

RURAL PARTICIPATION

The mobilization of village leaders and activists that accompanies rural modernization campaigns is a departure from the classic stereotype of the disenfranchised peasant. Still, meaningful voice or influence is difficult to achieve, particularly in an authoritarian context. The pressure on local officials to deliver results drives them to exert maximum control over the policy process. This exaggerated reaction to uncertainty is actually consistent with how they would normally behave. As previous research has shown, political elites often dismiss the participation of rural citizens as inefficient and illegitimate.[91] Campaigns may not be able to undo those prejudices, but they can sometimes challenge them by opening up new space for collective action.

Through the delegation of certain tasks to farmers' organizations and village leaders, and through villagers' own acts of negotiation and resistance, the state's goals can be brought into better alignment with rural citizens' needs. Popular mobilization can also help unseat the entrenched interests that stand in the way of change and lead to a greater commitment of local resources—thereby reducing the costs of central policy implementation, while at the same time modifying central policy to suit local conditions. Meaningful participation is more likely if there are rural organizations embedded in the village that can link up with higher levels of government. The ability to communicate with higher-level officials is critical, since it cannot be assumed that local authorities are more responsive to rural interests. They may have views of development that are grounded in urban bias, or they may be too divided or too weak to support the policy. Rather than joining an implementing coalition with the central government and rural citizens, they could form a kind of blocking coalition to support the status quo or reinvent the policy to suit their own interests.

OUTCOMES

In Taiwan, South Korea, and China, campaigns led to only marginal gains in agricultural production and rural incomes, but they changed the village environment in ways that had a profound impact on rural life. The village environment—defined as the quality of village infrastructure, sanitation, and housing—is an extremely important aspect of rural development that is generally underappreciated in scholarly accounts. There are surely good reasons to question the state's involvement in this area. Government officials may benefit politically from the creation of scientifically designed, beautifully manicured villages, which in reality amount to nothing more than vanity projects. Or worse, the state's reorganization of rural society into carefully planned villages may result in economic disaster, as was the case with Tanzania's Ujamaa village campaign of the 1970s.[92] In East Asia, however, campaigns have contributed positively to the village environment, bringing paved roads, electricity, clean water, and trash collection services to poor and isolated communities. Moreover, the success of small-scale projects to upgrade dilapidated and dangerous housing, a common outcome of the region's campaigns, contrasts starkly with the grand failures of authoritarian social engineering. This is not to say that campaigns are a better solution than private investment. But the promise of campaigns is that by stimulating all kinds of investment (private and public, labor and capital, material and nonmaterial), they can deliver greater change to more places in a shorter period of time than market forces alone would produce.

Variation occurs when campaigns and institutions meet: whether campaigns result in positive or negative changes to the village environment (or other areas) depends on the responsiveness of local governments and rural organizations to the goals of the central government and the needs of rural citizens. To briefly summarize how the cases vary, Taiwan's campaign was most successful because its institutions ensured a strong degree of central control and rural participation.

The impact of South Korea's campaign was more mixed because although the central government was able to exert effective control over local officials, the quality of rural participation was moderate compared to that in Taiwan. And in China's case, weak central control and low levels of rural participation resulted in many negative changes to the village environment, including the forced demolition of entire villages and the continuation of rural resource extraction in the form of land grabs. Stated differently, Taiwan's implementing coalition was strong, South Korea's was moderately strong, and China's was weak. In the following pages, I elaborate these points with a comparison of local governments and rural organizations.

Local Governments Compared

Taiwan, South Korea, and China share a similar administrative structure, with power distributed vertically from the central government downward, to the province, city, county, township, and village. After Taiwan and South Korea democratized (starting in the mid-1980s), lower levels of government became more powerful, but this basic structure did not change. Here the term "local government" refers to both the county and township levels. The village government is treated separately, since village officials are closer to the residents they govern and arguably more accountable to them than higher-level officials.

Of the three cases, Taiwan's local authorities were the most inclined to support rural development. In the 1950s–1970s, there were a large number of bureaucrats working on rural issues, and these positions were considered to be of relatively high status. Many local officials were recruited from the grassroots, having served as village leaders or having worked in the local branch of the Farmers' Association. During the course of one's career, it was not uncommon to move between the government and the Farmers' Association, acquiring both managerial and field experience. Taiwan also had favorable structural conditions for bureaucratic oversight. The KMT was a Leninist regime, a hierarchically organized one-party state, which extended its power directly into the villages. The state's successful penetration of the countryside derived from Japan's earlier state-building efforts as well as the KMT's decision to thwart communism through land reform, not to mention the fact that Taiwan is a small island, whereas China is the size of a continent. Central-local government coherence was therefore easier to achieve, and once the center rolled out the Community Development Campaign and definitively moved away from urban bias in the 1970s, there was already a strong pro-rural implementing coalition in place. Along with the Farmers' Associations, local governments in Taiwan not only supported the center's goals but also adopted a more bottom-up, flexible approach to policy implementation.

In contrast, South Korean officials were less inclined to support rural development. In the 1950s and 1960s, local governments had only a handful of people working on rural issues, in part because the Rhee and Park governments were slow to rebuild the agricultural bureaucracy. Agriculture's meager budget and position within the bureaucratic hierarchy made it an unappealing career choice for anyone with talent and ambition. Local officials tried to avoid becoming rural extension agents, which meant that on the whole their expertise was lacking. Nonetheless, South Korea's central government exerted strong control over local authorities for the same reasons just mentioned: the political system was highly centralized and dominated by a single party, state power expanded under colonialism and was consolidated during land reform, and there were just fewer agents to monitor than would have been the case in a larger country. When Park Chung-hee made the decision to prioritize rural development and launch the New Village Movement in 1970, local officials responded immediately, but they were motivated by political pressure much more than policy objectives or the needs of rural citizens. So, while they did join with the central government to form an implementing coalition, they took a more top-down, rigid approach to policy implementation.

In China, local officials' degree of interest and proficiency in rural issues declined as the reform era progressed and the task of urban-industrial development assumed priority. This problem was more serious in China than the other cases on account of reforms that gave rise to "GDP-ism": fiscal decentralization, by allowing local governments to retain a higher proportion of taxes, created strong incentives to grow local industry; and the personnel management system rewarded those officials who could deliver growth with promotions. While early scholarship attributed China's takeoff to these reforms, later work has emphasized the downsides of GDP-ism, ranging from damage to the environment and rural public goods, to corruption, to the difficulties of recentralization and redistribution.[93] Around the same time that the central government unveiled Building a New Socialist Countryside in 2005, it introduced reforms to the cadre evaluation system, with the aim of bringing local government incentives into closer alignment with the campaign's goals. Faced with new pressures, local officials could not just ignore the policy. China is a one-party, unitary state in which officials are accountable to those working at the level above them. And yet the government's mobilization capacity is not matched by a similar capacity for bureaucratic oversight. In other words, the center successfully spurred local authorities into action, but it could not adequately monitor their performance.

This unusual combination of strong mobilization capacity and weak bureaucratic oversight stems from the paradox of decentralized authoritarianism in

China. I borrow this term from Pierre Landry, who notes that China's share of subnational government expenditures, about 55 percent for the 1958–2002 period, makes it one of the most decentralized countries in the world.[94] To explain why decentralization has not given rise to regionally based competition with the center, he argues that the party-state uses its personnel system to build political loyalty. I use the concept of decentralized authoritarianism somewhat differently to explain why policy implementation is so difficult in China, an issue that Landry never really clarifies. It is true that local officials' political careers ultimately depend on their relationship with higher-level officials, if not the center itself, and that this condition of political dependency means they are likely to follow central orders minimally, or excessively in the context of campaign. However, monitoring is extremely costly because of decentralizing reforms, the enormous scale of the state, and the compartmentalization of local governments (known in China as the *tiao-kuai* system of dividing government offices into vertical, functional "lines" and horizontal, geographic "areas"). As a result, local officials can easily adjust or manipulate central policies to suit their own interests.

This level of discretionary local authority over how and what to implement did not exist in Taiwan and Korea. In those cases, the center achieved controlled decentralization. There were strong checks on local officials from above, combined with some checks from below, due to the mobilization of rural organizations and village activists. In contrast, the Chinese case is better described as co-opted decentralization or even decentralized chaos, with weak checks on local officials from above and virtually no checks from below. In many places, local officials blocked central efforts to promote balanced rural development by prioritizing only those goals that benefited the urban-industrial sector, such as housing construction and land consolidation. In addition, the fact that rural citizens were, for the most part, left out of the policy process made the aggressive pursuit of those goals that much easier.

Rural Organizations Compared (and a Theory of Farmers' Organizations)

East Asia has exceptionally strong farmers' organizations, perhaps some of the strongest in the world in terms of their commercial and political influence.[95] One oft-cited reason is the cooperative tradition of rice cultivation at the village level, but this explanation ignores the important role of the state in supporting farmers' organizations.[96] During the process of industrialization, farmers' organizations served as the key institutional link between the developmental state and rural society, and this legacy continues through the present.

The purpose here is not to provide a comprehensive account of the region's rural organizations, since there are simply too many to cover: state and non-state, traditional and modern, not to mention the various ties (lineage, religion) and functions (labor, defense) on which they might be based. Rather, the focus is on production-oriented organizations that were sanctioned and promoted by the state, including the Farmers' Association (FA or FAs) in Taiwan, the National Agricultural Cooperative Federation (NACF) in South Korea, and the Farmers' Professional Cooperatives (FPCs) in China. In addition, the activities of organizations involved in campaign implementation are analyzed. These include Taiwan's community development councils, South Korea's village development committees, and China's peasant councils.

Setting aside for a moment the issue of participation in campaigns, there are two hypotheses about rural organization effectiveness that can be derived from existing literature. The first is about linkage and the second about autonomy:

1. *Farmers' organizations are more likely to benefit small farmers if they have an extensive membership base, with strong ties to the village community, and are formally linked to higher levels of the state that control key developmental resources.*

2. *Farmers' organizations are more likely to be developmental, as opposed to primarily extractive agents of the state and big business, if their leaders are actual farmers, preferably selected by farmer members, and if they have financial and managerial independence, giving them a certain degree of voice, political power, and influence over rural policy.*

In an important 1970s study of rural organizations across sixteen countries in Asia, Norman Uphoff and Milton Esman found that linkage, which is often inversely related to autonomy, was actually more important for development. They write: "Of key significance was the extent and effectiveness of linkages between and among institutions, horizontally with other organizations at the same level and especially vertically between local organizations and structures at the center of government which set policy and allocate resources essential to success in rural development."[97] The study goes on to characterize effective local organization as having multiple channels linking the village with higher levels of government, leadership that is subject to controls from above and below, and institutional legitimacy among farmer members.[98] My research supports the Uphoff and Esman thesis about linkage but also pushes back on their claims about how it trades off with (and matters more than) autonomy. As the Taiwanese case demonstrates, farmers' organizations can exhibit both linkage and autonomy, the combination of which allows for meaningful participation in the policy process.

I should point out that this conceptualization is slightly different from Peter Evans's notion of embedded autonomy. Used to describe state-business relations, the basic idea is that state cooperation with the private sector (embeddedness) can keep predatory corruption in check, while state isolation from society (autonomy) can prevent state capture by private interests.[99] Although the language is similar, embeddedness, compared to linkage, conveys a stronger and more intertwined relationship. To clarify, I would not characterize Korean farmers' organizations as embedded in rural society, because even though they had an extensive membership base (one measure of linkage), they were not always in close contact with villagers. Nor would I say that Korean or Taiwanese organizations were embedded in higher levels of the state, since despite their having formal channels of communication (another measure of linkage), their representation at the top was actually very limited.

On a related note, the concept of corporatism is only somewhat useful for understanding East Asian farmers' organizations. Their corporatist features—the fact that they were created by the state, regulated from the top down, and granted a monopoly of representation over farmers—meant that they were more involved in rural policy implementation than is usually the case in developing countries.[100] However, the Chinese case did not conform to this pattern, and the other cases (though I do describe them as corporatist) were not as similar as one might expect.

I contend that the institutional characteristics of farmers' organizations, by shaping the distribution of resources, can determine the prospects for broad-based agricultural development. They can also affect the rural policy process itself—whether implementation is more flexible and participatory, or rigid and bureaucratic, as well as rural citizens' ability to push for policy change. Although the East Asian cases are often grouped together, I find that differences in their farmers' organizations account for why Taiwan had the strongest record of production (an area where campaigns had limited impact) and for why its government was the most responsive to rural citizens. South Korea was less successful because the NACF exhibited linkage but not autonomy, and China stands out as the weakest case, with the FPCs lacking both linkage and autonomy.

South Korea's organizations were structured in the same way as Taiwan's but were ultimately less effective. On the positive side, they both had an encompassing membership, integrated services (extension, credit, marketing), and close links with the agricultural bureaucracy, owing to their parastatal status and branches at each level of government. Land reform also meant that they were not dominated by large farmers. Yet the NACF was not subject to strong controls from below, which undermined its credibility as a service and advocacy organization. Comparing the two systems, Larry Burmeister and colleagues describe the

FAs as more autonomous and rooted in rural society. They were more democratic as well, because of US policy recommendations and the KMT's own need
to build its legitimacy among the rural population. Above the township, the system only allowed for indirect representation of farmers' interests (a committee
at each level selected delegates to the level above it), but township elections were
extremely competitive and served to increase farmers' sense of ownership over
the FAs. Significantly, elected leaders were native Taiwanese, not mainlanders,
further strengthening the public's perception of FA independence. In contrast,
South Korean farmers did not elect NACF leaders and viewed the organization
as part of the government. Moreover, top NACF leaders came from a military
background instead of farming, and they interacted with members infrequently.
Credit services were not really offered until the 1970s, and the majority of funds
came from central transfers rather than commercial activities. Taiwan was different in each of these respects.[101] By the late 1960s, the FAs had gained considerable
political power. They raised concerns about deteriorating rural conditions and
advocated against urban bias, pressuring the government to move away from
extractive policies.

The qualities that made Taiwan's FAs successful constitute a package that is
rarely found among farmers' organizations in the developing world. Instead, a
situation like China's is more common. Chinese FPCs, which only gained legal
status in 2007, are very decentralized, operating mostly within the boundaries of a
single township. In cases where commercial activities cover a broader geographic
area, it is usually because the cooperative is controlled by a large agribusiness
rather than small-scale producers. In general, FPC membership and functions
are very limited in scope. They have restricted access to capital, and their leaders
are recruited by the local government. Although they are tied to local authorities, they are disconnected from higher levels of government, so they have little
political influence and are only minimally involved in policy implementation.
The aggregate effect of the Chinese system is a kind of enclave development that
is uneven and unequal. In short, the FPCs hardly resemble their more powerful counterparts in Taiwan and South Korea, or Japan for that matter. And the
chances that they will evolve into a national organization are slim, since the CCP
does not want to risk empowering the "peasant majority."[102]

Returning to the subject of campaigns, in all three cases farmers' organizations and rural councils were involved in implementation but with varying
effects. Consistent with the above analysis, Taiwan's Community Development
Campaign was more flexible and participatory, resulting in major improvements to the village environment and fewer problems than in the other cases.
Villagers elected leaders to the community development council and could
choose which projects to implement. The FAs provided technical support for

production-related infrastructure, tailoring their recommendations to villagers' needs. Older homes were preserved and renovated instead of torn down and rebuilt, so there was much less displacement than occurred in China. Additionally, the campaign imposed a smaller financial burden on villagers: Taiwan's government covered over 60 percent of campaign expenses, whereas the Korean and Chinese governments covered less than 40 percent, even though more money was spent overall in those countries.[103]

The implementation of South Korea's New Village Movement was flexible in some ways and rigid in others. While certain projects were basically mandatory, for example the installation of tile roofs on village homes, there was also some leeway for villages to be innovative. Unlike China, where county and township officials made nearly every decision about project implementation, in Korea decisions were often made at the village level with clear input from local activists, who were elected to the village development committee. A major exception was the government's attempt to orchestrate a green revolution by forcibly distributing a high-yield variety of rice called Tong'il (unification). The NACF used a mix of carrots and sticks to boost production: it raised rice procurement prices and had its officers destroy the seedbeds of non-Tong'il varieties. However, by the late 1970s, the government could no longer afford its price support policy, and Tong'il was abandoned because of serious crop failures and the fact that consumers preferred other varieties. If the NACF had been more responsive to farmers' concerns about Tong'il and promoted it gradually, instead of getting swept up in the atmosphere of the campaign, then perhaps Korea's green revolution would have been more successful.

Finally, as part of Building a New Socialist Countryside, the Chinese government called for the creation of FPCs in order to stimulate production. They were essentially treated as a campaign objective rather than partners in its implementation. Local officials supported the establishment of hundreds of thousands of cooperatives within just a few years and required many of them to waive membership fees. This move was good for cooperative expansion but bad for sustainability. Chinese survey research shows that most FPCs have a short life span, typically less than five years, and are largely dependent on the government for financial support.[104] So while some gains in agricultural production were made during the campaign, the FPCs' contribution appears to be minimal. Other factors, such as subsidies and the growth of agribusiness, were probably more decisive. Furthermore, China's efforts to alter the village environment provoked a storm of criticism from officials and the public alike for being top-down and excessive. In contrast with Taiwan and Korea, where rural councils were formed in every village, many local governments in China did not even attempt to include villagers in the policy process. A few places supported the creation of peasant councils, but in practice they had little room to make decisions. Projects were handed down to them by the local government and enforced by cadre work teams, who often monitored implementation on a daily basis. The end result was a continuation of urban bias: applying industrial principles to agriculture and urban models of residential life to villages. Millions of villagers were forced to "move upstairs" into apartments, give up their livestock and vegetable gardens, and hand over their former housing plots to the government.

To reiterate an earlier point, saying that campaigns were important in East Asia is an empirical observation, not a normative statement. Campaigns are powerful, but they are also potentially disastrous. Moreover, tensions in the theory suggest that positive outcomes are highly contingent—that is, dependent on a combination of variables and mechanisms that do not necessarily go together. First, although the main explanatory variables, institutions and campaigns, follow different logics and make different contributions to development, campaigns need institutions to function. Second, campaigns work better with centralized bureaucratic control and decentralized rural participation, which can help reduce the risk of false or excessive compliance at the local level. Lastly, farmers' organizations are more effective if they possess linkage and autonomy. These qualities facilitate the transfer of resources between (and within) sectors and are critical for the articulation of rural interests, whether under normal circumstances or during periods of extraordinary change. To demonstrate how campaigns operated in a particular historical context, I now turn to the experience of Japan.

Broader Implications

Campaigns in Japan

As mentioned previously, Japan made significant gains in agricultural production in the prewar period, as a result of private and state efforts to build production-related infrastructure, spread new technologies, and organize society in such a way that most, if not all, farmers could access extension services. This legacy had a positive effect on postwar agricultural development, in addition to land reform, which improved the social and economic position of former tenants and stabilized the countryside politically. Yet Japan's institutions are only part of the story of its rural transformation. What is less well known is the history of state-led campaigns, beginning with the Local Improvement Movement at the turn of the twentieth century, continuing with the Rural Revitalization Campaign in the wake of the Great Depression, and then resuming after World War II with the New Village and New Life Campaigns. The Japanese case therefore illustrates the argument in brief, that in response to rural decline East

Asian governments turned to rural modernization campaigns to both protect and develop the countryside.

In launching the Local Improvement Movement (1900–1918), the Meiji government aimed to prevent the emergence of crippling social problems characteristic of Western industrial societies, including class hostilities, labor strife, and the destruction of the village. Such problems, officials believed, would hurt national unity and undermine the state's ability to finance industrialization and imperialism. As Kenneth Pyle explains, the campaign's intense focus on developing rural areas stemmed from practical considerations (four-fifths of the population was rural in 1900) as well as deeply rooted "traditions of Japanese political thought which predisposed leaders to regard agrarian society as fundamental."[105]

Several concrete programs were rolled out under the banner of local improvement: the expansion of elementary education; the transfer of hamlet common lands to the administrative village; the merging of local shrines into a single state Shinto shrine; the diffusion of agricultural innovations; the promotion of village financial and economic planning; and the integration of local citizens' groups into the state administration. All these programs were designed to reduce parochialism, build national loyalty, and further economic development. Even though the campaign fell short of fully realizing these goals—only about 10 percent of villages drafted plans for economic development, and the proposals for shrines and common lands were met with resistance—it did succeed at fostering emperor-centered nationalism and bringing local associations into closer contact with the state. In this way, the campaign marked a departure from the previous policy of laissez-faire to one of significant state intervention in the countryside. It also set a precedent for similar, more intense campaigns in succeeding decades.[106]

The origins of the Rural Revitalization Campaign (1932–1941) lie in two streams of social protest that preceded it: the tenant union movement and the agrarianist movement. Ann Waswo explains that a series of economic shocks in the Taisho era (1912–1926) led to increased conflict between tenants and landlords. The establishment of rice inspection programs caused landlords to impose quality standards on the rice tenants paid in rent, which disadvantaged small-scale tenants who farmed inferior land and bred resentment among large-scale tenants who wanted to sell their rent rice at market value. Additionally, the dramatic increase in rice prices during World War I affected not just urban residents but also farmers who had to purchase rice for their own consumption. After the war, crop prices dropped sharply and were unstable throughout the 1920s. In response, more than four thousand tenant unions were formed across the country, and the number of officially recorded tenancy disputes escalated from fewer than five hundred in 1920 to over sixty-eight hundred in 1935.[107]

Agrarianism (known as *nohonshugi* in Japanese) began much earlier but reached its culmination around the same time as the tenant union movement. Agrarianist writers in the late 1800s extolled farmers as gatekeepers of morality and were critical of the fact that villages had to bear the costs of industrialization.[108] During the Local Improvement Movement, the government popularized many agrarianist ideas, all the while extracting resources from the countryside. In the 1920s, agrarianism evolved into a popular, antiurban and antigovernment movement. Some agrarianists even joined forces with the military to assassinate Prime Minister Inukai Tsuyoshi in 1932. The movement's legacy, however, was far greater than this violent episode. It produced a generation of rural spokespersons who successfully lobbied the government for relief after the Great Depression devastated Japan's silk and rice markets, two mainstays of the rural economy. It was also a force behind local revitalization initiatives, which provided inspiration for the national campaign.[109]

By the 1930s, Japanese agriculture was in crisis, with farmers subject to exploitative tenancy conditions, heavy tax burdens, high levels of debt, and stagnant consumption. In August 1932, the government convened a "Village Rescue" session of the Diet, during which it committed 1.6 billion yen to rural relief over three years, an amount that signaled its prioritization of the countryside. Given the severity of conditions, however, it was still not enough, so the Rural Revitalization Campaign (formally called the Farm, Mountain, and Fishing Village Economic Revitalization Campaign) was launched to supplement government support with collective self-help.[110] This campaign was about charting a course out of the Depression and finding a way to bring middling farmers, who were the most active in the tenant union and agrarianist movements, "back into the fold."[111]

The Rural Revitalization Campaign was very broad in scope, eventually reaching 80 percent of Japan's villages. Coordinated by the Ministry of Agriculture and Forestry, general standards for revitalization were developed and passed down to participating villages. For example, there were guidelines for increasing production, strengthening cooperatives, restructuring debts, renovating kitchens and toilets, and educating villagers in the teachings of Ninomiya Sontoku, a nineteenth-century agricultural and political leader who stressed the importance of thrift, diligence, and self-sufficiency.[112] Despite the state's heavy hand in promoting the campaign, it was implemented in a very participatory way, with input from a wide range of local actors and organizations. In fact, every household was involved in village planning, and no two plans (for different villages or even for different households within the village) were exactly alike.[113] This flexibility diminished after 1937, when the campaign was repurposed to support Japan's war with China. Yet this fusion of rural revitalization and wartime mobilization,

Kerry Smith argues, is no reason to dismiss the campaign as regressive or fascist, since in its early years it was a grassroots movement that delivered many economic benefits to impoverished farmers. In the village where he conducted research, the campaign led to higher productivity, lower debts, greater savings, and improved public infrastructure.[114]

The New Village and New Life Campaigns of the 1950s–1960s represent a continuation of these earlier initiatives. Although the agricultural sector performed well after land reform, the rural-urban income gap grew wider, such that by 1960 rural households were earning 32 percent less than urban households. This income differential led most farmers to either migrate to the cities permanently or to seek part-time employment in the nonagricultural sector, once again prompting public concerns about rural decline.[115] In addition to a host of subsidies and price supports designed to protect farmers, the government's New Village Campaign stressed village planning, collective infrastructure projects, and training a new generation of leaders in self-help. Similarly, the New Life Campaign called on villagers, especially housewives, to be "frugal, rational, healthy, and mutually cooperative."[116] Neither campaign was very successful at reducing rural-urban disparities, but their connection to the prewar period is noteworthy. Simon Partner has suggested that they were part of a larger "Lifestyle Improvement Movement," lasting from roughly 1925 until 1965, which combined state and private efforts to achieve "hard" infrastructural and economic goals, as well as "soft" spiritual and behavioral goals.[117] Sheldon Garon similarly argues that such "moral suasion campaigns" have been used continuously by the Japanese state as a tool of social management from the early Meiji period onward.[118]

More so than the other cases, the line between state campaigns and social movements was often blurred in Japan, largely because of the strength and independence of its rural organizations. In spite of the expanding reach of the state, rural hamlets maintained a high degree of autonomy and a rich associational life. It was local actors who initiated the Rural Revitalization Campaign, and it was their efforts that sustained the campaign once it was scaled up. To take a different example, one reason the New Village Campaign fizzled out is that the national farmers' association, Nokyo, did not support it.[119] Structurally, Nokyo descended from the Meiji period's National Agricultural Association. Politically, it inherited the tenant unions' tradition of rural collective action. This history, combined with Japan's more open political system, made the state somewhat captive to agrarian interests in the postwar period.[120] With passage of the Basic Agricultural Law in 1961, the state finally moved away from self-help and adopted a sweeping set of benefits that essentially guaranteed income parity between farmers and workers, a point that underscores Nokyo's disproportionate political power.[121]

This overview of the Japanese case, though certainly incomplete, is suggestive of the argument I am making about institutions and campaigns. On a basic level, it highlights the centrality of campaigns in an unexpected context—a country that is not in a state of perpetual revolution and, to the contrary, is known for its technical-rational approach to policymaking. It also provides preliminary support for the contention that campaigns can have a positive effect on development, especially when the state partners with rural citizens. Finally, Japan is significant because of its connections with the other cases. While it is a well-established fact that Taiwan, South Korea, and China have, to a certain extent, regarded Japan as a development model, it is important to understand that campaigns are also part of that model. For instance, there are clear parallels between South Korea's New Village Movement of the 1970s and Japan's Rural Revitalization Campaign of the 1930s, which was actually implemented in Korea by Japanese colonial authorities. At the risk of oversimplifying what was surely a complex process of diffusion, learning, and innovation, the implication is that rural modernization campaigns may have originated in Japan before spreading to other countries in the region.

The idea that institutions and campaigns were both important in East Asian rural development is a departure from the developmental state literature and from previous scholarship that describes state intervention in rural society as predatory or even pathologically destructive. For Robert Bates and Michael Lipton, the main cause of rural underdevelopment is urban bias, as manifested in price and trade policies that sacrifice the interests of small farmers for the sake of the government, industrial producers, urban consumers, and large farmers.[122] East Asia was no exception. For several decades, Taiwan, South Korea, and China exhibited high levels of urban bias. Eventually all three countries reversed course, but this did not amount to a retreat of the state and the triumph of undistorted markets, as Bates and Lipton would prescribe. Rather, greater state intervention occurred in the form of rural modernization campaigns.

For James Scott, most state-led development schemes are doomed to fail because they are based on utopian, high-modernist visions of how nature and society should be ordered, and these failures are especially pronounced in places with strong authoritarian states and weak civil societies. While the tragedy of the Great Leap Forward may easily be explained by this logic, it is less useful for understanding cases like South Korea's New Village Movement, which resembled the Leap in many ways but turned out differently. This is not to dismiss the framework entirely—all the campaigns in this study were, to some extent, about making the countryside more legible, and perhaps the varied effects of campaigns ultimately comes down to the degree of "local knowledge" that was incorporated.[123] Still, the idea that state intervention, especially through campaigns, is inherently destructive (an idea closely associated with Scott) is something that my research does not support.

The fact that Park Chung-hee repeatedly called the New Village Movement a "great leap forward" raises some interesting questions.[124] Why, despite growing international awareness of the Leap's failure, would Park invoke this slogan unless he believed in the potential of campaigns to unleash forces for development? What does this language suggest about the Korean case, specifically its characterization as a prototypical developmental state? To put it simply, Park's regime was simultaneously technocratic and mobilizational. The same paradox is evident in Taiwan and China. It can be seen not only across different policy realms (i.e., industrial versus rural policy) but also within the domain of rural policy itself, with local governments drawing up meticulous plans for campaign implementation and using instruments like standardized performance evaluations to assess campaign outcomes.

Apart from technocratic governance, another theme of the developmental state literature is that state-society relations are best understood through the lenses of corporatism and embedded autonomy. While these concepts have mostly been used to explain state-business relations, they are also applicable to the rural sector. State power was extended into the villages through the creation of quasi-governmental farmers' organizations, which functioned more like parastatal institutions than representatives of civil society. They cooperated with the state to promote development and rarely voiced any kind of political opposition. Most accounts of state-society relations stop there, but as Atul Kohli explains, corporatism and mobilization went hand in hand to solidify state power: "Since corporatism may create only a quiescent exclusion and thus may not add to the state's overall power, the more ambitious cohesive-capitalist states [South Korea] even attempt controlled ideological mobilization of popular groups—say, in the name of the nation—so as to also harness their energies to pursue state goals."[125]

Relaxing certain assumptions about how developmental states operate reveals different strands of political culture and modes of politics that, examined together, provide a more complete understanding of how rural development unfolded in the region. It also promises to shed light on an understudied approach to development, which states throughout the developing world have used historically, and will continue to use, in order to tackle the problems of rural poverty and underdevelopment. The particular experiences of Taiwan, South Korea, and China, and the story of how institutions and campaigns interacted to affect development outcomes in those countries, constitute the subject of the next three chapters.

2

RURAL DEVELOPMENT IN TAIWAN, 1950s–1970s

In Taiwan, the defeated Kuomintang regime (KMT or Chinese Nationalist Party) sought to regain control of mainland China by transforming the island into a model province that would legitimize its right to rule. Knowing that the Chinese Communist Party (CCP) had established its rural base in large part through redistributive land reform, the KMT carried out a comprehensive land reform program in the early 1950s, which led to the creation of a smallholder farm economy with extremely low levels of inequality. In addition to land reform, the KMT built up a rural extension system to provide technical education and production inputs to farmers. These institutions resulted in nearly two decades of accelerated growth. According to Taiwan's former president Lee Teng-hui, who is perhaps the only agricultural economist to ever become a head of state, agriculture played a textbook role in Taiwan's development. It met the domestic demand for food, accounted for a substantial share of exports, and provided capital and labor for industrialization.[1] As one of the first countries in the post–World War II period to achieve industrialized nation status, Taiwan stands out as an exemplary case of successful development.

Taiwan's rapid transition from a poor, agricultural society to a wealthy, industrialized nation has received much scholarly attention. Robert Wade's research, for example, reveals how the government of Taiwan, like Japan, was able to effectively "govern the market" and promote development through well-formulated institutions and industrial policy.[2] While industrial policy is central to many accounts of East Asian development, the role of rural policy has been less emphasized. Moreover, among the scholars who have written about Taiwan's rural sector, there is a tendency to focus narrowly on production and present an instrumentalist view of agriculture. Consistent with Lee Teng-hui's assessment, the implication is that agriculture's value lies in how much it contributed to industrialization.

In this chapter, I explain Taiwan's impressive record of rural development as an important end in itself. First, I describe patterns of change in agricultural production, rural living standards, and the village environment. I show that uneven progress across these different areas—the fact that growth in production was greater and occurred earlier than improvements in the other areas—can be attributed to the siphoning of rural economic gains for urban-industrial development. Second, I link these outcomes with rural institutional arrangements, asserting that while farmers benefited from favorable initial conditions, US support, and land reform, the more crucial factor behind Taiwan's success was the quality of its farmers' organizations. The Taiwan Farmers' Association (FA or FAs) ensured that growth in agricultural production was achieved throughout the countryside instead of being concentrated in a few places. It was also the main actor behind policy changes that would advance the broader interests of small farmers. I contend that the FAs' power derived from somewhat contradictory attributes: linkage with the state and autonomy from it. The remainder of the chapter sheds light on what happened after the government's urban-biased policies were reversed in the 1970s. I examine Taiwan's Community Development Campaign and argue that the combination of appropriate goals, central control over local authorities, and rural participation led to several positive outcomes. Although the campaign did little to strengthen production or the relative income position of farmers (government pricing policies had a more direct impact), it did have a major effect on improving village infrastructure, sanitation, and housing.

This case study illustrates the conditions under which farmers' organizations and campaigns are more likely to promote development. To be clear, very few countries in the world have achieved the same level of success for the same reasons, which makes Taiwan something of an outlier but also an interesting case theoretically. In contrast with much of the peasant politics literature, which focuses on the negative effects of state intervention and the informal foundations of peasant resistance, Taiwan is an example of how small farmers can be actively involved in development through formal organizations with close ties to the state.[3] Related to this point, the FAs' power can only be understood in the larger political context of postwar Taiwan. Although the KMT was in some ways more Leninist and repressive than it had been on the mainland, it allowed local elections to take place for the entire martial law period (1950–1987).[4] After 1969, elections were expanded to include a few seats in the parliament, and this open-ing gave the FAs, which had been holding their own elections for over a decade, an opportunity to influence policy.[5] Without the associations and their ability to organize voters, it is unlikely that Taiwan's national politicians would have been as responsive to rural issues. Urban-biased policies would have remained in place longer, and change would have been initiated only after rural conditions had reached a point of crisis. In short, the FAs were Leninist transmission belt organizations that actually incorporated farmers' interests.[6] And while Taiwan's circumstances were unique, a general lesson is that bottom-up policy change is possible in competitive authoritarian regimes.[7]

The way the government responded is also significant. Of the three cases, Taiwan perhaps most closely conforms to the expectations of the developmental state model. Yet even there, at a time when the regime was becoming more tech-nocratic and institutionalized, mass mobilization was used to accomplish state goals. Chiang Ching-kuo, Chiang Kai-shek's son and successor, could easily have been mistaken for a mainland politician in this 1972 address to Taiwan's farmers: "Presently, as a result of the country's industrialization, numerous difficulties have befallen the agricultural sector. Although this may be an unavoidable part of the economic development process, the government must take responsibility for resolving these problems and improve your working and living conditions. We have therefore decided to accelerate rural construction by mobilizing all gov-ernment agencies and the power of the masses to help push forward this new campaign."[8] As this chapter demonstrates, the KMT's rural policies were both technocratic and mobilizational, and it was the combined effects of institutions and campaigns that contributed to Taiwan's success.

Changes in Taiwanese Rural Sector Development

The transformation of agriculture in postwar Taiwan occurred in stages: recov-ery (1945–1951), accelerated growth (1952–1967), and agricultural adjust-ment (1968–present). This section broadly describes rural sector change in the 1950s–1970s, the most significant decades for industrialization and rural development.

Taiwan's economic recovery from World War II was complicated by a major and violent political transition from Japanese to Chinese Nationalist rule. After fifty years of colonial governance (1895–1945), Taiwan was formally retroceded to the Republic of China (ROC) on October 25, 1945. The Taiwanese, who ini-tially celebrated the restoration of Chinese power, soon became disillusioned by government corruption, their exclusion from politics, and worsening economic conditions. Inflation, as measured by the Taipei wholesale price index, skyrocketed from 260 percent in 1946 to 3,500 percent in 1949.[9] Rising tensions between Taiwanese and mainlanders erupted in February 1947, when protests against police violence in Taipei escalated into an island-wide uprising against the KMT. The government responded by dispatching troops to round up and execute an estimated twenty thousand Taiwanese, including most of the intellectual and social elite. The uprising and its brutal suppression, known as the 2–28 Incident, badly damaged the KMT's legitimacy, but it also strengthened the regime's tenuous hold on the territory by silencing dissent. On December 9, 1949, as the CCP emerged victorious from the Chinese Civil War, Chiang Kai-shek relocated the ROC capital to Taipei, and by 1952 about two million refugees (including half a million troops) from the mainland had arrived in Taiwan.[10]

The KMT's immediate goals were to feed the army and the civilian population, stabilize prices, and speed up the process of industrialization. In the 1950s, more than half of Taiwan's population lived in rural areas (about 4.7 million out of 9.3 million people), and despite severe infrastructural damage from war, agriculture was the largest and strongest sector of the economy.[11] It was also the main source of exports and therefore a critical sector for earning foreign currency, which could be used to finance industrialization. Major export crops included rice, sugar, tea, fruits, vegetables, and citronella oil.[12] These circumstances pointed to an obvious policy agenda: to accomplish its goals, the KMT would have to develop agriculture. And by all accounts, it succeeded.

Agricultural production was restored to prewar levels by 1951 and then entered a fifteen-year period of accelerated growth, averaging 4.6 percent annually. Overall, between 1952 and 1967, staple crop production increased 82 percent, and livestock production increased 186 percent. Output of fruits and vegetables increased 476 percent and 107 percent, respectively, providing the basis for a large-scale food-processing industry. Agricultural exports grew 128 percent and constituted the majority of total exports until 1966, at which point the relative decline of agriculture had become apparent. Yet even as Taiwan confronted the problem of agricultural adjustment, the sector still performed strongly, averaging 3.2 percent annual growth between 1968 and 1979.[13]

Most economists agree that Taiwan's industrial takeoff would not have been possible without the resources supplied by agriculture. From 1951 to 1955, the net outflow of capital from agriculture constituted 75 percent of domestic capital formation, and it remained a key source of capital until about 1970, when the terms of trade shifted in favor of agriculture, meaning more money flowed into the sector than left it.[14] With respect to labor, migration from the countryside did not occur on a massive scale, but the transfer of surplus labor nonetheless accounted for about 47 percent of the increase in the nonagricultural workforce in the 1950–1960s.[15]

It is remarkable that Taiwan was able to generate a rural surplus given the constraints on agriculture, namely limited land resources and a high population density. Taiwan's topography consists mainly of rugged mountains and foothills that are unsuitable for agriculture. Less than one-third of its land is arable, and most of that land was brought under cultivation during the colonial era. In the postwar period, Taiwan's cultivated land area remained nearly constant, expanding only slightly from 23 to 26 percent between 1945 and 1975. Despite these limited resources, the rural population grew by about 65 percent during the same period, from 3.4 to 5.6 million.[16] According to Samuel Ho, agricultural growth was accomplished through the widespread adoption of intercropping (i.e., planting a second crop between the rows of the first crop before the latter is harvested), mechanization, and the intensive use of chemical inputs such as fertilizers, insecticides, and fungicides. His research shows that the contributions of land and labor were insignificant compared to increases in working capital or chemical inputs, which accounted for nearly 60 percent of all gains in production between 1951 and 1970.[17]

The government used several mechanisms to extract the surplus from producers, including monopoly control over the sale of fertilizers and compulsory rice purchases. Under the rice-fertilizer barter system (1948–1972), Taiwanese farmers were paid only 70 percent of world market prices for rice and were forced to pay about 40 percent more for fertilizer than Japanese, Dutch, American, or Indian farmers.[18] Such price distortions, also known as price twists or price scissors, had a negative effect on farm incomes, which increased slightly after land reform and then remained constant until the barter system was phased out. In fact, virtually all gains in rural incomes during this period can be traced to the rise of off-farm employment opportunities.[19]

Rural living standards and the village environment improved at a slower pace than agricultural production. Besides unfavorable pricing policies, another problem facing rural households was the declining size of Taiwan's farms. Although land reform drastically reduced tenancy rates and created a more equal society, it also resulted in very small landholdings, made even smaller by the postwar population boom. In 1952, the average farm size was 1.29 hectares (3.19 acres); by 1976, it was only 1.06 hectares (2.62 acres).[20] Significantly, about 42 percent of farmers actually cultivated less than 0.5 hectares (1.24 acres), an amount too small to support a typical family.[21] If it were not for Taiwan's decentralized pattern of industrialization, which started under the Japanese with the development of the food-processing sector, rural households probably would have struggled to survive. Unlike South Korea, where industry was concentrated in the cities, Taiwanese farmers could engage in part-time farming and supplement their incomes with factory work.[22]

Despite the rise of part-time farming and the diversification of incomes, most rural households perceived that their overall welfare was slow to improve. In 1964, sociologist Martin M. C. Yang conducted a survey of rural living conditions in Taiwan, collecting data on nutrition, water, housing, clothing, transportation, communication, and health care for a sample of 3,075 households. To assess the impact of land reform on different types of households, the survey targeted six groups: former tenants, tenants, original owner-cultivators, hired farm laborers, former landlords, and nonfarmers. With the exception of former tenants and nonfarmers, the majority of households from all other groups reported no improvement or even a deterioration of living conditions since land reform. In addition, over 38 percent of former tenants reported no improvement in living conditions, a surprising finding given that they had the most to gain from land reform. Yang asserts that cultural modesty, rising expectations, and population growth explain some of the dissatisfaction, as rural families incurred more debts related to an increase in marriages, new home construction, and education costs. Consumption patterns in some of the specific areas surveyed also reveal a story of gradual progress rather than decline.[23] While these explanations for the gap between perceived and actual living conditions are reasonable, one thing the analysis fails to mention is how economic policy during that time was designed to exploit agriculture.

Aside from the hidden taxes on rice and fertilizer just mentioned, several other measures also suggest that urban bias was a problem in Taiwan. For example, data on the intersectoral terms of trade, calculated as the prices received for farm products divided by the prices paid for nonagricultural commodities and services, show that conditions were unfavorable toward farmers until about 1975.[24] Similarly, the nominal and relative rates of assistance for agriculture (the NRA and RRA) were negative in Taiwan until about 1970, meaning that domestic farm product prices were well below international market prices and that government assistance to agriculture was far less than its assistance to industry.[25] Lastly, the distribution of gross fixed capital formation reflects how government investment was strongly skewed toward industry: while agriculture's share declined from 25 to 8 percent between 1951 and 1973, industry's share increased from 45 to 67 percent during the same period.[26]

As a result of this policy environment, farmers did not benefit as much as they should have from the gains in agricultural production, and the rural-urban income gap widened. The average rural household already earned 25 percent less than the average urban household in 1953. By 1968, the difference was

42 percent.[27] It was also in the late 1960s that Taiwan entered its agricultural adjustment phase. The primary sector's share of GDP, exports, and employment all dropped significantly, and the rate of out-migration increased.[28] Table 3 provides a snapshot of Taiwan's structural economic transformation in the 1950s–1970s and shows that by 1981 Taiwan had emerged as an industrialized country. What is unfortunately not revealed by this kind of macroeconomic data is that the 1970s was a good decade for farmers.

Following the passage of the Accelerated Rural Development Program (ARDP) in 1972, the rice-fertilizer barter system was abolished. This was a watershed event, marking a shift in government policy from squeezing the rural sector to protecting it. The nominal rate of protection for agricultural products increased

TABLE 3. Agricultural and Industrial Sector Change in Taiwan, 1952–1981

YEAR	1952	1957	1962	1967	1972	1977	1981
Population							
Total population (millions)	8.1	9.7	11.5	13.3	15.3	16.8	18.1
Rural population (millions)	4.3	4.8	5.5	5.9	5.9	5.6	5.0
Share of rural population in total population (%)	53.1	49.5	47.8	44.4	38.6	33.3	27.6
GDP[1]							
Share of agriculture in GDP (%)	35.9	31.7	29.2	23.8	14.1	12.5	8.7
Share of industry in GDP (%)	18.0	23.9	25.7	30.8	40.4	43.7	44.5
Exports							
Share of agricultural exports in total exports (%)	91.9	87.4	49.5	38.4	16.7	12.5	7.8
Share of industrial exports in total exports (%)	8.1	12.6	50.5	61.6	83.3	87.5	92.2
Employment							
Share of agricultural workers in economically active population (%)	61.0	58.2	55.3	49.4	39.9	33.8	28.0
Share of industrial workers in economically active population (%)	9.3	10.4	11.5	14.6	19.8	26.5	31.2

AVERAGE ANNUAL GROWTH RATES	1953–1962	1963–1972	1973–1981
GDP growth rate (%)	7.4	11.0	7.4
Agricultural production growth rate (%)	4.8	4.0	2.1
Industrial production growth rate (%)	11.7	18.6	11.0

Source: *Taiwan Statistical Data Book* 1982, 4, 8–9, 21, 34, 57, 60, 77, 189.

[1] GDP data based on constant 1976 market prices. Agriculture includes the farming, forestry, fishery, and livestock sectors. Industry includes the manufacturing, mining, and public utilities sectors.

rapidly in the 1970s, eventually reaching 52 percent in 1980 (14 percentage points higher than the average for Western European countries that year).[29] The rural-urban income gap, though it did not disappear, narrowed to 29 percent by 1983.[30] Because of their improved income position, many rural households were able to purchase modern appliances, such as televisions, washing machines, refrigerators, and telephones.[31]

The government also launched the Community Development Campaign to upgrade the village environment. Some progress was made in this area during the 1950s–1960s, but only on a limited, experimental basis. Local programs were scaled up to a national campaign in the 1970s, with dramatic effect. Millions of people benefited from housing renovation projects, including the installation of toilets, showers, and drainage pipes, as well as the paving of rural roads, the construction of rice drying areas, and the implementation of community sanitation programs, to name just a few of the campaign's achievements.

The rest of the chapter explains how Taiwan realized these various outcomes. It analyzes the institutions that facilitated rural development, examines the political logic behind the adoption of pro-rural policies, and discusses why the Community Development Campaign was ultimately successful.

Rural Institutions and the Farmers' Associations

In the 1950s, Taiwan's rural economy was transformed from one dominated by tenant farming to one of owner-cultivators with secure private property rights to land. This system of smallholder farming, combined with the Farmers' Associations and the extension services they provided, led to impressive gains in agricultural production. The importance of land reform in shaping these institutions is undeniable. It reduced tenancy and equalized the distribution of landholdings, which allowed Taiwan to avoid the problem of bimodal development—a dichotomy between wealthy, large-scale commercial farmers on the one hand, and poor, small-scale subsistence farmers on the other. Even more crucial than land reform, however, was the quality of the Farmers' Associations themselves. The FAs possessed both linkage and autonomy, which enabled farmers to meaningfully participate in the rural policy process. In terms of linkage, they had an encompassing membership base, strong ties to the village community, and close connections with higher levels of the state. In terms of autonomy, their leaders were professional farmers, who were elected by association members, and they had a certain degree of financial and managerial independence from the state. Because of these qualities, the FAs facilitated extensive, long-term agricultural development, and they eventually succeeded at lobbying the government for pro-rural policies that led to gains in other areas besides production. But before getting into how the FAs functioned and why they were so effective, it is necessary to address the influence of external actors on Taiwan's rural development.

Japan and the United States

Most scholars agree that Japanese colonialism had an overall positive impact on Taiwan's economic development. As explained in the previous chapter, Japan invested in modern systems of transport, taxation, finance, education, and administration. It controlled the most lucrative parts of the economy (the sugar industry) and extracted heavily from the rural sector, but it did not conform to the normal colonial pattern of neglecting agriculture. Because of Taiwan's subtropical climate, which allowed for the cultivation of several crops a year, it was designated as a base for agriculture that would supply Japan's domestic market with cheap food. In Tun-jen Cheng's words, "Japan took a high cost and high yield approach to colonizing Taiwan, pursuing extensive programs for economic growth before exploiting the proceeds."[32] A major component of this high-cost approach was the creation of state and community-based rural extension organizations. Although their operations were disrupted during the war, the KMT was able to quickly draw from these preexisting resources in setting up the Farmers' Associations.

Historical accounts of the FAs usually begin in the year 1900, when a group of tenant farmers in Sanxia Township, Taipei County, founded a formal association for mutual protection and assistance. By 1908, there were sixteen such organizations, which the colonial government promptly co-opted in order to facilitate agricultural development and resource extraction. Interestingly, the *Sanxia Famers' Association Gazetteer* challenges the common narrative that the association first emerged in opposition to colonial rule, providing evidence that despite anti-Japanese sentiment in the area, its purpose was to work with authorities to stabilize food production and maintain social order.[33] If this account is accurate, then co-optation was probably not difficult, a point supported by the proliferation of state-controlled farmers' organizations during this period. Eventually, all organizations related to irrigation, credit, and specific farm products were merged into a single organization, the Taiwan Agricultural Association. It consisted of one provincial-level association, eight county-level associations, more than three hundred township-level associations, and nearly five thousand village-level agricultural practice societies. The governor-general of Taiwan (the *sotokufu*) served as executive director of the provincial association, and Japanese officials were likewise in charge of the local associations. The size of this institution was second only to the government: by the early 1930s, it employed about forty thousand people.[34]

Through this system, the colonial government orchestrated a green revolution in Taiwan. Irrigated farmland expanded from 32 to 64 percent of total cultivated land, which meant that farmers who previously engaged in dry farming (the cultivation of wheat, soybeans, sorghum, sweet potatoes, etc.) switched to primarily growing rice.[35] Japan also simplified Taiwan's land tenure system by buying out large absentee landlords with government bonds and conferring property rights on smaller, cultivating landlords. Under pressure to meet regular tax payments, this new landlord class worked with colonial authorities and the agricultural associations to stimulate production by promoting new seed varieties, fertilizers, and cultivation techniques among their tenants.[36] The spread of chemical fertilizers and ponlai rice, in particular, helped to raise the average rice yield by 45 percent.[37]

As a result of these innovations, agricultural output climbed from 2.9 percent annual growth in the 1910s to 5.1 percent in the 1920s. It then slowed down a bit to 3.5 percent in the 1930s.[38] By comparison, agricultural output in Japan grew 2 percent annually between 1900 and 1920, and only 0.9 percent annually between 1920 and 1935.[39] Both the colonial state and farmers benefited from these changes. About 16 percent of Japan's total rice supply and more than 80 percent of its sugar supply came from Taiwan.[40] And while Taiwanese sources tend to emphasize the poverty and insecurity inherent in the prewar tenancy system, there are some reports that Taiwanese farmers may have enjoyed a higher standard of living than Japanese farmers in terms of housing, clothing, bank deposits, and other indices.[41] The ample availability of credit and technical services led many Taiwanese farmers to express, once the war was over, that they were better off under Japan, a sentiment that surely influenced the KMT's decision to rehabilitate the associations.[42]

Another key legacy of Japan was the development of Taiwan's rural industries. In 1930, the food-processing sector, which was geographically dispersed, accounted for 64 percent of all registered factories, 55 percent of factory employment, and 76 percent of total factory production. Additionally, as Japan became more involved in World War II, it moved several of its factories to Taiwan for security purposes. These included shipbuilding, oil refining, pulp, basic metals, textiles, and fertilizers. So, while Taiwan was still predominantly rural at the end of the colonial period, it nonetheless had a foundation for future industrialization.[43] Importantly, the continued development of industry after the war, especially food processing and light industry, helped to mitigate the negative effects of the KMT's developmental squeeze on agriculture by generating alternative sources of rural income. In 1958, more than 95 percent of rural incomes in Taiwan derived from farming; by 1979, about 85 percent derived from nonfarm sources.[44] The growth of rural industry, of course, did not prevent the issue of depressed farm incomes from becoming politically contentious in the late 1960s, but it did perhaps delay bottom-up demands for policy change.

As for the United States, its main contribution to Taiwanese rural development was to offer aid and policy advice to the KMT. In total, between 1949 and 1968 (the entire aid period), Taiwan received nearly US$4.2 billion in aid, of which approximately $2.4 billion went to the military and $1.8 billion to economic assistance. Within the budget for economic assistance, Public Law 480 food aid amounted to about $387 million, a small sum compared to South Korea's $1.7 billion in food aid.[45] Despite the negative effects of food aid on development—in Taiwan, US imports depressed the production of wheat, cotton, and soybeans—Hsin-huang Michael Hsiao suggests that US aid to agriculture was the most productive part of the whole aid program. Less than a quarter of all economic aid went to agriculture, but it financed nearly two-thirds of domestic capital formation in that sector. The Sino-American Joint Commission on Rural Reconstruction (JCRR) also operated on a relatively small budget, funding over six thousand projects with $366 million in grants and loans.[46]

The commission was originally made up of two Americans and three Chinese members. After the commission moved from mainland China to Taiwan in 1949, a number of leadership changes occurred, and the proportion of Chinese among the general staff increased, but there was always at least one American commissioner.[47] One theme that emerges from the oral histories of JCRR leaders is that the commission's success was related to its being run by technical experts who were not beholden to the American or Taiwanese governments, and it could directly cooperate with any public or private institution.[48] The JCRR was therefore more isolated from political pressure than an ordinary government agency. Yet, at the same time, it had access to central officials and participated in the drafting of several important policies, most notably land reform and the reorganization of the FAs.

Land Reform

When the Nationalists first arrived in Taiwan, tenant farming was the dominant form of agriculture. In 1949, only 36 percent of farm families were owner-cultivators. About 25 percent were part owners, part tenants, and 39 percent were full tenants. Population growth, exaggerated by the sudden influx of mainland refugees, had the effect of raising rents and reducing farm acreage to the point of threatening tenants' basic subsistence. Farm rents, typically 50 percent of the value of the main crop, had climbed to 70–75 percent during the political transition period. It was in this context that Wolf Ladejinsky, a US Department of Agriculture official, made the following observation about the countryside (the year was 1949): "Of all the farmyards I have seen in the Far East, Southeast Asia, and in the Middle East, that of the average Taiwanese tenant is among the worst, both in appearance and in equipment. Tenants' huts, so-called barnyards, equipment, and livestock, as well as their health point to nothing but poverty."[49] Ladejinsky had been invited by the JCRR to offer advice on land reform, a policy that he had just overseen in Japan. The recommendations, which the KMT took seriously and implemented, included the formation of democratically elected landlord-tenant committees to carry out the policy and a gradual progression of reforms, from rent reduction to the redistribution of public and private lands.

The KMT's responsiveness stemmed from a few considerations. First, the party was aware that its failed rural policies had cost it the mainland and could possibly cost it Taiwan if the communists managed to infiltrate the island. Second, the party's ideology supported equal access to land resources, as detailed by its founder Sun Yat-sen in his writings and speeches on the "people's livelihood" principle. The KMT's experimentation with rent reduction in Zhejiang, Fujian, Sichuan, and a few other places in the 1920s–1940s, though ultimately unsuccessful, was partly motivated by this idea.[50] Third, President Truman himself put direct pressure on Chiang Kai-shek to act on US recommendations, explicitly linking agricultural improvement to national security.[51] Finally, unlike the situation in China, Chiang's government had no previous ties to the landed classes in Taiwan, and this autonomy from traditional power holders prevented opposition to the reforms.

Land reform led to an immediate boost in household incomes and a significant redistribution of land resources. The rent reduction program capped all tenant rents at 37.5 percent of the value of the main crop (an amount intended to achieve a 25 percent reduction in rent based on the assumption that it was 50 percent under normal circumstances). The next step was selling off public lands formerly held by the colonial government and the Taiwan Sugar Corporation. While these two policies were both successfully implemented, by far the most consequential component of the whole land reform agenda was the Land-to-the-Tiller program. It placed limits on the scale of ownership (2.9 hectares or 7.2 acres) and strengthened tenant rights, yet its main effect was to dramatically reduce the rate of tenancy. In 1953, the majority of Taiwan's farm households became owner-cultivators, thus laying the foundation for a more equitable pattern of development (see table 4).[52] Former landlords were compensated with commodity bonds and shares in government enterprises, which turned out to be worth much less than the market value of their land, but nevertheless ensured that some of their wealth was shifted to the industrial sector.[53]

As already suggested, however, land reform was not a panacea for the rural economy. It resulted in extremely parcelized plots and an overall reduction in farm size, such that it became practically impossible for families to survive on farm income alone. Price distortions further stymied long-term growth in incomes, and even the medium-term effect on living standards was questionable. Bernard Gallin, in his classic study of a Taiwanese village, writes: "At the time of the research (1958) at least, this [Land-to-the-Tiller] act in itself had not brought about any noteworthy increase in the standard of living." He explains that besides landlords, two other groups were negatively affected. First, before the reforms, tenants of the Taiwan Sugar Corporation's holdings paid only 25 percent of the

TABLE 4. Extent and Impact of Land Reform in Taiwan

POLICY	(A) 37.5% RENT REDUCTION, 1949–1952	(B) SALE OF PUBLIC LAND, 1948–1958	(C) LAND-TO-THE-TILLER PROGRAM, 1953	TOTAL SHARE OF CULTIVATED AREA AND HOUSEHOLDS AFFECTED BY REDISTRIBUTION (B+C)
Share of cultivated area affected (%)	29.2	8.1	16.4	24.5
Share of farm households affected (%)	43.3	20	27.9	47.9

Total revised lease contracts: 377,364 (100%)

Total cultivated area affected by redistribution: 208,753 hectares (515,840 acres)

Total farm households affected by redistribution: 334,511

Total landlord households affected by redistribution: 106,049

YEAR	1949	1953	1965	1975
Share of owner-cultivators in total farm households (%)	36	55	67	82
Share of part owners–part tenants in total farm households (%)	25	24	21	9
Share of full tenants in total farm households (%)	39	21	12	9

Source: Data for the upper half of the table come from Ho 1978, 163; M. Yang 1970, 81. For the lower half see *Taiwan Agricultural Statistics* 1966, 9; *Taiwan Agricultural Statistics* 1977, 2.

value of the main crop in rent. The reforms thus did not generate any substantial savings for them, and given the taxes incurred as new owners and the rising costs of production, many families saw their yearly expenses increase. Second, jointly owned landholdings, which in his research site accounted for 62 percent of all land resources, were expropriated in the same way as property belonging to landlords. A single plot could have anywhere from two to hundreds of owners, and many joint owners suffered losses because of minimal or no compensation.[54] These findings indicate that the results of Yang's survey discussed earlier might in fact reflect real dissatisfaction with post-reform conditions rather than cultural modesty or rising expectations.

In short, the effects of land reform were mixed. Though in many ways it was an incredible achievement, it was not sufficient for sustained rural development. And while it reduced inequality within the countryside, it offered no solution to the growing rural-urban gap. For these reasons, the Farmers' Associations were more important in the long run.

The Farmers' Associations

After a few years of unsuccessful attempts to revitalize the Farmers' Associations, the KMT solicited help from the JCRR. The government tried, for example, to create separate extension and credit associations, but in practice they performed the same functions and wasted resources competing for membership. Coordination problems also emerged among different government agencies involved in FA work. To resolve these problems, in 1949 the government reverted to the Japanese model of having a single organization with branches at each level of the administration, and it entrusted one department, the Provincial Department of Agriculture and Forestry (PDAF), with all FA-related work.[55] Institutional streamlining was not enough, however, to restore operations. As a result of the war, over 50 percent of FA warehouses, fertilizer stations, and rice mills had been destroyed, and nearly all association managers and technicians had returned to Japan. Because of limited financial support from the ROC government, many associations developed sizable debts, which further hindered their ability to provide services.[56] The US entered into the picture in 1950, when JCRR consultant Walfred A. Anderson published a report containing several suggestions that remain the basis for FA organization today. The report's main finding was that nonfarmers (merchants, industrialists, urban workers, etc.) controlled the majority of local associations, a point confirmed by KMT documents estimating the share of nonfarmer members to be as high as 80 percent in some places. It advised that the FAs distinguish between associate and active members, with the latter defined as those deriving most of their income from farming, and that organizational control be given to active members.[57]

Around the same time as land reform, the government carried out a massive reorganization of the Farmers' Associations. First, in August 1952, it passed the "Provisional By-Law Governing the Improvement of Farmers' Associations of Different Levels in Taiwan." In keeping with Anderson's views, it defined regular (i.e., active) members as those deriving 50 percent or more of their income from farming and stated that only regular members could vote or stand for election to the FA board of directors. Associate members were eligible for election to the FA board of supervisors, a less powerful body in charge of internal audits, but were not allowed to hold more than one-third of supervisor positions.[58] Next, the PDAF and JCRR set about registering members, organizing elections, and training officials. These efforts, which were completed between October 1953 and March 1954, produced impressive results—372,000 existing members were downgraded to associate status; total membership at the township level expanded to about 590,000 households; and nearly 29,000 new officials were elected, of whom 95 percent were actual farmers. At the village level, the agricultural practice societies that had been active during the colonial era were revived (and renamed small agricultural units or SAUs), and they quickly expanded their membership base to over 720,000 households. By this measure, the FAs encompassed the entire farm population.[59]

The democratization of FA governance, together with land reform, solidified the position of smallholders in the rural economy and had a profound impact on development. Following some initial financial difficulties—caused by low membership fees and the withdrawal of savings by nonfarmers who felt alienated under the new system—revenues picked up as the associations took on various functions and earned people's trust. While skilled FA leaders were able to convince nonfarmers to reinvest in the associations, a lot of revenue came from regular member deposits and the collection of service fees.[60] Each township association was divided into four main departments: agricultural extension, credit, insurance, and supply and marketing. Since this last department was responsible for selling fertilizers and purchasing rice under the barter system, it is fair to say that the FAs, similar to marketing boards in Africa, were used to impose hidden taxes on agriculture. However, the associations were not purely extractive institutions. They supplied critical inputs to farmers and, beginning in the 1970s, were used to channel subsidies and other resources to the rural sector. Smallholder control also meant that services were more accessible than is usually the case in developing countries, where inputs are directed by the state to large farmers or to specific geographic areas chosen for political reasons.[61] Survey data from the

1950s confirms that FA services were very widely used. It also shows that farmers were in regular contact with FA staff. In 1959, over 74 percent of households surveyed by the JCRR reported receiving a home visit from an extension agent in the past year (see table 5).

To summarize just a few of the FAs' accomplishments: First, they spearheaded an enormous outreach and research program. They distributed radios, newspapers, and magazines to the village SAUs; set up thousands of farm discussion groups, home economics clubs, and 4-H clubs; and provided assistance to a large corps of agricultural researchers.[62] Samuel Ho writes: "In 1960 the number of agricultural research workers per 100,000 people active in agriculture was 79 in Taiwan, 60 in Japan, and only 4.7 in Thailand, 1.6 in the Philippines, and 1.2 in India."[63] Second, building on the prewar green revolution, they promoted intercropping, mechanization, high-yield varieties of rice, and chemical inputs. By the early 1970s, rice yields reached 3.5 tons per hectare, one of the highest levels in the world.[64] Third, they created a comprehensive livestock improvement program, equipped with the latest innovations in veterinary diagnostics, mass vaccinations, and scientific breeding.[65] Fourth, FA credit departments greatly alleviated the problems of rural capital shortages and high-interest money lending. Between 1949 and 1960, the amount of farm loans provided by the organized money market increased from 17 to 57 percent.[66]

The effectiveness of Taiwan's rural organizations stemmed from two essential qualities: linkage and autonomy. With regard to linkage, I have already

TABLE 5. Percent Households Receiving FA Services in Taiwan, 1952–1959[1]

YEAR	1952	1955	1959
Agricultural Extension Department			
Obtained improved seeds	48.3	45.5	70.6
Obtained crop protection assistance	24.1	61.3	91.3
Obtained hog vaccinations	36.2	76.1	83.7
Received home visit from extension agent	27.6	46.1	74.2
Credit Department			
Deposited savings	29.3	35	67.4
Obtained loans	46.6	57	75.6
Supply and Marketing Department			
Purchased goods from the FA	36.2	72.8	90.1
Sold goods through the FA	15.5	29.8	53.6
Total households surveyed	*n*=58	*n*=1200	*n*=1400
Share of households with FA membership	20.7	85.6	94.2

Source: Data compiled from JCRR surveys, available in Kuo 1984, 150–55.

[1] Insurance departments were added in 1963, so those services are not listed.

explained how the FAs had an encompassing membership base and an organizational presence in all of Taiwan's villages through the SAUs. As subsequent chapters will show, this was simply not the case in South Korea or China. Still, it would be a mistake to characterize the FAs as village organizations. They were, more accurately, parastatal institutions with close ties to the villages. Though technically separate from the government, they assumed responsibility for certain entrusted activities (maintaining the barter system, primarily) and were involved in virtually all aspects of rural policy implementation. Drawing from social and political theory, the FAs can be understood as having a corporatist relationship with the state. They were hierarchically structured, with only one association operating in a given territory. The provincial FA could dissolve any poorly performing unit in the system, and each association's program budget had to be approved by the unit above it. Farmers were also forbidden from forming alternative organizations. These rules were designed to facilitate top-down supervision of the FAs and to prevent the growth of civil society organizations that might challenge the state. In exchange for political loyalty, the FAs were given access to key resources, such as funding and new technologies, and they were granted limited representation in the Legislative Yuan. It seems that instead of being put off by this structure, many farmers actually welcomed the supervision by higher-level authorities because it reassured them that programs would be properly administered (for illustrations of the FAs' structural features, see the appendix).[67]

Of course, institutional linkage with the state does not guarantee political influence. Rather, the FAs' ability to provide feedback, channel discontent, and initiate change was a product of their autonomy. First of all, they were the only (quasi-) public institution in postwar Taiwan that was not controlled by mainlanders. Even though mainlanders composed 40 percent of the provincial-level FA staff, there was usually just one mainlander working for the local associations, a security agent in charge of guarding the granary and reporting on signs of unrest to the government.[68] Second, with the exception of a few spots on the board of supervisors, all FA leaders were professional farmers chosen by members of their own communities. At the village level, direct elections were held every four years for SAU leaders and township FA representatives. Above the villages, the principle of indirect representation was employed: assemblies of representatives would elect a board of directors, a board of supervisors, and representatives to the next level in the system. Third, the FAs not only chose their own leaders but also managed their own finances. Whatever funds they received from the government or the JCRR usually came in the form of loans instead of grants, and most revenues derived from their own commercial activities and services, not from government-entrusted activities. The FAs' (albeit limited) independence from the state in terms of finances and leadership is yet another way in which they differed from their counterparts in South Korea and China.[69]

FA elections were also highly contested, and despite some downsides such as intervention on the part of local factions and the KMT, the overall effect of elections was to increase farmers' participation in politics and sense of ownership over the associations. Joseph Bosco describes the FA system as "a semi-governmental organization that controls much patronage, so its political offices are sharply contested by local factions."[70] Indeed, factions competed fiercely for spots on the assembly of representatives and board of directors. The board would elect a chairman, who in turn appointed a general manager. The chairman's pick had to be approved by two-thirds of the board and could in theory be a capable nonfarmer, although the main criterion for selection was loyalty to the chairman. These individuals were in many ways as powerful as the head of the township government. They determined FA staffing and distributed such items as cash crop licenses, construction contracts, loans, and community development funds.

To prevent local factions from gaining too much power, the KMT recruited them to join the party. In 1954, during the first round of FA elections, temporary party organizations were created to recommend and enlist candidates. As a result, the KMT captured the majority of leadership positions, setting a pattern that continues through the present day (see table 6).[71] The regime also intervened by limiting campaign activities to the ten days leading up to the election, setting education and training requirements for general managers, and monitoring association activities through its own security agents.[72] While none of these measures necessarily eliminated clan-based corruption or the oppression of minority factions, the combination of near-universal membership and centralized supervision of the FAs meant that local leaders were less likely to engage in extreme forms of patronage.[73] In other words, the KMT superimposed its own patron-client relationship on the FAs as a way of mitigating local capture by dominant factions.

Moreover, factional and party interference did not detract from a general perception among farmers that the FAs were *their* organizations. According to JCRR survey data (the same used in table 5), the share of farmers who stated that "the farmers own the FAs" increased from 1.7 percent in 1952, to 56.1 percent in 1955, to 79.5 percent in 1959. The share of farmers who stated that "the chairman of the FA board of directors is determined by election" also increased from 20.7 percent in 1952, to 66.5 percent in 1955, to 80.2 percent in 1959. Farmers gave similar responses when asked about FA representatives. In addition to farmers' sense of ownership and control over the FAs, the survey data suggest that farmers were

TABLE 6.   Extent of KMT Representation in Taiwan's FAs (1954 FA Election Results)

	(A) TOTAL ELECTED	(B) KMT CANDIDATES[1]	(C) KMT RECRUITS[2]	SHARE OF KMT MEMBERS AMONG ELECTED FA OFFICIALS (B + C) / A
Village SAUs				
SAU head	4,875	1,939	1,642	73%
SAU vice-head	4,875	1,456	1,603	63%
Township FA representatives	16,916	6,421	4,141	62%
Township FAs				
FA directors	3,805	2,193	862	80%
FA supervisors	1,086	617	22	59%
County FA representatives	1,349	782	351	84%
County FAs				
FA directors	386	287	62	90%
FA supervisors	124	82	27	88%
Provincial FA representatives	89	69	0	78%
Provincial FA[3]				
FA directors	33	33	0	100%
FA supervisors	10	10	0	100%
TOTAL	**33,548**	**13,889**	**8,710**	**67%**

Source: Central Committee of the Kuomintang 1954, 59–60.

[1] Candidates who were members of the party before winning the election.

[2] Candidates who joined the party after winning the election.

[3] FA rules allowed for four representatives to the Legislative Yuan. Based on this data, it is reasonable to assume that all of them were KMT members.

at least minimally engaged in FA activities: in 1959, about 82 percent of farmers said they had attended a SAU meeting in the past year.[74] Yang's survey in the mid-1960s provides further evidence of a rich associational life in the countryside, with most farmers reporting that they voluntarily and regularly participated in local elections and community organizations.[75] In contrast, farmers in Korea did not elect leaders to the cooperatives and considered them to be just another arm of the government.[76]

Political Competition and Policy Change

Since farmers' regular electoral participation and engagement with the FAs prevented them from one-sidedly serving the state, it is worth considering why Taiwan's authoritarian regime allowed them to function the way they did. Clearly the United States, through the JCRR, was interested in promoting American democratic ideals, but the KMT's calculation was probably much more practical. They needed the Taiwanese to run the FAs because fluency in local dialects was critical for extension work. More importantly, elections were a way to create buy-in from farmers who might otherwise be tempted to form a rival (communist) political party or movement. Given Taiwan's close proximity to the mainland and the strength of local factions, the Nationalists decided it was better to permit open political competition than to drive it underground and risk losing control.

This same logic propelled the regime to expand the scope of local government elections. Party leaders gradually realized they would not be returning to the mainland, especially after China's 1964 atomic bomb test, so the only way to fill vacancies created by an aging political elite was to bring more Taiwanese into politics. They also knew that repression alone was not a long-term solution to governance. Regular elections for local government positions started as early as the 1950s and then expanded in 1969 to include a few seats in the parliament (most notably, the Legislative Yuan). This change marked the beginning of what Thomas Gold has called the "Taiwanization" of the political sphere. In 1972, Hsieh Tung-min became the first Taiwanese to assume the post of provincial governor. Chiang Ching-kuo later selected Hsieh to be his vice president in 1978, followed by Lee Teng-hui in 1984. These developments at the top were the culmination of aggressive party recruiting efforts at the grassroots: by the early 1970s, about 80 percent of the KMT's 1.25 million members were Taiwanese.[77] And within the FAs, recruitment was so successful that they functioned as voter turnout machines for the KMT during local elections.[78] This dynamic of political competition at the height of authoritarianism, within the Farmers' Associations and in the political system more broadly, makes Taiwan very different from the other cases. Even those politicians with no background in agriculture grew to care about the countryside because of Taiwan's highly organized rural electorate and the political influence of FA leaders.

Locally, political elites frequently moved between the FAs and the government during the course of their careers. As a typical example, Mr. Fan-Chiang's experience, recorded by Taiwanese scholar Huang Ta-chou, reveals how elections helped to build strong horizontal and vertical ties among local institutions: Born in 1926, Fan-Chiang attended school from the age of nine to fifteen. He was drafted into the Japanese military and served until the war ended in 1945, after which he returned to his village. Fan-Chiang was a skilled farmer and was selected by his peers to be a small agricultural unit leader in 1949. In the mid-1950s, he was elected to be a township FA representative and a member of the board of directors. He was then elected to the county government assembly, shortly after which he worked for the county party organization. Moving every few years between the government and the Farmers' Association, Fan-Chiang eventually became a township FA general manger in 1970. Reading his story and the recollections of others like him underscores the prestige associated with rural work in Taiwan, and it shows that the status of the FAs was similar to that of the government. Faced with various career options, many people chose to work for the associations. And given their political connections, they were uniquely positioned to provide feedback on rural policy. They also knew which leaders were more inclined to support farmers and could mobilize voters to back them.[79]

At the national level, the FAs transmitted farmers' grievances upward to central officials. Their voice was strengthened by the JCRR, which regularly conducted surveys of farmers and shared its findings with the government. Also important was a group of agricultural advocates in the Provincial Assembly and the Legislative Yuan. From existing content analysis of the meetings of these bodies, it is clear that official discourse about the countryside changed after 1969: the previous focus on agricultural production for the sake of government revenue shifted to greater concern for farmers' welfare. The advocates spoke about the shortcomings of land reform and painted a picture of worsening poverty. As one Legislative Yuan representative explained in 1970: "Agricultural policy is a problem that we have not resolved for many years. After the 37.5 percent rent reduction and the Land-to-the-Tiller programs were implemented, it seemed on the surface that farmers received many benefits. Yet in reality, once the farmers obtained land, their production costs never went down. After subtracting production costs, they have almost nothing left. Farmers' lives have therefore still not really improved . . . [they] are experiencing extreme suffering." Indeed, several politicians made passionate appeals to eliminate extractive policies, arguing that people could no longer subsist on farming and were abandoning it only to end up as slave-like workers, criminals, and prostitutes.[80]

In summary, the Farmers' Associations could not enact policy change on their own, but they did enable farmers to meaningfully participate in different stages of the policy process: implementation, feedback, and eventually agenda setting. The constituencies and political leaders they produced became increasingly powerful over time, as the regime moved toward including more Taiwanese voices in politics. The barter system, which for decades had required farmers to purchase fertilizers using in-kind payments of rice at exploitative, nonmarket prices, was finally abolished with passage of the Accelerated Rural Development Program in 1972. To be sure, there were other factors that affected the government's decision, such as the declining cost of agricultural protection. In fact, just a few years before the ARDP was adopted, the government had already started to lower the prices of fertilizers, pesticides, and farm machinery. Growing revenues from the industrial sector, along with rising urban incomes and changes in diet, also decreased the government's need for cheap rice and other kinds of rural taxes.[81] Without the emergence of a pro-rural coalition, however, it is unlikely that economic factors alone would have caused a substantial shift in policy. I have made the case that the FAs deserve credit for gains in production during the extractive phase of agricultural policy and for setting in motion changes that would effectively end that phase. Moreover, what most previous accounts of rural policy transition have failed to explain is that the government did not just end extraction—it transformed the face of the countryside.

The Community Development Campaign
Origins

The Community Development Campaign was launched around the same time as the ARDP. The latter represented a more typical agricultural adjustment program, calling for reduced taxes, increased spending, low-interest credit, better services, and scale agriculture. The government allocated at least 2 billion yuan to the ARDP annually between 1973 and 1979. Though a small percentage of total government spending (1–3 percent, depending on the year), it marked a decisive break from the past.[82] As previously noted, because of the ARDP and supplementary measures like subsidies and import restrictions, the nominal and relative rates of agricultural protection turned positive, and the rural-urban income gap shrank considerably. By itself, however, the ARDP was regarded as an insufficient solution to the rural problem. To achieve more immediate and visible results, the government embraced mass mobilization.

The Community Development Campaign cannot be understood without reference to past campaigns. In China, the Mass Education and Rural Reconstruction Movements of the 1920s–1930s focused on improving rural conditions through the development of autonomous village organizations. Led by Y. C. James Yen, Liang Shuming, and other activist intellectuals, these movements sought to provide an alternative to communism. Yen later served as a commissioner for the JCRR and moved to Taiwan, where his ideas about grassroots community building influenced the top leadership.[83] The New Life Movement was another campaign that took place in the 1930s–1940s to counter the influence of communism. Some scholars view it as linked to global fascism, whereas others emphasize that it was closely intertwined with state building and civilian relief during the war period. Importantly, because Chiang Kai-shek and Chiang Ching-kuo personally led the campaign, it provides a window into how they thought about the countryside. The main objective was to create an orderly and civilized society by using ideological education to reform the most basic aspects of rural life: clothing, food, housing, and behavior. Although thousands of New Life community organizations were established across the country, the campaign's momentum ultimately fizzled out because the communists proved more capable of providing people with real economic and security benefits.[84] Taiwan's countryside was similarly viewed as backward, but now the leadership understood that any campaign to reform it needed to deliver tangible change to be successful.

In 1955, the government launched the People's Livelihood Construction Campaign, which drew inspiration from Sun Yat-sen's ideology. It stressed ensuring equal access to land resources, sustaining high levels of production, and satisfying villagers' basic needs (as in the New Life Movement, these were defined as clothing, food, housing, transportation, education, and recreation). Taiwanese sources state that the campaign was intended to pick up where land reform had left off, and given the timing, it is possible the campaign was launched in response to China's collectivization drive. Even though farmers in Taiwan maintained control over their own land and production practices, laws on compulsory labor were invoked to support village improvement projects. An earlier law requiring men ages eighteen to fifty to take part in road building, irrigation, production, and defense work was revised to incorporate more projects related to village infrastructure. Campaign coordination committees were formed to bring together leaders from government, schools, the police, and the FAs. In addition, the government initiated a formal competition among local jurisdictions to mobilize labor and other resources. The policy lasted for ten years and affected less than 10 percent of all villages (there were 515 experimental sites in total), but its impact was nonetheless significant. Several hundred miles of roads, irrigation canals, and drainage pipes were added to existing infrastructure. Other improvements included the construction of embankments, water towers, pumps, bridges, rice drying areas, toilets, bathhouses, animal pens, compost houses, child-care centers, and community centers.[85]

The success of previous experiments, combined with international development trends, eventually paved the way for a more comprehensive campaign. In the 1960s, when the United Nations was supporting community development programs worldwide, UN consultant Chang Hung-chun introduced the concept to Taiwan. It quickly gained currency among officials who were eager to raise their government's status internationally, an issue that became even more pressing after Taiwan lost its UN seat to China in 1971. Local experiments were scaled up and repackaged as community development in a series of national policy documents that would serve as the foundation for the Community Development Campaign—the People's Livelihood Social Policy (1965), the Community

Development Eight-Year Plan (1969), and the Community Development Ten-Year Plan (1972).[86] The Chinese names of these policies are listed in table 7. Taiwan also took notice of South Korea's New Village Movement and modeled certain aspects of its approach after what was happening there, such as training village activists in order to change rural culture.[87]

Taiwan's bureaucracy, compared to that in Korea and China, was more inclined to support rural development, and groups representing urban-industrial interests were not as strong politically. This difference had to do with historically close ties between agriculture and industry and the fact that many local officials had started their careers in the FAs. The dismantling of urban-biased policies was consequently easier to execute. The bigger barrier to change, from the perspective of the leadership, was rural culture itself. They believed that land reform had created a society that was simultaneously more egalitarian and more individualistic. And if rural backwardness stemmed from a lack of community spirit, then a campaign would be more effective than a normal piece of legislation (like the ARDP) at delivering spiritual and moral change. Mass mobilization would not only advance the material well-being of the village, but it would foster a public ethos as well.

On a deeper level, it is clear that the KMT's favorable view of campaigns was driven by competition with the Chinese communists and political insecurity. Chiang Kai-shek had been fearful of an underground communist movement since arriving in Taiwan and viewed the countryside through the lens of his failures on the mainland. As virtually any rural policy document from that period shows, the regime was fixated on the question of how it lost the Chinese peasantry. Taiwan represented a second chance. The KMT studied the CCP and sometimes borrowed directly from the communists' tool kit, mimicking their organization and style of policy implementation.[88] It successfully executed land reform and penetrated the FAs. And yet it was never fully confident it could hold on to their loyalty. By the late 1960s, farmers had become a powerful interest group. They did not directly challenge Chiang's authority, but reports of rural decline and popular discontent deeply concerned him. Having experienced some success with campaigns in the past, Chiang's government had reason to believe that this approach could deliver greater change than market forces alone could produce. The campaign furthermore promised to transform rural culture and reassert state control over the countryside at a time when elections were expanding. It was also an important moment for Chiang Ching-kuo, who wanted to create a popular base of support as he prepared to take over from his father.[89]

In summary, campaigns were seen as a means of development and legitimation. They could overcome barriers to change, accomplish concrete goals, and

TABLE 7.   Community Development Policies in Taiwan, 1955–1981[1]

CAMPAIGNS AND SUPPORTING POLICIES	CHINESE NAME	YEARS
People's Livelihood Construction Campaign	基層民生建設運動	**1955–1965**
Compulsory labor	國民義務勞動	1947
Community Development Campaign	社區發展運動	**1965–1981**
People's Livelihood Social Policy	民生主義現階段社會政策	1965
Community Development Eight-Year Plan	社區發展八年計畫	1969
Community Development Ten-Year Plan	社區發展十年計畫	1972

[1] The ten-year-plan, which was supposed to conclude in 1978, was extended through the year 1981. Single years indicate the first year that a policy became effective.

engender loyalty among the population. The framework of community development in particular was also a way of signaling to international actors that Taiwan was progressive and open compared to China and that its leaders cared about helping those left behind by industrialization. As one might expect, scholars critical of the campaign lament the state's heavy involvement as running counter to international norms about community development.[90] However, I would suggest that if it is viewed as a state-led campaign, and not according to the ideals of community development per se, it was actually quite successful.

Goals and Implementation

The Community Development Campaign succeeded at producing policy compliance and positive outcomes because its overarching goal was rural development, rather than extraction, and because of the political-institutional context in which it was implemented. Taiwan's centralized political system and technocratic leadership facilitated bureaucratic monitoring, and although the FAs were just one of several groups responsible for campaign implementation, their strong presence in the villages prior to the campaign helped to normalize rural participation in the policy process.

In terms of goals, the Community Development Eight-Year Plan (1969–1976) described the policy as a "social movement" aimed at "eliminating dirt, disorder, and poverty, increasing production and welfare, and promoting a new morality." Accordingly, in this document and the revised ten-year plan (1969–1978), specific projects were divided into three categories: basic infrastructure; production and social welfare; and spiritual and moral construction. This last category called for community organizations and activities that would promote healthy living and a collective consciousness, for example the formation of Boy Scout troops and Chinese musical orchestras. "Life basics" courses on civilized behavior—standing in line, wearing clean clothes, eating at a table, etc.—were also commonly conducted during the campaign.[91] By most accounts, these projects were less successful than those focused on infrastructure and production, but the emotional appeal of making the community better was still a powerful call to action.

The elimination of taxes and disbursement of grants further bolstered popular enthusiasm for the campaign, though not without local costs. Initially, the government allocated 250,000 yuan to each community. This money covered roughly half the cost of community development, and residents were expected to provide matching funds to make up the difference. The poorest households had to borrow money or donate more of their labor to meet this requirement. To reduce their burden, the government later revised the policy. It assumed a greater share of the cost for every site (about 52 percent of the total), with even higher levels of support for poverty areas (about 84 percent). The ten-year plan also mandated that poorer villages be developed first so as to prevent local governments from channeling funds to the easiest cases, namely those villages near the township with a better baseline of development.[92]

To facilitate local compliance, campaign coordination committees were formed at the provincial, county, and township levels. The committees were composed of leading officials from nearly every institution, including the military and the police. They were charged with developing plans, disbursing funds (primarily through the FAs), and overseeing implementation. During the planning stage, village assemblies were held to solicit ideas from residents. Villages were legally defined as an extension of the township government and considered to be separate from communities, which were conceptualized as autonomous, service-oriented units. But in practice, the functions of these units overlapped.

The creation of communities gave rise to two changes in the local leadership structure. First, some villages were merged together so that each community was roughly the same size, about 350 households. When mergers did occur—the eight-year plan organized all of Taiwan's 6,215 villages into 4,893 communities—leaders from different villages had to negotiate the location of community projects, a process that was undoubtedly contentious and subject to the influence of local factions. In these cases, the campaign coordination committee was expected to play the role of mediator. Second, a younger generation of activists gained power through the establishment of community development councils. These were elected bodies of roughly ten people representing a mix of traditional and new elites. The empowerment of individuals in their twenties, thirties, and forties, who otherwise might have considered leaving the countryside, added to the campaign's momentum.

The community development councils operated at the village (or community) level. They were responsible for mobilizing residents and managing the day-to-day activities of the campaign. They were also in charge of community center operations and infrastructure maintenance. The village SAU leader and township FA representatives usually held spots on the council and took the lead on production-related projects. The township coordination committee frequently dispatched officials to consult with council members and to check on the campaign's progress. In addition, the provincial government arranged for outside inspection teams to evaluate and rank local governments based on the quality of the communities in their jurisdiction. Places that performed better were rewarded with media attention, medals, and other benefits. Taiwan's small size and centralized political system contributed to policy coherence among different levels of government. In conjunction with education and training, as well as fiscal and administrative regulations, all these mechanisms—the campaign coordination committees, community development councils, and competitive evaluations—were used to exert central control over local authorities and increase compliance. Stated differently, these policy tools effectively brought local actors into an implementing coalition with the central government.

On the issues of rural participation and accountability to villagers, scholarly assessments are mixed. Several ethnographic case studies assert that the community development councils were weak. They point out that projects were mostly passed down from the township and that the campaign relied on compulsory labor.[93] Still other studies reach the opposite conclusion, showing that the councils crafted and adjusted development plans based on local needs and feedback. They also claim that people were eager to contribute to projects that directly benefited the village, which was not necessarily true of other compulsory labor projects.[94] This discrepancy in the literature likely stems from real variation in local campaign experiences.

Nevertheless, there are good reasons to believe that, on the whole, the campaign was implemented in a relatively flexible and participatory manner. First, the example of the FAs demonstrates that villagers regularly voted in elections and treated them seriously. Council elections were probably treated the same way, especially given the influx of new resources tied to community development. There was an expectation that council members would advocate for villagers to higher levels of the state, which was reinforced by villagers' own ability to communicate with the FAs and outside inspection teams. Second, despite government claims to the contrary, the countryside already had a rich associational life. Besides the FAs, there were irrigation associations, credit cooperatives, labor exchange groups, temple associations, and a myriad of groups organized around lineage, neighborhood, gender, age, and profession.[95] These organizations surely had their own views on how to improve the community and wanted to see those reflected in the campaign. So, even if the community development councils were weak, there were still other groups that sought out partnerships with the government and offered their contacts and resources in exchange for influence. Third, in contrast to the other cases in this study, Taiwanese sources are filled with references to Western examples of community development and translations of phrases that evoke democratic norms of participation: civic organization, community action, inclusion of the poor in decision making, sense of belonging, and felt needs, to name just a few.[96] Since the intended audience of these materials was local officials and campaign activists, it seems the regime's embrace of these norms was not just about international posturing. It was also about a real commitment to grassroots engagement.

Outcomes and Legacy

Whereas Taiwanese sources suggest that the campaign was transformative, it has received almost no attention from Western scholars.[97] This is probably because the campaign had only a moderate effect on the agricultural economy. While, on the one hand, production-related infrastructure was successfully upgraded and expanded, on the other hand, efforts to develop new rural sidelines and scale up production fell flat. In fact, between 1960 and 1990, the share of households with farms smaller than 1 hectare (2.47 acres) increased from about 67 percent to 75 percent, and the share of households with farms larger than 3 hectares (7.41 acres) decreased from 3.3 to 2.5 percent.[98] The difficulty of scaling up agriculture in Taiwan, as in the rest of East Asia, was a product not only of land reform but also the FAs, which served to protect and entrench the position of small farmers in Taiwanese society.[99]

The Community Development Campaign's greatest impact was to change the village environment. It led to dramatic improvements in public infrastructure, sanitation, and housing. Most if not all of Taiwan's villages were affected, and the sheer scope of the campaign in terms of the number of projects implemented was impressive (see table 8). Official statistics also reveal an unevenness to project implementation, meaning that different communities experienced different kinds of change. Apart from variation in resources, which certainly existed across communities, another explanation for this unevenness is that the campaign did not impose a one-size-fits-all vision of modernity on the countryside. Villagers had some degree of choice over which projects to implement, and there were fewer negative outcomes as a result. For instance, older homes were preserved and renovated instead of torn down and rebuilt, so there was very little

TABLE 8. Results of the Community Development Campaign in Taiwan, 1969–1981

Total number of communities	4,025
Total number of community residents	7,328,074 (about 1.3 million households)
Total cost of community development	6,082,449,911 yuan
Government expenditures	3,687,463,819 yuan (about 61%)
Community expenditures	2,394,986,092 yuan (about 39%)
Basic infrastructure projects	
1. Water towers	9,274
2. Toilets	172,307
3. Showers	37,107
4. Drainage pipes	10,395,456 meters
5. Pathways	21,055,140 square meters
6. Parks	1,520
7. Playgrounds	913
8. Athletic fields	1,016
9. Activity centers	3,531
10. Home sanitation improvement	335,307 households
11. Township roads	71,023 kilometers
12. Village roads	57,132 kilometers
Production and social welfare projects	
1. Rice drying areas	2,101,259 square meters
2. Animal pens	55,831
3. Compost houses	39,478
4. Technology training classes	3,898
5. Farm improvement stations	1,577
6. Child care centers	1,725
7. Agricultural cooperatives	122
8. Home renovation for the poor	20,262 households
9. Home construction for the poor	25,481 households
10. Employment assistance	33,405 people
11. Community production funds	1,063
12. Cooperative farms	49
Spiritual and moral construction projects	
1. "Life basics" courses	12,706
2. Cultural and athletic activities	20,383
3. Recognizing good people/deeds	4,343
4. Elderly associations	1,909
5. Boy scout troops	389
6. Classes for mothers	2,945
7. Sports tournaments	494

Source: Taiwan Provincial Government Social Affairs Department, cited in Liu J. 1991, 69–72.

displacement, and the government rather than villagers shouldered the majority of campaign expenses.[100]

After the more concrete, infrastructure-related goals were achieved, the campaign began to lose steam and eventually petered out. By the late 1970s, the state had retreated from playing an activist role in community affairs, and rural policy had returned to normal. The agricultural bureaucracy resumed its regular work, as did the leaders of other departments and institutions who had been mobilized during the campaign. Although the state intended for the community development councils to exist indefinitely, its withdrawal had the effect of demobilizing them. These organizations, while composed of nonstate actors, had been created and managed by the state. Their mission was to promote development, not to advance a broader political agenda, and they rarely if ever acted independently. Taiwan had a strong state, and the leadership knew that so long as rural conditions were improving, there was little chance the community development councils or any other organizations would present a challenge. The campaign had served the purpose of stabilizing the countryside, and once Chiang Ching-kuo had consolidated power, the state's strategy shifted from mobilization to less interventionist policy measures like subsidies.

Following Taiwan's transition to democracy, President Lee Teng-hui (1988–2000) resurrected the idea of community development. The new program was different from the old in that it targeted urban areas and did not take the form of a campaign. Still, one point of continuity was that the state supported the creation of community development associations as an alternative to what Lee saw as an overly bureaucratic approach to neighborhood governance. State-sponsored activism or what Benjamin Read has called administrative grassroots engagement—a process whereby the state creates, sponsors, and manages organizations at the most local level—thus continued under democracy and represents a long-standing feature of governance in Taiwan.[101]

In conclusion, the use of campaigns to spur development stands out as being quite different from the conventional wisdom. The developmental state model as described by Wade and others is correct in its portrayal of Taiwan's institutions, but it does not fully account for what happened in the countryside. The state did not "pick winners" and let the market do the rest. Instead, it launched a modernization campaign to speed up the pace of rural transformation, a decision that had more in common with Maoism or Leninism than Japanese industrial policy. At the same time, this portrait of the campaign as a top-down policy with genuine societal participation makes the Taiwanese case diverge from a purely Leninist system.

The Community Development Campaign succeeded at improving rural conditions because it occurred in a particular context that prevented the campaign from working against farmers' interests. It was meticulously planned and implemented by a technocratic bureaucracy operating in a highly centralized political system. Frequent inspections and crosscutting coordination agencies stopped government support from being diverted to other purposes. More importantly, Taiwan's strong rural organizations provided a critical check against campaign excesses. The community development councils and the FAs, with their extensive organizational reach and politically influential leadership, were crucial for shaping local plans and generating mass participation. Without them, the use of compulsory labor alone would have most likely failed to sustain the campaign.

While this case study has highlighted the interplay between institutions and campaigns, perhaps the bigger lesson is that the Farmers' Associations, in their own right, were incredibly effective agents of development. The FAs exhibited an unusual combination of linkage with the state and autonomy from it, with small farmers occupying most of the leadership positions. Because of these qualities, the FAs were able to achieve extensive, long-term gains in agriculture, and they ushered in pro-rural reforms that fundamentally changed the state's relationship with the countryside and led to gains in other areas besides production. The FAs today remain encompassing organizations (current membership is about 1.8 million), and they are still the key actors for implementing rural policy. Their power has been reduced, however, by the continued decline of agriculture and, arguably, by the democratization process itself, which led to the empowerment of new social classes and new political parties (because of their close historical ties, the FAs remain largely supportive of the KMT).[102] A few studies have also shown increased levels of corruption as the agricultural sector became more heavily subsidized by the state.[103] Despite these changes, it is no exaggeration to say that Taiwan's Farmers' Associations were the principal contributor to rural development from the 1950s onward. This research thus confirms the view that Taiwan represents a "farmers' association approach" to development.[104] Through the comparative analysis in the chapters that follow, it becomes even more obvious just how much these institutions mattered.

3

RURAL DEVELOPMENT IN SOUTH KOREA, 1950s–1970s

South Korea's industrialization was accomplished in just two decades. Between 1962 and 1981, the economy grew at an average annual rate of 8.4 percent, with a peak average of 10.2 percent for 1972–1976.[1] Only a small number of countries have ever achieved such spectacular growth. To explain South Korea's rise, scholars have stressed the role of Japanese colonialism in creating an effective state bureaucracy, the advantages of late industrialization, especially the borrowing of technology from early innovators, and the presence of internal and external threats that caused the country's leaders to equate growth with national security.[2] While these same factors contributed to Taiwan's economic success, Korea's development experience was actually quite different: agricultural development did not precede industrial takeoff, and the impact of government policy on the countryside was more mixed.

Despite the successful implementation of rural land reform, South Korean agriculture was neglected for most of the 1950s and 1960s. President Syngman Rhee devoted nearly all of the country's resources to the industrial and military sectors. The government made little effort to strengthen rural institutions or to ensure that farmers had access to seeds, fertilizer, and other inputs. The National Agricultural Cooperative Federation (NACF) was not established until after Park Chung-hee took power in 1961. It proved to be much weaker than similar organizations found in Japan and Taiwan, partly because Park's initial commitment to rural development was short-lived. After early experiments with rural debt relief and price supports led to inflation and budget deficits, macroeconomic policy shifted in the direction of squeezing agriculture to develop Korea's urban-based export industries.[3] Rural economic growth was hindered by limited investment, unfair pricing policies, and cheap food imports from the United States. As a result, Korean agriculture lagged far behind other sectors, and it did not provide many resources for industrialization, with the exception of surplus labor.

In the 1970s, President Park broke with the previous pattern of urban bias by launching the New Village Movement (also known as the New Community Movement or Saemaul Undong). The campaign attempted to raise farm output and incomes in at least two ways. First, the state orchestrated a green revolution by requiring farmers to grow a high-yield variety of rice called Tong'il (unification). Rice prices were also adjusted such that rural incomes actually surpassed urban incomes in 1974.[4] However, by the late 1970s, the government could no longer afford its price support policy, and Tong'il production was abandoned because of crop failures and the fact that it was unpopular with consumers. Second, the state promoted the development of rural industry as an avenue for off-farm employment, but this effort, known as Factory Saemaul, failed to curb a rural exodus to the cities. Between 1970 and 1990, more than half the rural population (nearly eight million people) migrated to urban areas.[5]

Neither Tong'il nor Factory Saemaul was very successful, but in the area of rural infrastructure, the campaign produced enormous changes. Through local village development committees, the government mobilized villagers for the construction of roads, bridges, irrigation channels, sewage systems, warehouses, and community centers. Village homes were renovated with the installation of water taps, electricity, telephones, and tiled roofs. Critics assert that, despite all these improvements, the campaign did not help the rural economy and was ultimately a waste of resources, since so many people left the countryside. Yet, even to this day, the South Korean government claims that the New Village Movement was a major achievement, an essential part of Korea's modernization, and that it remains a useful example for other developing countries to emulate.

The development trajectory of South Korea strongly resembles W. Arthur Lewis's dual-sector model in which agriculture's contribution to industrialization is limited to the supply of surplus labor. This model assumes that because agriculture is an inherently backward economic sector, only successful industrialization can make it more productive.[6] Most economic historians believe that Korea reached the Lewis turning point in the early 1970s. They also generally agree that while Korean agriculture was advanced by global standards, its impact on development was minimal. In the end, industrialization did more to improve the lives of rural Koreans than any innovations in farming or policies targeting the countryside.[7] Still, why did the government intervene precisely when the problem of rural underdevelopment should have resolved itself, and why did intervention take the form of a campaign? The academic literature on Korea's development has not paid adequate attention to the New Village Movement or to the more general question of why Korea followed a path different from Taiwan's.

This chapter explains South Korea's mixed record of rural development. I begin with an overview of rural change in the postwar period and show that agriculture did not contribute much to the overall economy or to rural household incomes because of an adverse policy environment. The situation improved in the 1970s, with noticeable gains in production, incomes, and infrastructure, although progress was uneven in each of these areas. Next, I discuss rural institutions and the shift away from urban bias. I argue that agriculture underperformed because land reform was insufficient for long-term growth and because South Korea's rural institutions were relatively weak. The Ministry of Agriculture was low in the bureaucratic hierarchy, and its extension agencies never developed deep roots in society. The NACF in particular was qualitatively different from its counterpart in Taiwan. It was an appendage of the state that exhibited linkage but not autonomy. Rural policy was implemented in a more rigid, top-down manner, with less participation from small farmers and fewer people advocating on their behalf. Support for pro-rural policies, instead of emerging gradually, was triggered by fears of a political crisis. Many farmers voted against Park at the ballot box and with their feet, supporting opposition candidates in the 1967 and 1971 elections, and moving to the cities where anti-Park sentiment was on the rise. The termination of US food aid added to the problem. Domestic output could barely keep up with urban demand, and higher food prices promised to incite unrest. This context is essential for understanding the New Village Movement. In the last part of the chapter, I analyze the campaign in detail and assert that, even if it was primarily about sustaining Park's rule, the campaign still had a positive effect on rural development, especially in terms of improving the village environment. Park's personal commitment to the campaign, combined with strong controls from above, ensured that local officials complied with central policy. The campaign would have been more successful, however, if it was less ambitious and more participatory.

The South Korean case illustrates both the strengths and weaknesses of a campaign approach to development. The New Village Movement essentially reset the priorities of every branch of government, temporarily overriding other work. The government devoted significant material and administrative resources to rural development, and it used various tactics to induce collective action, such as training village activists and distributing selective assistance to high-performing villages. Compared to a more market-driven development strategy, the campaign delivered greater change to more places in a shorter period of time. Yet it also set unrealistic goals and created a highly politicized environment. Local officials were under extreme pressure to deliver results, which necessarily limited the space for popular feedback and led to several negative outcomes. The existing literature on the campaign contains a range of views that are difficult to reconcile. Western scholars tend to emphasize its authoritarian politics and economic failures; Korean scholars are more varied in their opinions; and the Korean government focuses almost entirely on its achievements. My analysis challenges extreme views of the campaign, showing that it was not a misguided experiment in social control any more than it was a grassroots movement that brought an end to crippling poverty. To really understand it requires attention to the payoffs and costs of campaigns and the way those were shaped by Korea's political-institutional context.

This case study also adds to a growing body of scholarship on modern Korea that questions the validity of the developmental state model.[8] It highlights the importance of mobilization in the Park era, which coexisted with the regime's technocratic style of governance. Moreover, it qualifies the claim that Korean development can be attributed to the strength of its institutions. Korea actually had a strong state but weak rural institutions compared to Taiwan. Korean agriculture was also more statist, in the sense of being subservient to and dominated by the state. Rural policy decisions were made at the top with little input from society or even the scientific community. Of course, if the baseline of comparison were a poor country with a weak state, Korea's rural institutions would seem strong. Relative to Japan and Taiwan, however, the lack of institutional autonomy is striking.

The concepts of state and societal corporatism may be useful here. At the societal end of the spectrum, Nokyo in Japan was built out of preexisting, independent farmers' organizations that were co-opted and reorganized by the state. While on the one hand it was subject to top-down regulation and expected to carry out state policy, on the other hand its political power was so great that the state often found itself captive to agrarian interests. The NACF in Korea sits firmly on the statist side of the spectrum, as it was built by the state and imposed on society, and Taiwan's FA system falls in the middle, shifting over time toward societal corporatism. Without taking a detour into theories of state-society relations, this characterization of the three systems echoes the argument that institutions with linkage and autonomy are better for development.[9]

Changes in South Korean Rural Sector Development

After Japanese colonial rule (1910–1945) ended, Korea entered a tumultuous period of occupation by foreign powers, division, and war. In the South, the

Korean War (1950–1953) resulted in over one million civilian casualties and left up to a quarter of the population homeless.[10] The prospects for economic recovery were bleak, since the cities were basically destroyed and most colonial-era industries were located in the North. Although agriculture in South Korea was more developed, the North cut off fertilizer supplies, which exacerbated the problems of diminished production and food shortages. President Syngman Rhee (1948–1960) relied on the United States to obtain fertilizers and grain.[11] Production experienced a one-off boost from land reform and then slowed considerably. Easy access to food aid meant the government had little incentive to develop agriculture and could direct its resources elsewhere. Rural neglect evolved into a pronounced policy of squeezing agriculture under Park Chung-hee (1961–1979). Early on, Park presented himself to the public as a "son of the soil," yet it took a full decade before a more balanced development strategy was seriously pursued. In short, rural policy can be roughly divided into three phases: land reform (1950–1953), unbalanced growth (1954–1971), and agricultural adjustment (1972–present).

Agriculture played a small part in Korea's economic takeoff. Most gains in production during the 1950s occurred immediately after the war. In the wake of cease-fire talks and land reform, total production grew 10.9 percent annually from 1952 to 1954, surpassing prewar peak levels in 1954. The annual growth rate then dropped to 2.4 percent for the remainder of Rhee's presidency, from 1954 to 1960. The sector's performance improved under Park, growing about 3.8 percent in the 1960s and 3.6 percent in the 1970s (see table 9). Even though these rates were above the global average (about 2.7 percent for 1952–1971), agriculture's impact on the larger economy was modest. In the mid-1960s, its share in gross national product (GNP) started to plummet, while the manufacturing sector boomed. Industry and related services accounted for nearly 70 percent of the increase in GNP between 1964 and 1975. For this same period, the outflow of capital from agriculture constituted only about 10 percent of domestic capital formation, owing to several years of negative cash flow and low savings rates among rural households. The outflow of labor was a different story. The farm population reached its peak in 1967 and then declined rapidly. By 1975, an estimated nine million farmers-turned-migrants had joined the nonagricultural workforce.[12]

South Korean agriculture was hardly a backward economic sector, but it never received enough support to realize its potential. Rhee was concerned primarily with maintaining the military, which had expanded during the Korean War from about sixty-five thousand troops to over seven hundred thousand.[13] Economic policy was a secondary priority. Beyond encouraging some degree of import substitution, there was no coherent strategy for growth, much less a plan for agriculture. Rhee engaged heavily in patronage politics and surrounded himself with those most loyal to him. Corruption and political repression eventually gave rise to an opposition movement that toppled the regime. The interim government led by Chang Myon was ineffectual and short-lived. On May 16, 1961, Park successfully staged a military coup and two years later was elected president. He campaigned on an agriculture-first platform, in part because he believed that increasing farmers' purchasing power was key to building a market for manufactured goods. More importantly, Park wanted to exploit his rural identity—he was one of seven children born to poor farmers—to create a reliable base of support in the countryside that would counterbalance the more contentious political climate of the cities. Soon after the election was over, however, he wavered on economic policy and decided to prioritize industry.[14]

The first and second five-year plans (spanning 1962–1966 and 1967–1971) outlined an ideology called "guided capitalism" and endorsed strategic state intervention in the economy to support export-oriented industrialization. Grain self-sufficiency was also identified as an important goal, but in practice it was ignored because of continued access to US food aid. For the Rhee and Park eras, the total value of imports from the Public Law 480 "Food for Peace" program was US$1.7 billion (versus $387 million for Taiwan). Grain imports amounted to over 12 percent of domestic production in the late 1960s and to over 20 percent in the early 1970s. Although some aid was probably necessary to meet consumption needs, comparing the data on P.L. 480 with estimated shortages in domestic production strongly suggests that excess imports were used to keep food prices and urban wages down.[15] Sadly, even with a grain surplus, pockets of the countryside were still regularly affected by "spring hunger," a four-to-six-week period occurring after the winter food supply was exhausted.[16]

Besides cheap food imports, low levels of investment and unfavorable terms of trade also worked against the rural sector. Agriculture consistently received less than 9 percent of total government investment in the 1960s, a small share considering its size.[17] As in Taiwan, a rice-fertilizer barter system was used to extract resources from the countryside. The government purchase price for rice was below the cost of production for the entirety of Rhee's presidency. It rose above the cost of production under Park but remained below market prices until 1972.[18] More aggregate data on the prices received and paid by farmers confirm that the intersectoral terms of trade were unfavorable toward farmers between 1964 and 1972.[19] Additionally, the nominal and relative rates of assistance for agriculture were negative in South Korea until about 1970.[20]

The intention behind discriminatory pricing policies was to enable the transfer of resources from agriculture to industry, but in reality, the main effect was to depress production and enlarge the rural-urban income gap. Rice was (and still is) the most important farm product in Korea. Despite increases in average yields, rice production grew only 2.1 percent per year for 1954–1973, which was lower than the population growth rate and lower than production levels in the 1930s.[21] Supplementing incomes with specialty crops or local off-farm employ-ment was difficult, since land resources were scarce and most industries were concentrated around the cities of Seoul and Pusan. Owing to land reform and a high population density, the average farm size in Korea remained below 1 hectare (2.47 acres) until 1978, with over 30 percent of rural households farming less than 0.5 hectares (1.24 acres).[22] This amount of land was too small to adequately support a family. And while the rural standard of living may have improved in absolute terms (poverty data actually give a mixed picture), it clearly declined in relative terms.[23] The average farmer's income dropped from being 16 percent higher than the average urban worker's in 1963 to 35 percent lower in 1969. Looking at just agricultural income (excluding other sources), the gap was even larger: compared with urban wages, farm incomes were 5 percent lower in 1963 and 50 percent lower in 1969.[24] Survey data on real per capita consumption show a similar decline. Farm households consumed about 14 percent less than urban households in 1963. By 1968, the difference was 55 percent.[25]

Korea's rapid transition to an advanced industrial economy is reflected in agriculture's diminishing share of GNP, exports, and employment (again, see table 9). Underlying these structural changes was a deliberate strategy of unbal-anced growth. The discussion so far has focused on how that strategy hurt the countryside, though surely there were benefits too. Fast-paced industrializa-tion provided a market for farm products, an outlet for surplus labor, and an increased supply of production inputs such as chemical fertilizers and farm machinery.[26] Moreover, the developmental squeeze on agriculture and related rural-urban disparities could have been much worse.[27] As one scholar described the situation, rural areas were left in a state of "benign neglect."[28] Of course, none of this mattered to farmers who resented the palpable improvements in other Koreans' lives. Worried about their economic and social position, many people who had supported Park Chung-hee in the 1963 election voted against him in 1967.[29]

In the years that followed, Park started rolling out more favorable pro-grams for agriculture, although it was not until the third five-year-plan period (1972–1976) that P.L. 480 imports were terminated and agricultural adjust-ment goals were formally incorporated into national development policy. These included promoting high-yield varieties of rice, increasing the purchase price for grains, improving access to rural credit, investing in village infrastructure, and developing major river basins into large-scale farming areas. The New Vil-lage Movement, launched in 1970, became the ideological and organizational framework for the third five-year plan, and eventually all rural programs were subsumed under the campaign. To be clear, the state's strong emphasis on industrialization was not abandoned, as it was also during this time that Korea shifted from light manufacturing to heavy and chemical industrialization. The key difference with the previous period was that industry and agriculture were developed simultaneously. According to Young Jo Lee, these changes amounted to a "politically timely but economically unsustainable Bismarckian alliance of 'rye and steel.'"[30]

Certain aspects of Korea's agricultural adjustment strategy were indeed unsustainable. Park insisted on subsidizing both producers and consumers, ordering that rice and barley be purchased at above-market prices and sold at below-market prices. It also subsidized the cost of fertilizer. These interventions were financed through extra-budgetary accounts, the Grain Management Fund and the Fertilizer Fund, which quickly accumulated large deficits (about 2 percent of GNP in 1974) and generated inflationary pressures.[31] Eventually, fertilizer subsidies were scaled back, and price supports for Tong'il were discontinued. These changes translated into better terms of trade and an improved income position for farmers in the early 1970s, followed by another period of relative decline. Between 1968 and 1973, the ratio of prices received to prices paid by farmers increased 20 percent. It held steady (and was equal to 1.0) for about three years, then dropped 13 percent between 1976 and 1981.[32] Data on consumption and incomes exhibit the same pattern. Farm income even surpassed that of the average wage earner in 1974–1975, only to fall behind again in the late 1970s.[33] Interestingly, in spite of these particular adjustments, the overall level of agricultural protection increased rapidly during this time. The nominal rate of protection soared from -4 percent in 1965 to 117 percent in 1980 (versus 82 percent for Japan, 52 percent for Taiwan, and 38 percent for Western Europe in 1980).[34] Still today, Korea has one of the most protected agricultural sectors in the world. My research does not attempt to explain this fact, except to suggest that it reflects just how small and uncompetitive the sector is.

Similar to the up-and-down movement of rural incomes, gains in agricultural production were short-term and uneven. In general, the growth rates of major crops in the 1970s were lower than in the 1960s. One exception was rice, which grew about 3.9 percent per year from 1970 to 1979.[35] Most of this growth was due to the diffusion of Tong'il. Its yield was over 30 percent higher than traditional japonica varieties. By 1976, South Korea had achieved the second-highest total rice yields in Asia (after Japan). The next year, Park declared that rice self-sufficiency had been realized and the country was prepared to extend food aid to the North. Serious problems soon emerged, however, as crop disease and cold weather led to failed harvests in 1978–1980. Farmers were hit hard, since at its peak 85 percent of all paddy land was dedicated to Tong'il, and cultivation of the crop required costly chemical fertilizers and farm machinery.[36] Rural indebtedness and relative poverty levels began to rise, tenant farming returned, and millions of people gave up farming altogether.[37] Once it became clear that efforts to scale up agriculture and promote rural industry had also failed, the state's development plans were scrapped in favor of more food imports, protective tariffs, and price supports for the small number of farm households left. Korea is still a net food importer, and high levels of agricultural protection are justified on food security grounds.[38]

The New Village Movement's biggest impact was on the village environment. Korean sources often characterize rural conditions before the campaign as "life with a kerosene lamp under a thatched roof." In 1970, about 80 percent of rural homes had thatched roofs made of rice straw, and only 20 percent had electricity. Less than 10 percent of all roads were paved, and approximately 40 percent of villages were inaccessible by car.[39] In just these three areas—roofs, electricity, and roads—the campaign brought about dramatic changes. By 1978, almost 100 percent of thatched roofs had been replaced with tiled roofs, 98 percent of households had installed electricity, and nearly 100 percent of villages could be reached by road.[40] Whereas some observers lamented the new roofs as damaging to traditional aesthetic values (they were usually bright blue), for many people, they were a welcome symbol of modernity, since the old ones had to be replaced every year.[41] Consumption of electricity and ownership of electrical appliances increased at a staggering rate, enabling all kinds of improvements in productivity and quality of life.[42] And with the rapid construction of bridges and roads (about eighty thousand small bridges and 105,000 kilometers of roads were built), the traditional A-frame wooden carrier, used to transport heavy loads along narrow pathways, virtually disappeared.[43] Once the iconic image of rural poverty, the A-frame was replaced by hand-drawn carts, bicycles, and motorized vehicles. In addition to these achievements, the campaign facilitated the upgrading of irrigation, sewage, and drinking-water supply systems. All types of infrastructure, at the household and community levels, were affected.

The government's drive to make the countryside look modern was also problematic, to be sure. It imposed uniform standards on villages and required residents to shoulder most of the costs. It probably diverted resources and attention away from projects that could have effected broader economic change, such as the development of village sideline industries. For these reasons, there are few scholars outside Korea who assign any role to the New Village Movement in fostering rural development. Yet within Korea, the campaign is remembered as a kind of golden age for rural advancement. In 2008, to mark the sixtieth anniversary of the Republic of Korea, the *Chosun Ilbo* published the results of a Korean

TABLE 9. Agricultural and Industrial Sector Change in South Korea, 1954–1981

YEAR	1954	1957	1962	1967	1972	1977	1981
Population							
Total population (millions)	21.5	23.0	26.5	30.1	33.5	36.4	38.7
Rural population (millions)	13.2	13.6	15.1	16.1	14.7	12.3	10.0
Share of rural population in total population (%)	61.2	59.1	57.0	53.5	43.8	33.8	25.8
GNP[1]							
Share of agriculture in GNP (%)	48.0	44.4	36.6	30.1	26.4	23.0	18.0
Share of industry in GNP (%)	7.6	10.3	16.2	20.6	23.4	28.5	30.9
Exports							
Share of agricultural and marine exports in total exports (%)	n/a	n/a	45.0	19.4	10.5	11.5	6.5
Share of industrial and mining exports in total exports (%)	n/a	n/a	55.0	80.5	89.5	88.4	93.5
Employment[2]							
Share of agricultural workers in economically active population (%)	n/a	n/a	63.1	55.2	50.6	41.8	34.2
Share of industrial workers in economically active population (%)	n/a	n/a	8.7	12.8	14.2	22.4	21.3

AVERAGE ANNUAL GROWTH RATES	1954–1961 (1954–1960)	1962–1971	1972–1981
GNP growth rate (%)	4.4 (4.3)	8.8	8.0
Agricultural production growth rate (%)	3.6 (2.4)	3.8	3.6
Industrial production growth rate (%)	11.3 (12.4)	17.1	14.0

Source: Data for 1954–1961 come from *National Income of Korea* 1975, 146–47, 248–49, 256–57. Data for 1962–1981 come from *Major Statistics of the Korean Economy* 1982, 3–4, 7, 19, 58, 64. Population estimates for 1954 and 1957 taken from Ban, Moon, and Perkins 1980, 14.

[1] GNP data for 1954–1961 based on 1970 constant market prices; data for 1962–1981 based on 1975 constant market prices. Agriculture includes the farming, forestry, and fishery sectors. Industry includes the manufacturing and mining sectors.

[2] Employment data for 1962 are actually for 1963.

Gallup poll about the country's greatest achievements. The New Village Movement topped the list for over 40 percent of respondents, receiving more votes than any other event, including the 1987 democracy movement and the 1988 Olympics.[44] While public memory is admittedly subjective and often unrelated to actual historical events, what this poll suggests is nonetheless important: that perhaps the campaign has been judged unfairly and its impact, on balance, was more positive than negative.

The rest of this chapter deals with the questions of how and why these various outcomes occurred. Following an examination of rural institutions and the NACF, it returns to the subject of the New Village Movement, offering insight into the reasons the campaign was successful in some areas but not others.

Rural Institutions and the National Agricultural Cooperative Federation

Japan and the United States

Any discussion of South Korea's postwar institutions must consider how they were shaped by Japan and the United States. In the early twentieth century, Japan transformed the Korean peninsula. Colonial authorities built modern political and economic institutions, developed both hard and soft infrastructure, and greatly expanded state control over society. On the basis of a cadastral survey conducted between 1910 and 1918, property rights and a system of land taxation were formalized, allowing the state to effectively penetrate the countryside.[45] After World War I, with a surplus of industrial capital and plans to extend its empire into China, Japan intensified its development efforts. In the northern part of Korea, where there were more mineral resources, the colonial state partnered with private capitalists to promote industry, while in the south it introduced new agricultural technologies and farming practices.[46]

Rice production took on greater urgency following the Japanese Rice Riots of 1918, a series of mass demonstrations that broke out across Japan against soaring rice prices. The government suppressed the riots and provided emergency relief, but these were stopgap measures, as structural changes in the Japanese economy meant domestic food supplies would only become more constrained. The solution was to increase supplies coming from abroad. By the 1930s, imports from Korea and Taiwan accounted for about 20 percent of Japan's domestic rice consumption.[47]

In the Korean countryside, the colonial state implemented a series of rice production increase plans. It built up a network of farmers' organizations, which facilitated the distribution of advanced farm inputs. Consumption of chemical fertilizers, for instance, increased thirteen times between 1916 and 1936, from about 400 metric tons to over 522,000 tons. Improved seed varieties were also widely adopted, affecting 85 percent of paddy land by 1936.[48] These changes, combined with major improvements in farmland and irrigation, led to significant gains in production. Rice yields rose from 1.7 tons per hectare in 1920 to 2.5 tons in 1940, and total rice output grew on average 3 percent per year.[49]

Despite these achievements, exploitive tenancy conditions and high levels of extraction impoverished Korean farmers. In 1932, the landlord class accounted for less than 4 percent of the population but owned approximately 64 percent of all farmland. Japanese landlords, in particular, controlled nearly 40 percent of farmland, including the most prime areas. Under the tight supervision of the colonial agricultural bureaucracy, one-third of the rice crop was shipped to Japan. Because this amount exceeded the gains in output, per capita rice consumption in Korea dropped 35 percent, and total grain consumption dropped 20 percent between 1915 and 1933.[50] Landlessness and starvation drove many people to migrate to Japan and Manchuria. Citing Japanese sources, Albert Keidel reports that well over half the rural population suffered from spring hunger, and more than one million people left Korea because of food shortages in the 1930s.[51]

As previously explained, Taiwan had a very different experience under colonialism. Agriculture was developed earlier and more fully. The situation of tenant farmers was not as precarious, owing to a lower population density and fewer absentee landlords. Farm size remained stable over time (whereas Korea's declined), suggesting that the expansion of cultivated land kept pace with population growth. The availability of local off-farm employment in the food-processing sector stemmed migration rates and minimized rural-urban imbalances. Living standards improved in step with increases in production, and people's overall evaluation of the state's agricultural institutions was positive.

These differences between Taiwan and Korea were mirrored in their postwar development trajectories. Korea's leaders did not see the same potential in agriculture that Taiwan's leaders did, so they prioritized other sectors. Industrialization continued the way it started, with state and private capital concentrated in a few cities. The result was greater disparities between rural and urban areas and higher rates of long-distance migration.[52] Korea's leaders were also much slower to revive the agricultural technologies, infrastructure, and institutions that Japan had left behind. Colonial-era farmers' organizations and rural extension agencies withered away during the Rhee administration. After they were revived in the 1960s, they were used primarily for resource extraction, causing distrust and alienation among farmers who already associated them with past exploitation. Thus, the effect of colonialism on South Korea's rural development was mostly negative. Agriculture probably would not have recovered as quickly from wartime destruction without the advances made in the 1920s–1930s, but compared to Taiwan, Korea fared worse under colonialism and inherited less favorable initial conditions.

South Korea also benefited less from US assistance than Taiwan, even though it received substantially more support. For the entire aid period (1946–1976), Korea received about $13 billion, making it one of the largest foreign aid recipients in American history. At the time, only Israel and South Vietnam had received more.[53] While most of this money went toward the military, about $5.6 billion went toward economic assistance. Within the budget for economic assistance, allocations for agriculture and natural resource programs were minimal, adding up to about $110 million. As already mentioned, over fifteen times that amount, or nearly $1.7 billion, was transferred to Korea in the form of P.L. 480 surplus imports, negatively affecting rural production and incomes. This type of assistance was phased out starting in 1971, the first year Korea was required to purchase the imports with foreign exchange instead of local currency.[54] In contrast, Taiwan allocated more funding to agriculture and received less in food aid.[55] It also had a more influential group of rural policy experts advising the government through the Joint Commission on Rural Reconstruction. Perhaps because of differences in leadership and aid priorities (and the larger market for surplus commodities), the US mission to Korea was less engaged in rural issues. US officials made no effort to rehabilitate or democratize the farmers' organizations, and their enthusiasm for land reform was wanting.

Land Reform

Before serious attempts were made at land reform, rural conditions in Korea were extremely volatile. In 1949, more than 16.7 million people, or 83 percent of the total population, lived in the countryside, and Korea's rural population density was among the highest in the world (around seven hundred people per square kilometer).[56] Approximately 76 percent of farms were smaller than 1 hectare (versus 25 percent for Taiwan), and 42 percent were smaller than 0.5 hectares (versus 10 percent for Taiwan).[57] As is common in densely populated societies, tenant farming was the dominant system of agriculture. Prior to reform, around 80 percent of farm households were engaged in full- or part-time tenant farming. Rents ranged from 45 to 80 percent of the main crop, and debts were commonplace, occurring in 75 percent of households.[58]

Tenancy disputes were a regular feature of rural life. They escalated quickly during the colonial era, propelled by an activist peasant union movement. Japanese authorities described the unrest as a "constant phenomenon," recording over 4,800 disputes in the 1920–1932 period, and more than 136,000 disputes in the 1933–1939 period. Attempts were made to regulate landlord-tenant contracts, but the overall class structure remained intact through the end of World War II. After the war, local peasant unions and so-called people's committees took matters into their own hands, enacting land reform measures to address the grievances of tenants. News of successful land reform in the Soviet-controlled North bolstered these efforts and fueled demand for reform in the American-occupied South. In the fall of 1946, a major agrarian rebellion erupted, involving 2.3 million participants across forty counties. The US response was to suppress the rebellion. Some one thousand protesters were killed, and another thirty thousand were arrested. The occupation government also came down more firmly on the side of land reform, and in 1948 it redistributed a portion of tenanted land formerly owned by the Japanese.[59]

Up until the 1946 rebellion, the US Army Military Government in Korea (USAMGIK) had no clear position on land reform. Some directives were issued in 1945, but many administrators viewed land reform as antithetical to American capitalist values, smacking of communism, and were lukewarm about the idea at best. Still others pointed to the example of US-backed reforms in Japan and argued that similar policies were necessary if South Korea was to avoid falling prey to communism.[60] General John Hodge, the military governor of Korea, miscalculated the extent to which farmers would become disillusioned by the Americans' failure to act. For poor farmers, the delay fueled their suspicion that former Japanese holdings would be divvied up among wealthy Korean landlords who supported the occupation.[61] As for why the US was less proactive in Korea than Japan, it is important to remember that land reform was just becoming part of American foreign policy. Hodge was also less familiar with the issue than his counterpart in Japan, General Douglas MacArthur. As Wolf Ladejinsky noted of MacArthur: "He remembered the failure of the Philippine government in 1945 to act upon his advice to fight farm unrest among the Filipinos through more widespread ownership of land. He understood that any real chance of cutting the political ground from under the feet of the Communists, of bringing even a semblance of democracy to Japan, depended on the improvement of the lot of those who worked the land. He knew that there was no point to preaching democracy to empty stomachs."[62] In Korea, it took a major rebellion before Hodge learned the same lesson, and even then, the reforms were limited.

American ambivalence carried over into the Rhee administration, which was faced with a politically more difficult task: since most Japanese farmland had already been redistributed, the question now was what to do about Korean-held properties. Initially, Rhee was rather intransigent about land reform, objecting to proposals from the National Assembly that he deemed too inequitable toward landlords, many of whom supported his presidency.[63] After much back and forth, legislation was finally passed in March 1950. It called for a comprehensive redistribution of land resources, placed limits on the scale of ownership (of about 3 hectares or 7.41 acres), and outlined the terms of tenant payments and landlord compensation. However, ongoing objections to the bill delayed its implementation until the outbreak of the Korean War three months later. At that point, the suppressed people's committees reemerged. With help from the North Korean army and party organizations, the committees rushed to take control of the land slated for redistribution. These developments induced the South Korean government to take decisive action and prompted many landlords to preemptively sell off their holdings. As soon as the North Korean army retreated, the reforms were implemented without resistance. In light of these details, it is difficult to argue that land reform was an external policy imposed on Korea by the United States. Rather, as Gi-Wook Shin has persuasively argued, it was a product of agrarian conflict.[64]

South Korean land reform finally materialized at the height of the Korean War. Altogether, more than one million hectares of farmland were redistributed to tenants through government and private sales. Although tenancy was not eliminated, the vast majority of farmers became owners of their land. By 1964, the share of full owner-cultivators had risen to 72 percent, up from 14 percent in 1945 (see table 10). The government compensated landlords with land bonds, more than half of which went toward the purchase of vested enterprises previously owned by Japan. Land reform thus aided the process of industrialization, as former landlords became private entrepreneurs.[65] More importantly, it destroyed the old rural class structure and created a smallholder farm economy with extremely low levels of inequality. Despite Korea having a larger rural-urban gap than Taiwan, the income distribution among rural households was similar: the rural Gini coefficient was about .31 in 1970, down from .50 twenty years earlier, and the bottom 40 percent of the population received around 20 percent of national income.[66]

Land reform provided immediate relief to former tenants and gave a short-term boost to agricultural production, but it was not a solution for long-term growth. The fall in production after 1954 and the laggard growth performance described earlier testifies to its limitations.[67] For all the problems with the old system, landlords at least invested in farmland development and provided easy access to seeds, fertilizers, and farm equipment. After land reform, the government was slow to take on those functions, and price distortions made it difficult for farmers to do so themselves.[68] Moreover, there was virtually no change in the size of Korean farms.[69] Families struggling to make ends meet on their tiny plots either left the countryside or reentered into tenancy agreements, a trend that

TABLE 10. Extent and Impact of Land Reform in South Korea

POLICY	(A) VESTED FARMLANDS SOLD BY USAMGIK, 1948	(B) LAND REFORM ACT, 1949 (APPROVED IN 1950)	(C) PRIVATE SALES, 1945–1951	TOTAL SHARE OF CULTIVATED AREA AND HOUSEHOLDS AFFECTED BY REDISTRIBUTION AND PRIVATE SALES (A+B+C)
Share of cultivated area affected (%)	10.6	14.3	24.7	49.6
Share of farm households affected (%)	29.6	37.0	n/a	66.6

Total cultivated area affected by redistribution and private sales: 1,140,800 hectares (2,818,978 acres)

Total farm households affected by redistribution (excluding private sales): 1,646,945

Total landlord households affected by redistribution and private sales: 169,803

YEAR	1945[1]	1947	1964	1965
Share of owner-cultivators in total farm households (%)	13.8	16.5	71.6	69.5
Share of part owners–part tenants in total farm households (%)	34.6	38.3	23.2	23.5
Share of full tenants in total farm households (%)	48.9	42.1	5.2	7.0

Source: Data on cultivated area and the distribution of owners and tenants come from Ban, Moon, and Perkins 1980, 286. Data on the number of farm and landlord households come from Pak 1956, 81–82, 131, 192 (shares based on a 1950 estimate of 2,473,833 farm households). These two sources provide different figures for the area affected, with Pak's estimates being slightly lower.

[1] The columns for 1945 and 1947 do not add up to 100 percent. For those years, 2.7 and 3.1 percent of households were classified as "farm laborer and burnt field farmer."

increased over time (the proportion of full- and part-time tenant farmers rose from 30.5 percent in 1965 to 64.7 percent in 1985).[70] While the conditions of tenant farmers were certainly no worse than before land reform, concerns about their welfare nevertheless provided fodder for activist farmers' movements in the late 1970s.[71] As explained below, these movements were a reaction to disappointment with the New Village Movement and the NACF.

The National Agricultural Cooperative Federation

During the Rhee and Park administrations, the Ministry of Agriculture was a relatively weak institution.[72] Sung Hwan Ban and colleagues write that after 1945, the agricultural research and extension service built by Japan was dismantled. The Rhee regime "did almost nothing to replace it," and Korean farmers expressed "no regrets," given their experience under colonialism. Some guidance programs and cooperatives continued operating at the village level, but these were limited in scope. By the early 1960s, USAID officials were convinced the Ministry of Agriculture was too elitist and corrupt to run an extension service, so they supported the creation of the Office of Rural Development (ORD). Founded in 1962, the ORD was housed within the Ministry of Agriculture but functioned as an independent agency. Like other line ministries, it had representative branches at the provincial, county, and township levels. These were known as Rural Guidance Offices. The NACF, established by Park one year earlier, had a similar status and structure. It was a separate, centralized agency attached to the Ministry of Agriculture.[73]

Although the Ministry of Agriculture, the ORD, and the NACF were the main institutions charged with managing rural affairs, they were effectively subordinate to other, more powerful agencies: the Economic Planning Board and the Ministry of Home Affairs. Also established by Park, the Economic Planning Board was responsible for drafting national development policy. In the 1960s, it went up against the Ministry of Agriculture on the issue of grain prices and successfully pushed for an industry-first development strategy. Given that the Economic Planning Board had budgetary power, the Ministry of Agriculture's only real choice was to acquiesce.[74] The Ministry of Home Affairs was in charge of the police and local administration, appointing the heads of each level of government below the center (9 provinces, 140 counties, 1,473 towns and townships, and 36,000 villages). It challenged the Ministry of Agriculture for control of certain programs, including, for example, the New Village Movement.[75] What this shows is that even during the 1970s, when rural development became a national priority, the status of the agricultural bureaucracy was marginal.

Indeed, agriculture's meager budget and position within the larger economy and bureaucracy made it an unattractive career choice for talented, ambitious officials. Finding personnel who were competent and enthusiastic about agricultural matters was a persistent problem. The ORD Guidance Offices had an especially difficult time recruiting and retaining staff because of low salaries, few promotion opportunities, poor working conditions, and inadequate logistical support.[76] The same could be said for the NACF, which had the additional problem of being negatively associated with Japanese rule.

The NACF was formed through the merger of preexisting village cooperatives with the Korea Agricultural Bank. Despite what its name implies, as Ban and colleagues note, the only cooperative feature about it was that farmers purchased shares to become members.[77] It was not rooted in any kind of independent, grassroots movement; on the contrary, it was a parastatal institution that was founded by the state, organized along corporatist lines, and designed to prevent grassroots initiatives. It was also not really a federation, as lower-level units within the system were subject to the authority of the central headquarters in Seoul. Furthermore, its tiered structure paralleled the government, enabling easy manipulation by state actors. More than 90 percent of Korean farmers belonged to the NACF because it was their only source of fertilizer and low-interest credit. Besides these functions, the NACF handled all government purchases of grain. It sold production inputs and consumer goods and, to a lesser extent, was involved in agricultural extension, marketing, and insurance services. Larry Burmeister observes that after land reform, "a relatively egalitarian distribution of land plus agro-ecological uniformity (minimal commodity differentiation across farms) generated a potentially unified farm bloc." The NACF was therefore "created to insure that a politically docile countryside could be harnessed to the industrialization drive."[78]

The NACF was similar to the Farmers' Association in Taiwan in terms of its structure, functions, and origins. However, the FAs were far more effective agents of development. For starters, they had much more interaction with farmers and were more seriously engaged in agricultural extension work. The NACF actually had no regular presence in the villages, and it was not until the 1970s that the most basic units, known as primary agricultural cooperatives (PACs), were fully operative at the township level. Below them, there was no formal equivalent of Taiwan's small agricultural units.[79] It seems the consolidation of preexisting village cooperatives into township PACs was an intentional decision made by Park: since the township was not a natural social unit, farmers were less likely to identify with the cooperative and use it to advance their collective interests.[80]

The NACF also had a smaller extension staff than the ORD, and the way services were delivered by both institutions was top-down and disconnected from farmers. Rural guidance officers summoned the village heads to the township, with the expectation that they would go back and share information with others.[81] Guidance officers did not have much contact with the ORD's researchers and scientists, either, because of differences in education and social status. And ORD researchers were even more isolated from farmers.[82] In contrast, Taiwanese villages were like well-equipped laboratories of experimentation in the 1950s–1960s, with around 60 percent of FA income invested in extension work.[83] Close cooperation among officials, researchers, guidance workers, and farmers was the norm. Again, drawing from Burmeister's research, such cooperation led to "induced innovation" in the cases of Taiwan and Japan. In Korea, on the other hand, it was predominantly the state that directed the course of technological change in agriculture, without strong regard for scientific or market considerations, much less the interests of affected social groups. A prime example, addressed below, was the Tong'il campaign.[84]

The NACF had different rules of governance as well. Most critically, Korean farmers did not choose their own cooperative leaders. Those working at the township level were generally from the local area, but they were appointed, not elected (NACF elections were not instituted until after democratization in 1988). At the higher levels, it was often active or retired military officials calling the shots. In contrast, Taiwanese farmers voted every four years for representatives to the township FA, who in turn elected representatives to the level above, and so forth. Despite some problems with factional and party interference, the process was largely viewed as democratic and legitimate. Elected leaders were professional farmers and ethnically Taiwanese, which made farmers feel like they had ownership over the FAs. The perspective of Korean farmers was entirely different. They used the terms "government" and "agricultural cooperative" interchangeably, reflecting a distance between the NACF and its members. Additionally, the system was more rigidly hierarchical. Higher-level units were not constituted by representatives from below, and township PAC staff rarely moved up in the organization. The overall effect of these rules was to impede the flow of information, both horizontally and vertically, and to create gaps between the supply of services and actual demand. For instance, the way fertilizer was distributed was not based on information that farmers provided to the cooperative (as it was in Taiwan). Instead, it was determined at the central level using aggregate data from the Ministry of Agriculture and state-controlled fertilizer plants.[85]

Another point of divergence was that local cooperatives in Korea were heavily dependent on central fiscal transfers. Banking operations were not functional until the 1970s, and with limited capacity for self-financing, the cooperatives were unable to make their own decisions about what activities to pursue. Transfers also undermined the quality of services, since there were no hard budget constraints to ensure efficiency.[86] Data on agricultural marketing channels illustrate how this may have affected farmers' confidence in the NACF. Apart from accessing fertilizers and farm chemicals, over which the cooperatives had near-monopoly control, farmers preferred going through private commercial channels to buy and sell the items they needed. In the early 1970s, the private sector handled most purchases of farm implements (60 percent of total business) and animal feed (80 percent), as well as most sales of fruits and vegetables (60 percent), rice (73 percent), and other grains and potatoes (90 percent). Moreover, the delayed introduction of township banking operations meant that farmers borrowed mainly from private sources (over 65 percent), which had significantly higher interest rates (59 percent per year on average, compared to 13 percent for the NACF).[87]

This analysis supports the hypotheses about linkage and autonomy outlined in chapter 1. The NACF had an extensive membership base and was linked to higher levels of the state, giving it access to developmental resources. Land reform eliminated the possibility of landlords or large farmers controlling the cooperatives, which in theory was beneficial for small farmers. However, the NACF did not have strong ties to the village community. In addition to not having an organizational presence there, it also lacked formal mechanisms of accountability connecting cooperative officials to farmer members. Township leaders and staff, despite being from the areas they served, were not in frequent contact with farmers. Officials at the upper levels were not even necessarily familiar with farming, yet they exercised managerial and financial authority over the lower levels. For these reasons, the NACF was more extractive than developmental. It could effectively carry out state policy, but in a top-down manner that did not lend itself to feedback or participation. It was an appendage of the authoritarian state, not a vehicle for advancing farmers' interests.

Perhaps if the US had advocated for democratic reforms as it did in Taiwan, the NACF would have been more successful, although the larger political climate in Korea would have needed to be different as well. Because of how colonialism and the war period unfolded, there was a lingering distrust of rural institutions among the public and the government. In the early 1950s, local administrators were suspected of being colonial collaborators or communist sympathizers. Rather than trying to reconstitute these institutions in a way that would create buy-in from farmers, President Rhee neglected them, and President Park turned them into instruments of control. Park's government also became more authoritarian over time, as evidenced by the transition from the Third Republic (1963–1972) to the repressive Yushin regime (1972–1979). The Yushin reforms (*yushin* meaning "restoration" or "renewal") dissolved the National Assembly, eliminated popular elections, abolished presidential terms limits, and instituted martial law.[88] Needless to say, these circumstances were hardly conducive to the NACF adopting a more open or consultative model of governance, which raises the question: why did policy change occur?

The Shift toward Pro-rural Policies

In the 1967 and 1971 presidential elections, opposition candidates captured the votes of farmers who were dissatisfied with the government's squeeze on agriculture. Young Jo Lee reports that fertilizer prices rose 80 percent in 1964 alone, followed by a 44 percent increase in 1965. Farmers complained about not receiving the types of fertilizers they wanted at the times they needed them. Low grain prices, enforced by government purchasing quotas, acted as a ceiling on rural incomes. The opposition candidate in the 1963 election, Yun Po-sun, had lost by a slim margin (41.2 percent to 42.6 percent). In the end, it was rural voters who handed Park the victory. In 1967, Yun ran again, and even though this time Park won decisively, carving out a ten-point lead over Yun, rural voters in the southwestern Cholla provinces turned against him. In this region, known as the rice bowl of Korea, Park lost twenty-three of thirty-four counties, a shocking defeat considering that just four years earlier he had won all of them. What happened in Cholla was a clear referendum on agricultural policy and a warning that rural voters' support for the president could not be taken for granted. In 1971, Park found himself running against Kim Dae-jung of South Cholla (who would later serve as president from 1998 to 2003). Kim faced serious political and financial obstacles, but he still managed to carry 45 percent of the vote. Park's victory was marred by the failure of his attempts to win back farmers' loyalty through price adjustments, high-yield-variety seeds, and cement for rural infrastructure—the beginnings of what would become the New Village Movement. This time it was regionalist mobilization driving support for Kim (and for Park in the southeastern Kyongsang provinces). The loss of Cholla showed Park that he could neither command nor purchase the rural vote, especially at a time when regionalism was catching fire politically.[89]

While the specific factors affecting policymaking in Korea and Taiwan were obviously different, examining the two cases together is nonetheless suggestive of a theory of sectoral change, that is, of when countries might shift from urban to rural bias. In both cases, the top leaders were concerned about a looming rural crisis. The deterioration of farmers' economic position because of exploitative policies created an undercurrent of social and political discontent. In Taiwan, a pro-rural coalition emerged gradually, comprising the FAs, the JCRR, and members of the Provincial Assembly and Legislative Yuan. Expansion of the electoral process after 1969 and Chiang Ching-kuo's personal commitment to including more Taiwanese in politics were a big part of the story.

In Korea, the institutions most likely to advocate for farmers were weak, and the National Assembly was completely dominated by urban socioeconomic interests (professional bureaucrats, soldiers, educators, and businessmen accounted for 76 percent of members in 1967, while farmers accounted for only 0.6 percent).[90] The process of change was therefore not as incremental. Instead, there were two triggering events that precipitated a shift in policy: the presidential elections and the abrupt cancellation of US food aid. In response to changes in the global economy, including the decline of American postwar hegemony, the Nixon administration began to stress the export earning potential of agriculture. The US announced it would be scaling back the amount of food aid, altering the terms of assistance to dollar-repayable loans, and eventually cutting the P.L. 480 program altogether. Reluctant to tap into foreign exchange reserves for the purchase of imports, the Korean government decided to focus on increasing

domestic production, a strategy that could potentially engender political support in the countryside and appeal to nationalist concerns about food self-
sufficiency.[91] The experiences of Taiwan and Korea thus show that the adoption
of pro-rural policies is more likely when farmers can express their grievances at
the polls and when food security is threatened.

A third important factor in the Korean case was exceptionally high rates of
migration to the cities. As Jeremy Wallace has demonstrated, there is a strong
correlation between urban concentration and regime change, since cities tend to
promote collective action. Furthermore, a major cause of urban concentration
is urban bias.[92] A corollary to this argument is that agricultural adjustment policies may slow the rate of migration and contribute to regime stability. Park was
certainly worried about his standing in the cities, where he was consistently losing ground to his political opponents (in 1963, for example, Yun won 57 percent
of the urban vote).[93] Migration was threatening because it expanded the pool of
disaffected urban voters, while simultaneously reducing the size of the electorate
in the countryside, the president's stronghold.

Still another consideration was the connection between migration and food
security. The influx of migrants meant greater urban demand for food and fewer
rural producers. The old strategy of keeping food prices down by exploiting
farmers was becoming less viable. Even without the shock of aid withdrawals,
the government needed farmers to produce as much as possible in order to
keep pace with the country's shifting demographics. And according to the logic
of collective action, a smaller farm sector only improved the chances of farmers organizing against unfair prices and other discriminatory policies. It was
also becoming costlier to subsidize the growing population of urban consumers.
Given this set of conditions, the continuation of urban-biased policies would
have risked food shortages and surging prices. Shifting toward rural bias would
mean higher food prices as well, but at least gains in production might keep
prices from rising too quickly.

The conventional wisdom about sectoral change asserts that as farmers become
wealthier and more specialized, their capacity and determination to affect policy
increases. The government's reliance on cheap food to maintain social order also
diminishes as consumers become richer.[94] To these points I would add the following: it is not necessary that farmers be the ones pushing for change, so long as
the government somehow realizes their economic and political relevance. Korean
farmers were excluded from the policy process. They had virtually no influence
over the substance or implementation of rural policy. Yet they were still valuable
to Park because of his desire to create a political counterweight to the cities. The
elections provided a small opening for farmers (who were not well organized)
to express their dissatisfaction, and the results laid bare the problem of regime

legitimacy. After minor policy adjustments failed to shut out the opposition in 1971, Park doubled down on rural development.

Finally, in addition to the variables already mentioned—elections, food security, and migration—it is possible that Korea and Taiwan were copying each other and Japan. Mick Moore makes this argument, explaining that the timing of the switch to rural bias was similar in these countries because of policy emulation. This practice was quite common, arising from physical proximity, frequent exchanges, and the history of colonialism. He further suggests that the manufacturers of farm inputs and the agricultural bureaucracy itself may have influenced events, lobbying for change to protect their own interests in the face of rural decline.[95]

Although it is difficult to pinpoint the main impetus for reform without more information about the inner workings of these governments, the fact that Korea and Taiwan had competitive authoritarian regimes was extremely important. I hesitate to describe it as a necessary condition because, for Korea, changes in economic policy occurred at the same time popular elections were abolished, which made the president less beholden to farmers. And as explained in the next chapter, elections were clearly not a relevant factor in China, where farmers' grievances found expression through mass protest instead. That kind of situation is precisely what Park was trying to avoid with the New Village Movement: he wanted to prevent voter discontent from escalating into active protest, which, if unleashed, could be harnessed by his opponents to take down his presidency. The word "reform" understates what happened next. To counter such a threat, Park launched an ambitious mass mobilization campaign, an all-out effort to transform the countryside and consolidate authoritarian rule.

The New Village Movement

The New Village Movement has always been controversial because of its association with the Yushin regime. Beginning in October 1972, the government passed a series of emergency measures that effectively eliminated all legal constraints on Park Chung-hee's power and made him president for life. The New Village Movement, which started a few years earlier, was expanded and infused with an ideological component. The entire population was called on to fight communism, support modernization, and sacrifice for the nation-state. Building richer and stronger villages (and later cities, factories, and schools) was seen as essential to building a richer and stronger nation. In the context of Yushin, which otherwise depended heavily on the state's coercive apparatus, the campaign employed a mix of ideological indoctrination and material rewards to create a foundation for populism.[96]

There is some disagreement in the existing literature about whether the New Village Movement accomplished anything besides increasing support for Park. Several Western scholars have described it as overly political, top-down, and trivial in terms of its effect on development.[97] However, this characterization is only partially accurate. The 1970s was by far the most important decade for rural infrastructure development, and the historical evidence overwhelmingly suggests that gains in this area can be directly attributed to the campaign. A growing number of studies by Korean scholars also highlight the genuine enthusiasm and bottom-up initiative that occurred in many communities.[98] In addition, the New Village Movement's significance in terms of its scope and duration is undeniable. It affected the whole country for the better part of ten years. It even outlived Park, who was assassinated in 1979, and has since been repurposed by various political and social actors. Most notably, it has been used by the South Korean government as a source of soft power, upheld as a model of success and incorporated into the country's official development assistance. For all these reasons, the campaign merits more serious attention than it has been given previously.

Origins

The New Village Movement was not an ordinary agricultural adjustment policy. It aimed to solve Park Chung-hee's legitimacy problem by producing immediate, visible changes in the quality of rural life. It also sought to reshape rural culture, which was believed to be a major barrier to progress. Park subscribed to a cultural theory of modernization. In a 1971 speech to provincial governors, he remarked that villagers' construction of a bridge, for instance, "must be viewed from the psychological angle," and that "modernization starts with the spiritual modernization of individual farmers."[99] He often referred to Saemaul as a movement for "becoming prosperous" or "better living," but above all else, it was about spiritual enlightenment. At a national campaign event in 1972, he explained: "The Saemaul movement is a spiritual enlightenment campaign, a spiritual revolution, a philosophy of action. When our rural communities are overflowing with the Saemaul spirit, all our farm villages will become well-to-do in a short while, and the task of rural modernization will pose no problem."[100]

The Saemaul spirit was promoted as a concept that combined modern and traditional values. It consisted of three parts: diligence (a modern value), self-help (a traditional value), and cooperation (a traditional value). These were frequently contrasted with the "backward" cultural tendencies of indolence, dependency, and factionalism.[101] The campaign's message was thus somewhat contradictory. On the one hand, rural traditions were a source of hope and national renewal. On the other hand, farmers were trapped in a culture of poverty that had to be fundamentally altered. In the words of Kim Joon, director of the National Saemaul Leadership Training Institute (SLTI), the movement's primary goal was to "cure the sickness of our minds in order to regain the pure traditions of our forefathers."[102] Interestingly, the Saemaul spirit was also conceived as something akin to the Protestant ethic famously described by Max Weber.[103] Once farmers were awakened by the Saemaul spirit, their work ethic would improve, and Korea would quickly catch up with the West. Park was not a Christian, but he was apparently inspired by the work of Kim Yong-ki, founder of the Canaan Farmers' Training School, which taught Puritan values and became a model for SLTI.[104] Even today, Korean missionaries engaged in development projects abroad talk about this history and the affinity between Christianity and the New Village Movement.[105]

The official narrative of the campaign traces its origins to a village in North Kyongsang Province that had been affected by heavy rainstorms and flooding. In August 1969, Park visited the village while touring the disaster area and was impressed with how quickly its roads and housing had been repaired by the residents. The quality of construction was also better than average. The villagers' example of diligence, self-help, and cooperation formed the basis of the Saemaul spirit.[106]

From a broader international perspective, Japan stands out as the most likely source of inspiration for the New Village Movement. Park was obsessed with turning South Korea into a "second Japan." He was born during the colonial era and educated in Japanese. He attended the Manchurian Xinjing Officers School and the Japanese Military Academy, after which he served in the Imperial Army. This experience greatly shaped his personality and perspective on modernization. He believed that Yushin was comparable to the Meiji Restoration, a revolution designed to expedite economic development and realize the ideal of "rich nation, strong army." His faith in rural mobilization was also tied to Japan.[107]

As explained in chapter 1, in the 1930s, Japan launched the Rural Revitalization Campaign to provide relief to communities affected by the Great Depression. A similar government initiative took place in colonial Korea from 1932 to 1940. Village five-year plans were devised to address food shortages and household indebtedness. The campaign stressed spiritual regeneration as well, promoting the values of social harmony, collectivism, and self-sufficiency. Politically, Korea's Rural Revitalization Campaign was intended to cultivate consent for Japanese rule and to bring rural society into closer contact with the state. Young people were recruited to become "mainstays" of the campaign, and numerous village organizations were created, empowered, and co-opted by the state. Although the campaign's economic achievements were modest, it succeeded in strengthening state control. Gi-Wook Shin and Do-hyun Han write that when the New Village Movement is examined historically, "the parallels to the colonial campaign are unmistakable." Both campaigns emphasized the "economic and spiritual aspects of rural improvement, including such objectives as crop diversification, improved seed selection, simplification of traditional rituals, respect for traditional norms like filial piety, and loyalty to the nation."[108]

Competition with South Korea's communist neighbors was another factor that shaped the New Village Movement. Going by official statistics, during the 1950s–1970s, North Korea not only achieved the fastest rate of industrial-sector growth in the socialist world, but also the fastest rate of agricultural-sector growth in the entire world.[109] It was feared that if the North continued to perform better economically, then the communists would reemerge as an opposition force in the South. Reports attributing North Korea's success to the Chollima Movement—an economic modernization drive that resembled China's Great Leap Forward—may have motivated the decision to launch Saemaul. In fact, similarities among all three campaigns suggest that the Park regime was mimicking communist mobilization tactics.

Throughout the 1970s, Park repeatedly called the New Village Movement a "great leap forward."[110] He encouraged the competitive emulation of advanced villages as well as the construction of communal kitchens to free up women's labor so they could help with the campaign. Millions of people took part in training that stressed military discipline, and life in general became more regimented. Every day at 5:45 a.m., villagers were awakened by loudspeakers playing the "Song of Saemaul." Supposedly penned by Park himself, the lyrics urged villagers to "work while fighting" and "fight while working." Photographs from the period show people sitting or working together, often in perfect rows, listening to lectures, planting rice seedlings, or building bridges underneath the Saemaul flag.[111] In light of these details, it is no wonder that scholars have drawn comparisons with Maoist China and the interwar fascist regimes of Europe and Japan.[112] Just as Japan was considered a model and a rival power, the application of communist tactics to fight communism represented two sides of the same coin.

In the 1950s–1960s, the UN and USAID provided limited support for community development in Korea, although the initiative never really took off because of a lack of government commitment.[113] A more direct precursor to the New Village Movement was something called the People's Movement for National Reconstruction, which took place during the junta years (1961–1963). This campaign aimed to instill farmers with the values of hard work and frugality. It provided debt relief and grain price supports to raise incomes and involved the co-optation of rural organizations. An estimated four hundred thousand loudspeakers were installed in the villages, enabling the Ministry of Home Affairs to broad-cast propaganda, state policies, and Park's speeches. The Ministry of Education undertook similar efforts in the schools. The campaign helped Park mobilize votes in the 1963 election but then fizzled out as the direction of economic policy shifted in favor of industry.[114]

The revival of these methods and ideas nearly a decade later was motivated by politics. While there were surely good economic reasons to promote rural devel-opment (food security, domestic consumption, etc.), a large-scale campaign like the New Village Movement made little sense, given how small the rural sector had become. The timing and causes of policy change have already been discussed. As for why it took the form of a campaign, a key thing to understand is that Park, like Mao, came from a rural, military background and trusted in the power of mass mobilization. The third five-year plan by itself was unlikely to affect cultural change or to help him build a populist base. Park therefore pinned his hopes to the New Village Movement, believing it would address the political fallout caused by the relative decline of agriculture and turn Korea's peasants into loyal, industrious citizens. He also perceived it to be a viable approach to development, not unlike the strategies pursued in North Korea, Japan, and colonial Korea. The Great Leap Forward comparison is interesting, since by that time news of the famine had spread beyond China. Still, there is no reason its failure would have precluded Park from embracing mass mobilization. After all, the basic premise of these campaigns was different. Whereas China's campaign was about extracting as many resources from the countryside as possible, the New Village Movement marked the end of Korea's developmental squeeze.

Goals and Implementation

The impact of the New Village Movement was mixed because of the way its goals were defined and the political-institutional context in which it was implemented. Owing to Korea's highly centralized political system, the government successfully mobilized local officials to back the campaign, many of whom had no previ-ous experience or interest in rural development. Frequent inspections and mass supervision, facilitated by public announcements about how assistance would be distributed, worked to ensure that resources were not diverted to other pur-poses. The government also succeeded at generating significant popular support by empowering local activists, focusing on village improvement, and aiding a large number of villages (as opposed to a few models). However, the campaign's objectives became less clear and more ambitious over time. The high-profile status and ideological nature of the policy caused local officials to respond in an exaggerated manner that was not conducive to feedback. And even though many villagers had a favorable view of the campaign overall, it became apparent when problems arose that they were powerless to make meaningful changes. The quality of rural participation was ultimately lacking. The rest of the chapter elaborates these points.

With respect to the campaign's goals, the initial focus on the village environment was somewhat random, resulting from a cement surplus and the government's desire to dispose of it. Between October 1970 and June 1971, every village in Korea received 335 bags of cement to be used for infrastructure development. Following inspection, only those villages deemed to have made substantial progress (about sixteen thousand villages, or slightly less than half the total) were given an additional 500 bags of cement and one ton of steel rods.[115] This method of competitive, selective assistance continued throughout the campaign, as did the emphasis on infrastructure.

After 1973, agricultural production, rural industrialization, and other schemes intended to raise rural incomes took on greater importance. At the heart of these efforts was Tong'il production, the cornerstone of Korea's green revolution. Ideological work also intensified, and the target population for training (at SLTI and local sites) was expanded from Saemaul leaders, to farmers in general, to a broad spectrum of elites: professors, priests, monks, journalists, artists, doctors, judges, lawyers, accountants, industrialists, diplomats, congressmen, and even presidential bodyguards. Many of these actors became involved in various sub-campaigns, each with its own set of projects and goals. The main ones were known as Urban Saemaul, Factory Saemaul, School Saemaul, Military Saemaul, and the New Spirit Movement.[116]

The proliferation of campaign objectives was indicative of the policy's ideological character. According to Stephen Quick, ideological policies are vague, utopian, highly politicized, and basically immune from criticism. They usually have too many goals, a number of which are immeasurable, and no clear hierarchy of goals. For these policies, political popularity is a liability, since it "inhibits the feedback process and reduces the capacity of the implementing agency to respond creatively to problems."[117] In Korea's case, the campaign's popularity stemmed from its close association with the president. Local officials went to extreme lengths to exceed Park's expectations, often at the expense of what farmers really wanted or needed. Surely for many people, the cultural objectives of the campaign were questionable, based largely on prejudiced assumptions about farmers' attitudes and behavior, but there was no space to challenge the government's narrative in the context of Yushin. The promotion of scientific agriculture was problematic as well. This goal was technically too complex to be achieved through mobilization, especially at the accelerated pace that the campaign demanded. In the early 1970s, scientists raised concerns about disseminating Tong'il too widely, but they were overruled by the director of the ORD and Park, who elevated Tong'il to a matter of national security.[118] The result of such a politically charged environment was excessive compliance with central directives.

The way the policy was framed was not the only reason officials became swept up in the campaign. Placing the Ministry of Home Affairs, rather than the Ministry of Agriculture, in charge of the New Village Movement signaled the policy's importance and had the effect of mobilizing the entire bureaucracy. Saemaul promotional councils were established at every level of the administration, bringing together leaders from major public and private institutions to plan and coordinate campaign activities. Full-time Saemaul officers and departments were added to local governments, and all personnel, including the police and the military, were required to contribute to the campaign.[119]

This reshuffling of responsibilities was crucial because local officials in Korea were not automatically inclined to support rural development. Compared with Taiwan, fewer people were working on rural issues, and as a consequence of agriculture having been neglected for so long, urban bias was more deeply entrenched. Vincent Brandt and Ji Woong Cheong assert that the campaign successfully changed Korea's "status quo oriented bureaucrats" into "relatively enthusiastic activists dedicated to a transformation of the countryside."[120] After years of weak and fragmented efforts, rural policy coordination was achieved, but because of the intensity of mobilization, local officials were still primarily concerned with how to handle pressure coming from above. The top-down, statist orientation of rural policy remained unchanged.

Below the township, the village development committee was the focal point for campaign mobilization. This committee consisted of ten to fifteen members, including traditional village leaders (the village and neighborhood chiefs) and local activists known as Saemaul leaders. Surveys from the period show that Saemaul leaders had a higher education and income status than most farmers. Although they were engaged in farming, they also had experience in other careers. The majority were in their thirties and forties (about 84 percent), and the average length of service was four to five years. Around half of Saemaul leaders (48 percent) were chosen by election, while the rest were appointed or volunteered.[121] It was common practice to have two leaders sit on the committee at the same time, one male and one female. Estimates of the total number of Saemaul leaders active in rural areas during the 1970s range from 170,000 to 200,000.[122]

The empowerment of Saemaul leaders altered village authority relations. Park Jin-hwan, special adviser to the president and architect of the campaign, writes that women's participation "was a new concept for a country embedded in the Confucian cultural tradition," and that female Saemaul leaders "induced rural women to organize for the first time in the history of rural Korea." While his view is perhaps overstated, women's associations were indeed actively involved in the campaign. They organized against gambling and drinking, promoted birth control, and encouraged the use of "rice savings jars" to fund community projects.[123]

Saemaul leaders in general were also very different from traditional village elites. They were younger, self-made men and women. They were not paid for their work, but they benefited from significant state backing. They wore caps and armbands emblazoned with the campaign's logo, a green-and-yellow three-leaf bud representing the three parts of the Saemaul spirit. They had special postcards they could send to the minister of home affairs in case of any difficulties, a privileged channel of communication that bypassed local officials. Most importantly, they were publicly exalted by President Park. Many leaders received an honorary medal for their work, and the most outstanding ones were invited to present their "success cases" at SLTI, the National Saemaul Leaders' Convention, and the televised monthly meeting of the Economic Planning Board. Seung-Mi Han observes that by empowering this group, the campaign accelerated changes in governance that had been under way since the 1961 coup: "The Confucian rule by village headmen, which silenced the young and kept them from active participation in village affairs, was dismantled."[124]

The success cases of Saemaul leaders shared certain predictable elements—coming from humble beginnings, encountering some kind of difficulty, struggling alone to overcome that difficulty, feeling encouraged by the Saemaul movement, winning the trust of fellow villagers, and finally achieving collective prosperity. Many of the leaders recounted moving to the city for school or work, and then deciding to return home to make a difference. The themes of self-sacrifice, patriotism, and egalitarianism pervaded these narratives. Small details about mulberry trees, strawberry harvests, gravel collection, etc., made the stories sound authentic and relatable. At the same time, they contained lofty proclamations that sounded like propaganda, even if they were genuinely felt. To give an example, Mr. Lee Wan-suk of Kyonggi Province concluded his success story as follows: "Saemaul leaders! I am happy and honored to play the role of a single drop of oil in the flaming torch of the Saemaul Undong and would like to urge you to work together to make our fatherland more prosperous and radiant under the leadership of His Excellency President Park! Let us gather and unite our strength and move forward vehemently in the construction of an ever-expanding renovation of our fatherland!"[125]

In all likelihood, competition with other villages did more to motivate ordinary farmers than the emotional pleas of Saemaul leaders. In 1972, the government evaluated all villages based on standardized criteria for infrastructure, production, and incomes. It then grouped them into three categories, listed here from least to most advanced: basic (53 percent of the total), self-help (40 percent), and self-reliant (7 percent). Aid was directed to self-help and self-reliant villages, with greater amounts awarded to those demonstrating a strong commitment to the campaign, as measured by residents' labor, cash, and material contributions. The dramatic and highly visible transformation of villages receiving aid induced neighboring villages to participate, if only for the sake of keeping up appearances. Eventually, resistance gave way to competitive emulation. By 1977, there were no more basic villages. One-third had moved into the self-help category, and two-thirds were classified as self-reliant.[126]

To summarize, the government used several mechanisms to mobilize the bureaucracy and the population: Saemaul promotional councils and departments; village development committees and Saemaul leaders; intensive training and propaganda; standardized evaluations and inter-village competition. Mobilization was so effective that it is almost meaningless to speak of an implementing coalition. Everyone was part of it. There were no passive onlookers. Faced with enormous pressures from above and rising expectations from below, local officials had no choice but to comply. Farmers, for their part, were also more engaged with policy and had more interaction with officials than ever before. By the mid-1970s, most farmers were supportive of the campaign. It tapped into their desire for a better life and produced tangible improvements in village conditions. At least for a while, the sense of excitement was contagious.

However, despite the more egalitarian, participatory atmosphere created by the campaign, villagers' power vis-à-vis the state was limited. Park's assertion that the New Village Movement was a "training ground for Koreanized democracy" was contradicted by the Yushin reforms.[127] In practice, participation meant faithfully executing government policy. Specific project ideas were conceived at the apex of power and passed down the bureaucratic chain of command. Villagers worked under the close supervision of local officials, who at the height of the campaign visited several times a day. Saemaul leaders used a variety of tactics to achieve compliance, including demonstration, peer pressure, self-sacrifice, and in some cases violent confrontation.[128] Because villagers were expected to cover the majority of project costs and labor, they presumably had some bargaining power. Still, Saemaul leaders rarely opposed state directives or acted as policy innovators. According to one report, 90 percent of projects were "handed down" and only 10 percent were locally initiated.[129] Furthermore, while the campaign intentionally linked up with traditional organizations for mutual aid, rural associational life was not exactly robust. The state's penetration and atomization of Korean villages, which was reinforced by competition among villages, prevented the grassroots articulation of rural economic and political interests.[130]

Outcomes and Legacy

The top-down, one-size-fits-all approach to implementation was reflected in the campaign's outcomes. Even in the area of village infrastructure, the most popular and successful dimension of the campaign, things got carried away. National-level data show that the targets for major projects were often exceeded by a large margin (see table 11). Of course, the government may have wanted the official statistics to reflect a better-than-expected performance and just reported the targets and outcomes accordingly. Alternatively, it can be interpreted as evidence of excessive compliance. Take, for instance, the construction of village halls (community centers). This project supposedly originated at the village level; it was a creative choice made by farmers themselves rather than a mandate. Yet, assuming the data are correct, by the end of the campaign, there were actually more halls built than there were villages in Korea. In other words, the same projects were implemented everywhere and frequently taken to the extreme. Through the dissemination of visual propaganda and official guidelines for village beautification, the campaign produced a kind of rigid uniformity among villages. Indeed, the government's commemorative Saemaul pictorials are filled with images of nearly identical-looking communities.[131]

Related to this point, the government was heavily involved in designing, planning, and constructing rural housing. After 1976, when the roof replacement program was completed, the focus of village environmental improvement shifted from basic renovation to new home construction. The government called for the reconstruction of all dilapidated housing within ten years (an estimated 544,000 homes out of 2.9 million).[132] The Korean National Housing Corporation and the Ministry of Construction started releasing "standard designs for rural homes," which were said to resemble European villas. The NACF disbursed home loans through construction companies as a way of controlling expenses and building materials. In a comprehensive study of rural architecture, Seong-jun Jang explains that because of high rates of migration, there was little voluntary or private-sector reconstruction of housing, so almost by default the growing stock of dilapidated homes became the government's problem. During the 1970s, housing was increasingly treated as a "factor in the administration," something that had to be "finished" instead of allowed to develop organically. It was also regarded as a redistributive good. Jang writes: "The underdevelopment of the rural area legitimized a paternalistic control over every detail ostensibly for the public good, for the enlightenment of the people and for a just distribution of national wealth."[133]

TABLE 11.   Results of the New Village Movement in South Korea, 1971–1980

PROJECT	TARGET	OUTCOME	SHARE OF PROJECTS COMPLETED (%)
Village roads (km)	26,266	43,558	166
Farm feeder roads (km)	49,167	61,797	126
Small bridges	76,749	79,516	104
Small reservoirs	10,122	10,742	106
Small irrigation channels	22,787	28,352	124
Irrigation raceways (km)	4,043	4,442	109
Irrigation embankments (km)	17,239	9,180	53
Village halls	35,608	37,012	104
Public warehouses	34,665	22,143	64
Dilapidated housing improvement	544,000	225,000	42
Village layout improvement		2,747	
Sewage systems (km)	8,654	15,559	179
Electricity (households)	2,834,000	2,777,500	98
Telephone lines		345,240	
Saemaul factories	950	727	75
Reforestation (hectares)	744,354	347,153	47

Source: National Council of Saemaul Undong 1999, 24; S. Park 2009, 120.

Apart from the issue of uniformity, another problem was the financial burden placed on villagers. Between 1971 and 1979, the government covered only 37 percent of campaign expenditures (about 1.03 out of 2.75 trillion won), and with the exception of 1975, it never spent more than 5 percent of its tax revenue on the campaign (the average for the decade was 2.5 percent of tax revenue and 0.7 percent of GDP).[134] Since these figures include expenditures for the subcampaigns mentioned earlier, the actual burden on villagers was probably much higher than 63 percent. In fact, some scholars estimate it to be around 78 percent, with most contributions taking the form of unpaid labor.[135] In a four-village survey by Vincent Brandt and Man-Gap Lee, poor farmers expressed reluctance to work on projects that would bring advantages to wealthier households, and many complained that the New Village Movement only helped the rich.[136] Jang furthermore reports that in some places, poor people who could not afford to renovate or rebuild their homes ended up leaving the village. And as more people in general moved to the cities, the market value of rural homes decreased, making it hard to pay off housing-related debts.[137]

On the whole, however, the effect of the campaign on the village environment was positive. The problems described here were minor compared to the campaign's achievements. According to Brandt and Lee's survey, a strong majority of farmers (80 percent) said their standard of living was better in 1976 than 1971, citing Saemaul as the main reason. Farmers reported that they were very satisfied with the changes in roofs, roads, sewage systems, and electricity.[138] The impressive gains in these areas have already been discussed. It is important to remember that before the New Village Movement, most villages had received very little, if any, development assistance from the government, so the arrival of free cement and other supplies was a welcome change.

The campaign was much less successful at realizing its production and income goals. As previously explained, the government's promotion of Tong'il resulted in significant increases in rice output, but then later ran into major problems: growth in extra-budgetary expenditures, reliance on costly production inputs, and vulnerability to crop disease and low temperatures. It was also unpopular with consumers. Despite the promise of higher yields, farmers did not like the taste of Tong'il, which was no small matter, considering that they consumed about half of the rice they produced. Still, politicization of the issue led the government to ignore farmers' preferences as well as scientists' apprehensions about the risks of rapid diffusion. Local officials applied coercive methods, such as making repeated visits to farm households (in one county, the slogan "visit farmers ten times" was adopted) and destroying non-Tong'il varieties. Owing to poor demand, the government purchased Tong'il for use as military rations and had retailers sell it at discounted prices to low-income city dwellers.[139] Widespread diffusion, facilitated by intense administrative pressure and the homogeneity of Korean farms, made its collapse in 1978–1980 much worse than if it had been rolled out gradually and selectively. The program badly damaged the reputation of the agricultural bureaucracy (the ORD and NACF had led the effort) and, more seriously, put millions of farmers in financial jeopardy.

The push to industrialize the countryside also fell flat. As part of Factory Saemaul, the government provided companies with incentives to set up shop in rural areas. These included preferential loans, tax breaks, priority installation of electricity and telephone lines, and product purchasing contracts with government agencies and firms. Unfortunately, the supply of labor and infrastructure was simply not competitive with the cities. Between 1973 and 1976, the government authorized the development of 693 Saemaul factories. Only about half of them survived, and those that made it were tied to urban centers. In 1977, out of a total of 361 factories in operation, 240 were located within thirty miles of Seoul, Pusan, and Taegu. Additionally, factories in the provinces where these cities are located accounted for 79 percent of production and 73 percent of employment among all Saemaul factories.[140]

Lastly, the government attempted to create large-scale farms in major river basin areas. In total, about 369,000 hectares (912,000 acres) of paddy fields were consolidated to increase mechanization and efficiency.[141] Medium-size "joint farms" of five to ten hectares were also promoted. This program encouraged farmers with adjacent plots to coordinate management and labor (property rights stayed the same). Although the government claimed that its efforts were successful, many of the farms existed on paper only.[142] Except for some concentration in the livestock sector, average farm size hardly changed in the 1970s, and mechanization proceeded on a small scale, with usage of machinery limited mostly to the household or village level.[143] Perhaps because the New Village Movement was so focused on modernizing individual villages, it proved difficult to achieve broad-based regional development. Or maybe these were just unrealistic goals. By the time Park realized the benefits of scale agriculture and rural industrialization, it was too late, and mass mobilization, though powerful, could not alter existing patterns of production without accompanying changes to economic institutions.

By the late 1970s, rising levels of debt, poverty, tenancy, inequality, and migration—all symptoms of agriculture's decline—fueled activist farmers' movements. The Catholic Farmers' Union and the Christian Farmers' League staged local protests against the NACF and eventually turned against the New Village Movement. While some of the core members of these groups embraced the campaign in the beginning, they increasingly felt that it had not delivered on its promises. After a period of state crackdown, they reemerged in the 1980s as radical, antigovernment organizations.[144]

The New Village Movement was further weakened in 1979, when the head of the Korean CIA assassinated Park. It nevertheless continued under President Chun Doo-hwan (1980–1988), who placed his younger brother, Chun Kyung-hwan, in charge of the Central Headquarters for Saemaul Undong, a reconfigured semiprivate organization. In 1985, Chun Kyung-hwan was criticized for negotiating a deal to import cattle from New Zealand that would threaten domestic livestock producers. Coinciding with the democracy movement, the deal set off mass demonstrations. Then, in 1988, he was indicted for corruption, fined, and sentenced to seven years in prison. The scandal severely tarnished Saemaul's image, and virtually all its activities came to a halt.[145]

Given this checkered history, one of the most surprising things about the New Village Movement is that it was resurrected in the 1990s. Visitors to Korea can still occasionally see the green-and-yellow Saemaul flag displayed outside community centers and other public buildings. For many older people, the flag is a reminder of a simpler (albeit politically repressive) time, when everyone came together to achieve a just and prosperous society. Among young urbanites, knowledge of the movement is generally limited to kitsch portrayals of peasant life. Restaurant-goers may have been to the barbecue chain Saemaul Sikdang, where customers can enjoy rustic dishes and listen to the "Song of Saemaul" on request, and movie lovers may have seen the 2006 comedy *Mission Sex Control* about a fictional village that became a Saemaul success case for achieving zero births (the Korean title *Live Well* is much less racy). To this generation, the campaign is an unfamiliar historical episode, a relic of the old pre-democratic Korea.

Still for others, the Saemaul movement, while connected to the past, has taken on new meaning. Especially in rural areas, where it remains active as a community service organization, volunteers have focused on protecting the environment and narrowing the digital divide. In 2008, Lee Myung-bak became the first president since the 1980s to attend the National Saemaul Leaders' Convention, and he was instrumental in launching what is known as Green Saemaul.[146] As to be expected, Saemaul also received support from Park Chung-hee's daughter and now-former president Park Geun-hye. It is too soon to tell whether her impeachment in 2017 and subsequent imprisonment will have any effect on the organization, but the chances of it disappearing are slim. This would not be the first time it got caught up in political controversy, and it has already survived far longer than anyone predicted.

The turn against Saemaul and its resurrection are both embodiments of the campaign's popular legacy. It was not a democratic movement, and to the contrary, it highlights the limits of mobilized participation as a vehicle for advancing the public's interest. Nevertheless, farmers' genuine enthusiasm for the campaign triggered unforeseen reactions to its demise—protesters trying to remedy its failures and volunteers trying to salvage its successes. To dismiss the campaign as an exercise in social control misreads the degree to which people were invested in it. The New Village Movement was a central part of Korea's rural transformation, and despite its many flaws, it led to an improved quality of life for millions of people.

Finally, it should be noted that since its inception, the New Village Movement has been upheld as a model for developing countries. In the 1970s, foreigners in Korea were regularly shown around SLTI and exemplary villages in hopes that they would publicize the campaign's accomplishments abroad. Saemaul leaders were also sent to Africa for development work, making the campaign one of the country's first political exports.[147] In the 2000s, Saemaul became a formal part of South Korea's official development assistance. It has been recognized by numerous international organizations (the OECD, the Asian Development Bank, the World Bank, and several UN agencies) and was personally endorsed by the former UN secretary-general Ban Ki-Moon and the World Bank president Jim Yong Kim. In 2004, the Korean government started the "Knowledge Sharing Program," an effort to relate Korea's development experience to other countries through the publication of English-language materials about Saemaul and other topics.[148] And in 2009, the Korea Saemaul Undong Center launched Global Saemaul, an initiative that involves training community leaders from all over the world and developing pilot villages overseas. As of December 2017, the center claims to have supported 243 villages in 33 countries and to have trained over fifty-nine thousand people from 147 countries.[149] All of these actions have conferred legitimacy on a campaign that scholars writing in the 1980s believed was dying.[150]

Unfortunately for countries trying to learn from Korea, it is not clear what the New Village Movement has to offer. The official narrative is so watered down that it misrepresents what happened. There is almost no mention of authoritarian politics, state-led development, or negative outcomes. Instead, it stresses the importance of helping farmers to help themselves through spiritual and practical training.[151] Korea is not the best example of a country that prioritized agriculture or developed strong rural institutions. The campaign tried to make up for decades of neglect, and it did achieve success, but not in all areas, and certainly not just for the reasons cited by the Korean government. The simplest explanation for the New Village Movement's success is that Korea's political system shared more in common with Taiwan than Maoist China. The campaign was meticulously planned and implemented by a technocratic bureaucracy that was forced to accept the mobilization tactics Park so valued. In other words, it was run by "experts" instead of "reds."[152] There were strong checks on local officials from above, reinforced by a certain degree of horizontal supervision and very limited checks from below. It was a "big push" policy directed by a highly effective state more than an exercise in self-empowerment.[153] This makes it incredibly hard to replicate, even for a place like China, which in the 2000s took a keen interest in the New Village Movement. As the next chapter shows quite plainly, campaigns are inherently risky and work only under a narrow set of conditions.

4

RURAL DEVELOPMENT IN CHINA, 1980s–2000s

Since the initiation of reform and opening in 1978, China's economy has undergone tremendous changes. Rural decollectivization and market reforms generated impressive growth in agriculture, and the creation of special economic zones gave rise to a booming export sector that enabled China to "grow out of the plan."[1] Deng Xiaoping's policies set China on a path to become the fastest-growing economy in world history, but its development has also been extremely uneven. Coastal provinces are significantly wealthier than provinces in the interior. Urban residents earn at least three times more than rural residents, and high levels of inequality can be found within a single municipality or even between neighboring villages.

Before the 2000s, China's reform-era agricultural policy could be summed up as decollectivization followed by resource extraction and neglect. Between 1978 and 1984, the replacement of the people's commune system with household contract farming resulted in historic poverty reduction. Agriculture grew about 10 percent annually, and the number of people living in absolute poverty dropped from 250 million to 128 million (from 31 percent to 15 percent of the rural population).[2] After 1984, however, central government investment and growth rates in agriculture started to decline. As was the case during the Maoist period, local governments were expected to be self-reliant and raise their own funds for development. Township and village enterprises allowed some places to flourish, but industrialization proved to be more difficult for resource-scarce areas in central and western China. Under pressure to impress higher-level officials with economic achievements, many local governments resorted to imposing heavy taxes on farmers. These went toward developing industry instead of providing public goods. The quality of roads, schools, and clinics declined, and the rural-urban gap widened. By the late 1990s, heavy "peasant burdens" had become a source of widespread rural unrest.

Worried about the political risks of inaction, President Hu Jintao's government made unprecedented efforts to ameliorate rural conditions. In 2004, the State Council released a "number one document" proclaiming that rural development was the "most important work of the party." China had entered a new era in which "industry should nurture agriculture, and the cities should support the countryside."[3] Two policies in particular came to embody this principle. First, after a period of experimentation with rural tax reform, the central government decided in 2006 to completely eliminate agricultural taxes. Second, a policy called Building a New Socialist Countryside was introduced as the top domestic priority of the eleventh five-year plan (2006–2010). Its official motto outlined broad goals: "develop production, enrich livelihood, civilize rural habits, tidy up the villages, and democratize management."[4]

For the first time in China's history, the state began supporting agriculture without taxing it in return. Significant resources were channeled to the rural sector as household subsidies and earmarked transfers for public goods. The main function of local officials shifted from tax collection to service provision, and the notion of growth-first or industry-first development was challenged. The government aided farmers' cooperatives and agribusinesses to stimulate production. It expanded access to public education, established a cooperative medical care system, and strengthened social insurance programs for the poor. It also invested heavily in rural infrastructure. The New Socialist Countryside seemed to represent a "new deal" for farmers, a long overdue corrective to decades of institutionalized inequality.[5] Yet over time, the goal of "tidying up the villages" became the primary focus of local initiatives, eclipsing the policy's broader economic and social objectives; and despite an initial emphasis on rural participation and moderate change in this area, the policy evolved into a top-down campaign to demolish and reconstruct villages. Rural resource extraction continued in the form of land grabs, the rural-urban gap grew larger, and problems with the quality of public goods surfaced.

The New Socialist Countryside is not well understood outside China. Previous research has examined the state's capacity and tools for policy implementation, usually in one or a few localities, and there are only a handful of in-depth treatments of the subject.[6] Many scholars are skeptical about whether the policy did anything to really improve rural conditions and have focused instead on other issues affecting the countryside, such as migration and urbanization.

In contrast, within China, there is no question that the New Socialist Countryside was a historic turning point. Although it fell short of achieving its goals and created some serious problems, it fundamentally altered state-society relations and marked the beginning of China's agricultural adjustment period.

This chapter analyzes Chinese rural development in the reform era. I start by describing changes in production, living standards, and the village environment. I show that while tremendous gains were made in all these areas during the first half of the 1980s, the prospects for long-term progress were diminished by a national development strategy that prioritized the urban-industrial sector. The attempt to chart a more balanced path in the 2000s, though successful in some ways, could not solve the intractable issue of rural-urban inequality or protect farmers from local governments bent on acquiring more land. Embedded in this overview is a discussion of how rural institutional change affected these outcomes. Decollectivization, marketization, and decentralization unleashed powerful forces for growth. However, the dual nature of China's economy remained intact, and these same forces reduced the state's capacity and will to provide public goods and develop agriculture. Next, I highlight an understudied dimension of this problem: the largely failed effort to promote Farmers' Professional Cooperatives (FPCs). Unlike in the rest of East Asia, where farmers' organizations have been crucial for rural development, Chinese FPCs have been ineffectual, owing to their tiny membership base, weak links to the agricultural bureaucracy, and limited autonomy from local elites. I then build on this analysis and argue that the New Socialist Countryside's mixed outcomes can be attributed to ambiguous and shifting goals, weak central controls, and low levels of rural participation.

From a theoretical perspective, this study sheds light on how China sees itself relating to the East Asian model, by which "rural construction" is said to be "led by the government" and carried out by a "comprehensive farmers' association." While there is little chance that China will develop a national organization for farmers—the CCP has rejected that idea several times before—the decision to expand FPCs and launch the New Socialist Countryside was inspired by the East Asian cases, particularly South Korea. In the mid-2000s, tens of thousands of Chinese officials went to Korea to study the New Village Movement, and many more in China learned about it as part of their official duties. Chinese scholars took an interest in the campaign as well, writing extensively about why it succeeded and how this approach made sense for the region. The implication is that China not only engages in policy learning but also thinks about the East Asian model differently from the existing scholarship on developmental states.[7]

Furthermore, this research adds to the literature on campaign politics in China. To be clear, the central government never called the New Socialist Countryside a campaign because of the Maoist connotations of that term, but most local officials understood and implemented it that way. Plans were drawn up that emphasized speed and hard targets, special committees were formed to realign the interests of various departments, and cadre work teams were sent down to the villages. Propaganda slogans and images appeared in newspapers, on billboards, and along the sides of buildings and fences. Even the phrase "building a new socialist countryside" could be traced back to the revolutionary days of the 1950s. The resonance with past campaigns was unmistakable, except for one key element: the absence of mass participation.

A more restrictive form of campaign politics, in which the party-state's own agents are the chief targets of mobilization, is something the majority of post-Mao campaigns have in common. And while Deng Xiaoping's pledge to end mass campaigns and focus on economic development was indisputably a positive change, campaigns without mass support have their own pathologies. A basic tenet of Maoism was direct consultation with the masses as a prerequisite for governance. Referred to in party doctrine as the "mass line," remnants of this tradition can still be seen in the petitioning system and the party's ideological work.[8] At the same time, many Chinese feel that the party has abandoned the mass line and that institutions such as village elections have failed to improve accountability. Some villagers have even expressed nostalgia for mass campaigns, asserting that they were effective at curbing cadre corruption.[9] Herein lies the main problem with post-Mao campaigns. By leaving the masses out, local officials essentially have free rein over policies that are meant to be transformative. The risk is not that officials will ignore campaign directives, but rather that they will manipulate them to suit their own interests and carry them to extremes. As this case study illustrates, the combination of intense political pressure, weak checks from above, and virtually no checks from below greatly increases the likelihood of things spinning out of control.

Changes in Chinese Rural Sector Development

At first glance, it appears that China's economic takeoff was not led by agriculture. For the period 1978–1996, the industrial sector's contribution to GDP was higher than that of agriculture in every province (about 54.5 percent versus 16.5 percent). Industrial sector growth also exceeded GDP growth in all but five provinces (about 11.2 percent versus 9.2 percent). While numerous studies have confirmed that industry was indeed the main driver of the economy, a somewhat different picture emerges when the analysis is limited to the years 1978–1984. During this earlier period, the contribution of agriculture to GDP growth was higher than industry in over half of all provinces, including most of the poor inland provinces and a few along the coast, such as Fujian and Shandong. For China's poorest areas, the role of agriculture in jump-starting growth and reducing poverty was crucial.[10]

Agriculture's performance after 1984 was not as strong. Comparing the periods 1981–1984 and 1984–2006, the average annual growth rate of total agricultural output slowed from 10.6 percent to 3.9 percent. Farm output (excluding forestry, livestock, and fishing) likewise slowed from 9.5 percent to 4.3 percent, and grain production dropped from 6.8 percent to 1.0 percent. Interestingly, the lower growth rates for agricultural output and farm output were only one percentage point higher than those of the pre-reform period of 1963–1981, when collective agriculture dominated, and grain production was more than two points lower. These figures suggest that, in the long run, the change from collective to household farming did not lead to significantly higher levels of production. They also reflect the rapid diversification of agriculture, especially the shift to non-grain crops, and of the rural economy more generally.[11]

With regard to the causes of growth in the early 1980s, there are two main schools of thought. The first emphasizes political-institutional changes. In December 1978, at a meeting known as the Third Plenum, the Central Committee of the Chinese Communist Party adopted a sweeping set of policy reforms. A coalition led by Deng Xiaoping and senior economist Chen Yun proposed shifting government investment from heavy industry to light industry and agriculture, raising state procurement prices on farm products, and encouraging agricultural specialization based on market principles. In the months and years that followed, the reforms became more radical, and eventually the people's communes and the unified purchase and marketing system, the hallmarks of the planned economy, were dismantled. According to Daniel Kelliher, the reforms went far beyond what central leaders originally envisioned because it was actually the peasantry who led the reform process, enacting changes on the ground that induced policy revisions at the top and generated momentum for growth.[12]

The second school of thought stresses technological advancements made during the late Maoist period, including the spread of chemical fertilizers, new seed varieties, and irrigation infrastructure. Representing this view, Chris Bramall argues that decollectivization simply cannot account for the gains in production before 1980 (there was a noticeable increase between 1976 and 1980) or for the huge jump that occurred thereafter, since it was not until 1983 that the transition to family farming was completed.[13] Decollectivization, like land reform, had a short-term, positive effect on agricultural incentives and production, but was insufficient for long-term growth.[14] Furthermore, as research on land conflict has shown, since farmers were only granted land contract and usage rights, not ownership rights, they have faced ongoing problems with tenure security.[15]

Setting aside debates about the efficiency of collective versus family farms, or the importance of institutions relative to technology, a noteworthy point of convergence for these scholars is that the role of Deng and the central government, while pivotal, was secondary to other factors.

In line with this idea, a major reason for agriculture's decline after 1984 was that central support for pro-rural policies was only temporary. Despite the new government's rejection of Maoist economics, it similarly chose to prioritize industry over agriculture. This preference was reflected in its spending patterns. Central government investment in agriculture as a share of total investment declined from 9.3 percent in 1980 to 3.0 percent in 1988, and it stayed around that level until 1995. It rose slightly in the late 1990s but did not return to what it was at the start of reform until 2008.[16] The same thing happened with pricing policies. The rise in procurement prices after the Third Plenum had a direct and positive effect on production and incomes, so much so that the central government found it necessary to limit the amount of grain farmers could sell to the state out of concern for its own finances. It readjusted prices to fall below market rates and, in some years, below the cost of production. As production inputs grew more expensive, the intersectoral terms of trade worsened for farmers. During most of the 1990s, they paid more for goods and services than they received for their products, and in many instances, the state failed to compensate farmers at all, issuing "white slips" or IOUs on the items it purchased.[17] Data from the World Bank also confirms a strong anti-agricultural bias in China. The nominal and relative rates of assistance to agriculture hardly changed during the 1960s–1980s, and they remained negative until 1995 and 2000, respectively.[18]

It should be noted here that China under Deng was not a typical case of urban bias. It differed from other developing countries in that rural industrialization was an enormous success. By the mid-1990s, township and village enterprises (TVEs) employed over 135 million people, or nearly one-third of the rural labor force, and were producing more than half of the country's total industrial output and exports.[19] Before 1996, TVEs were the most dynamic sector of the economy, a wellspring of entrepreneurship and a vital source of income for rural families.[20] Jean Oi explains that decentralizing fiscal reforms, by giving local governments greater control over taxes and other funds, transformed rural officials into growth-promoting developmental agents. They treated local enterprises as "components of a larger corporate whole" and protected them because of the revenue streams they generated.[21]

However, in much of what Thomas Bernstein and Xiaobo Lü call agricultural and subsistence China, located in the central and western parts of the country, the factors that had enabled TVE growth on the eastern coast (i.e., market access, skilled labor, and overseas investors) were lacking. Local officials in these areas were more predatory than developmental, or rather, they engaged in predation in order to develop the local economy. The same fiscal policies that had created incentives for growth also reduced Beijing's capacity for redistribution, and conditions of resource scarcity meant that local officials often had to choose between supporting industry and providing public goods.[22]

A major tax reform implemented in 1994 unintentionally made this problem worse. Central revenues increased, enabling the transfer of funds to poorer provinces, but the regulation of fiscal transfers was inadequate. Meanwhile, local governments saw their budgets shrink by more than 30 percent. They cut spending on public goods and agriculture, and they turned their energies to the collection of extra-budgetary fees and land expropriation, causing peasant burdens to rise faster than incomes. Even though farmers blamed local officials, not Beijing, for their predicament, the central government was ultimately responsible for urban-biased policies that massively subsidized city residents. The provision of low-cost food and housing in particular was intended to prevent urban households from mobilizing against the regime. From the perspective of central leaders shaken by the Tiananmen Square uprising of 1989, that scenario was indisputably more threatening than localized rural protests.[23]

China thus resembles Taiwan in the sense that rural industry was an essential engine of growth in many areas, but it also resembles South Korea in terms of the way the government neglected agriculture. Rural resource extraction and urban bias occurred in all three cases. Yet in China, the rural-urban divide was larger and more rigid. Under the planned economy, restrictions were put in place on the circulation of land, labor, and capital. The household registration system, or *hukou*, divided the population between rural and urban and attached individuals' citizenship—their livelihood and welfare—to a specific locale. Over time, it became more difficult to traverse the rural-urban boundary, and society became increasingly dualistic and cellular.[24] Still, within the rural and urban sectors, incomes were distributed fairly equally. In 1981, China's overall Gini coefficient was .29, an exceptionally low value for a large developing country, on par with egalitarian societies like Sweden and Germany. The rural and urban Gini coefficients, estimated at .25 and .17, were even more unusual. The situation began to change almost immediately, though, as the reforms took effect, and inequality has risen steadily ever since. In 2004, the national Gini coefficient was .44 (the rural and urban coefficients were .37 and .32), meaning that China was more unequal than most of Asia and most other middle-income countries.[25]

The uneven growth of markets and TVEs, combined with the state's unwillingness to eliminate the institutions separating rural from urban citizens, led to the deterioration of China's income distribution. To use another measure, between 1984 and 2004, the ratio of urban to rural incomes jumped from 1.9:1 to 3.2:1, and the consumption gap increased from 2.3:1 to 3.3:1.[26] Farm incomes actually experienced negative growth in the late 1990s (about -3.3 percent for 1996–2000), causing wage labor to become more important. In places without many opportunities for off-farm employment, families resorted to long-distance migration. By the year 2000, nearly 145 million people had joined China's so-called floating population.[27] This group's impact on the economy was transformative, but its prospects for upward mobility were hindered by an experience of second-class citizenship in the cities.[28] And despite some experimental efforts at integrating the migrant workforce, whose numbers are fast approaching three hundred million, they remain largely excluded from the urban public goods regime.[29]

Problems related to the relative decline of agriculture, as reflected in its diminishing share of GDP, exports, and employment, intensified in the late 1990s and early 2000s (see table 12). Rural reform had resulted in less state control over agriculture but a continuation of the developmental squeeze. Both Deng Xiaoping and his successor Jiang Zemin (the CCP general secretary from 1989 to 2002) had presided over policies that privileged the urban-industrial sector and treated GDP growth as the key metric for official promotions.[30] There were moments when agriculture received significant support (after the Third Plenum and then intermittently to strengthen irrigation and grain output), but the overall effect of economic policy was to perpetuate unbalanced growth.[31] To make matters worse, during the ninth five-year plan (1996–2000), structural reforms were adopted that adversely affected TVEs. The government imposed strict constraints on rural credit and cracked down on private and informal sources of finance. It lifted restrictions on foreign firms, and it privatized many smaller state-owned enterprises, while hugely increasing investments in larger ones. Faced with reduced access to capital and heightened levels of competition, the TVE sector contracted and many firms went bankrupt, dealing another blow to rural incomes.[32]

The countryside was "becoming hollow." In a literal sense, this phrase referred to the loss of village labor and the growing stock of empty and dilapidated housing, especially in poorer provinces with high rates of outmigration. As young people left the villages in places like Anhui and Guizhou, the tasks of farming and child rearing often fell to older family members. Migrant remittances went toward caring for those left behind, and the remainder was usually invested in housing. However, because of the absence of formal housing markets, migration also led to a significant rise in empty dwellings and what the government calls idle construction land. Based on a 2006 national survey of more than twenty-seven hundred villages, the Development Research Center of the State Council concluded that around 45 percent of China's villages had large numbers of abandoned homes and that at least 10 percent of rural construction land was idle.[33]

In another sense, becoming hollow referred to the poor capacity of local governments to deliver public goods and services. The dismantling of the people's communes, along with the work point system, gave farmers greater control over their incomes, but it also caused collective welfare funds to dry up. Local officials found it increasingly difficult to provide services (e.g., "barefoot doctors" for basic health care) or enforce policies.[34] Even with the benefits of decentralization and economic growth, the quality of public goods suffered because the formal institutions required to ensure accountability were weak. Local officials lacked not just resources but incentives to provide decent roads, schools, and running water.[35] Moreover, Beijing's solution to the peasant burden problem—personnel and budget cuts—effectively turned local governments into hollow administrative shells, and insufficient fiscal transfers compounded the decline of public goods.[36] My own fieldwork in Jiangxi Province further revealed that the inferior quality of rural public goods deterred many families from investing in housing, which is to say, the hollowing-out of the local state and villages were interrelated processes.[37]

Protests and other "mass incidents" escalated toward the end of the Jiang era. The meaning of this term is vague and includes any collective action that violates the law, disrupts social order, threatens security, or damages property. National-level statistics on mass incidents are notoriously incomplete and unreliable, but they can still provide a general picture of change. In 2005, the Ministry of Public Security reportedly investigated a total of eighty-seven thousand incidents, a tenfold increase from 1993. Data on lawsuits and petitions exhibited a similar upward trend. While it is difficult to ascertain how much of this contentious activity was concentrated in the countryside, case studies and surveys suggest that the frequency and scale of rural protest were significant.[38]

In 1997, Jiang's second-in-command, Premier Zhu Rongji, warned officials that "underestimating the strength of the peasants would be a historic mistake." That same year, several major uprisings occurred in Anhui, Henan, Hubei, and Jiangxi, involving hundreds of thousands of farmers across dozens of townships. Protesters rallied against IOUs, grain and fertilizer prices, and excessive taxes. They attacked and burned down government offices and even seized firearms, causing numerous deaths and injuries.[39] Land-related conflicts also began to multiply, as village land was gobbled up by the construction of development zones and new cities. Between 1996 and 2006, China lost around 8.3 million hectares (20.4 million acres) of farmland, or 6.4 percent of the total. Tens of millions of farmers became landless (one study estimated eighty-eight million since 1990), and grain production plummeted 17 percent in 1999–2003, triggering concerns about food security.[40]

Demands for central government intervention and more equitable policies found expression in the growing literature on *sannong*, or three rural issues, the Chinese shorthand for peasants, villages, and agriculture. Books like *China along the Yellow River* (2000), *I Tell the Truth to the Premier* (2002), and *China Peasant Survey* (2004) depicted a rural society in crisis and brought the struggles of farmers to the forefront of national attention.[41] This turn in public discourse coincided with changes in the global economy that caused people to view the countryside differently. First, although China emerged from the Asian Financial Crisis of 1997–1998 relatively unscathed, the episode led many to conclude that the country was too dependent on exports and that higher levels of domestic consumption, especially in rural areas, would be necessary to prevent future shocks.[42] Second, China's entry into the World Trade Organization in 2001 raised concerns that greater import competition would hurt farmers and that the government's ability to protect them would only weaken as WTO regulations took effect. The time for intervention was ripe.

In the words of Chen Xiwen, the former office director of the Central Leading Group on Rural Work, Hu Jintao's ascendency, like Deng's before him, ushered in a "second golden age of rural reform."[43] At the top of the agenda was fiscal policy. Previous efforts to contain peasant burdens—establishing burden reduction offices, mobilizing inspection teams, and allowing farmers to seek redress through the petitioning and legal systems—had mostly failed. The only option left was deeper institutional reform. During the Hu administration (2002–2012), township and village governments were streamlined, and a big push was made to convert fees into regular taxes, a policy known as rural tax-for-fee reform (RTFR). After continuous implementation setbacks, however, the center decided to abolish agricultural taxes altogether in 2006. The move was widely trumpeted as an end to over two thousand years of "imperial grain taxes" and the beginning of a new era of rural development.[44]

Furthermore, as part of Building a New Socialist Countryside, the government started subsidizing farmers and pledged that all new increases in central and local spending would be primarily allocated to rural areas.[45] The Ministry of Finance began tracking central level investment with a measure called *sannong* expenditures. Official data show an average increase of 23 percent per year between 2002 and 2012, starting at 158.1 billion yuan and rising to 1.2 trillion yuan. These figures represented 7.2 and 9.8 percent of total expenditures, respectively, a dramatic reversal of the decline in central investment described earlier.[46] Of course, similar to the 1994 tax reforms, the fiscal health of local governments was made worse by the termination of agricultural taxes. Dependency on transfers increased, and to compensate for lost revenues, many governments turned to illegal debt financing, using land as collateral. In addition, transfers were often diverted, and subsidies were disproportionately channeled to wealthier (and presumably better connected) households. Yet, despite these challenges, existing research confirms that *sannong* funds did in fact reach the villages.[47]

The outcomes of the New Socialist Countryside were mixed. On the positive side, the fiscal shift resulted in an uptick in agricultural production, improved access to public goods, and higher incomes. Agriculture grew 4.2 percent per year in 2002–2012 (well above the global average of 2.8 percent), and grain output has risen steadily since 2004, owing to farmland protection measures and subsidies targeting major grain-producing areas.[48] Subsidies also went toward funding massive social welfare programs. About 835 million people obtained low-cost health insurance by enrolling in the New Cooperative Medical Scheme (NCMS), and 130 million schoolchildren benefited from Two Exemptions–One Subsidy (TEOS). The latter program waived school tuition and miscellaneous fees, provided free textbooks, and subsidized the cost of boarding. Within just a few years, health care and free compulsory education were extended to nearly every rural family.[49] Social insurance programs for poor and landless farmers were established as well. Taking the whole range of subsidies into account, one study estimates that their contribution to rural net incomes increased from 0.5 percent in 2003 to 4.7 percent in 2009.[50] Moreover, the overall growth rate for rural incomes reached its highest level since the early 1980s, averaging 8.0 percent per year for 2002–2012.[51]

On the negative side, the quality of these programs varied enormously, and there were still significant rural-urban differences in life expectancy, infant and maternal mortality, and access to secondary education, to name just a few indicators.[52] The growth in incomes was likewise not enough to narrow the urban-to-rural income ratio, which registered 3.1:1 or higher for the entire Hu era.[53] And while grain production increased by nearly 30 percent between 2002 and 2012, so did the country's reliance on grain imports, which grew by an astonishing 400 percent.[54] The government also attempted to upgrade the quality of farmland and enlarge the size of China's farms, which in 2006 averaged 0.6 hectares (1.5 acres), but these initiatives were fraught with conflict over how to scale up production in a way that would not exploit smallholders.[55] The development of cooperatives, discussed below, did not offer much of a solution.

Lastly, the New Socialist Countryside resulted in extraordinary changes to the rural built environment. Spending on infrastructure, as measured by rural fixed asset investment (from public and private sources), rose from 801.1 billion yuan in 2002 to over 3.9 trillion yuan in 2011.[56] Most of this money went toward roads, bridges, schools, irrigation, and drinking water. Survey data from the mid-2000s show a positive correlation between the quantity and quality of new infrastructure, as well as growing villager satisfaction.[57] Similarly, another study that

TABLE 12. Agricultural and Industrial Sector Change in China, 1978–2012

YEAR	1978	1982	1987	1992	1997	2002	2007	2012
Population								
Total population (billions)	.9626	1.017	1.093	1.172	1.236	1.285	1.321	1.354
Rural population (billions)	.7901	.8017	.8163	.8500	.8418	.7824	.7150	.6422
Share of rural population in total population (%)	82.1	78.9	74.7	72.5	68.1	60.9	54.1	47.4
GDP[1]								
Share of agriculture in GDP (%)	28.2	33.4	26.8	21.8	18.3	13.7	10.8	10.1
Share of industry in GDP (%)	47.9	44.8	43.6	43.5	47.5	44.8	47.3	45.3
Exports[2]								
Share of agricultural (primary) exports in total exports (%)	62.6	45.0	50.6	20.0	13.1	8.8	5.3	4.9
Share of industrial (manufactured) exports in total exports (%)	37.4	55.0	49.4	80.0	86.9	91.2	94.7	95.1
Employment								
Share of agricultural workers in economically active population (%)	70.5	68.1	60.0	58.5	55.2	50.0	40.8	33.6
Share of industrial workers in economically active population (%)	17.3	18.4	22.2	21.7	23.7	21.4	26.8	30.3

AVERAGE ANNUAL GROWTH RATES	1978–1991	1992–2001	2002–2012
GDP growth rate (%)	9.3	10.4	10.4
Agriculture, value added, growth rate (%)	5.3	3.8	4.2
Industry, value added, growth rate (%)	10.4	13.0	11.5

Source: Average growth rates come from the World Bank 2017. Export data for 1978 and 1982 come from Perkins and Yusuf 1984, 22. All other figures obtained from *Zhongguo tongji nianjian* [China Statistical Yearbook] 2013, 44–45, 95, 123, 225.

[1] GDP data based on 2012 prices. Agriculture includes the farming, forestry, livestock, and fishery sectors. Industry includes the manufacturing, mining, and construction sectors.

[2] Export data for 1987 are actually for 1985.

surveyed the same set of villages in 2002 and 2010 found that state-society relations had greatly improved as a result of better infrastructure and public goods provision.[58] However, these surveys do not capture the whole story. Village modernization became more extreme over time. Many families were compelled to move into shoddily constructed apartment buildings, often at their own expense. Since the new housing occupied less land than the old, local governments profited from the transfer and sale of "freed up" land quotas for urban use. These transactions frequently occurred without villagers' knowledge, adequate compensation, or change in *hukou* status. Village renovation thus exacerbated the problem of rural land grabs and created new peasant burdens in the form of housing-related debts. By the end of the Hu era, the campaign had become associated with mass relocations and the wholesale demolition of villages.[59] The remainder of this chapter deals with how and why these various outcomes occurred.

The Farmers' Professional Cooperatives

There is a well-established literature on the transition from Maoist agriculture and the institutional foundations of economic change in the reform era.[60] And yet, scholars have paid little attention to the development of farmers' organizations, or the lack thereof. Despite the Chinese government's push to strengthen them, they are still among the weakest in Asia. Compared to their counterparts in Japan, Taiwan, and South Korea, the Farmers' Professional Cooperatives in China have played a minimal role in development. In some ways, this outcome represents an unintended consequence of the reform process, that is, the decline in local governments' capacity and will to organize rural society in the wake of decollectivization and market reforms. In other ways, it reflects a strategic compromise, an acknowledgment of these organizations' importance in development and a desire to constrain them politically. This section provides some background on farmers' organizations and analyzes the FPCs comparatively in order to highlight a key point of institutional divergence between China and its neighbors.

Farmers' Organizations in the Mao and Reform Eras

For most of its history, the CCP has treated the development of farmers' organizations as foundational to its power. After 1927, when Chiang Kai-shek's forces began rounding up and killing thousands of communists in Shanghai and other cities, the CCP retreated to the countryside and began organizing peasant "soviets" to expand its base. While some party members were skeptical of this strategy, since it went against the orthodox Marxist belief in proletarian revolution, Mao, on the other hand, embraced it. In his 1927 "Report on an Investigation of the Hunan Peasant Movement," Mao famously argued that the peasants, by organizing themselves to overthrow landlordism, had demonstrated their revolutionary consciousness and would therefore be key to China's national liberation. The choice facing the party, he explained, was whether to lead them, trail behind them, or oppose them.[61] The entire Jiangxi Soviet period (1927–1934) can be interpreted as an experiment in leading the peasantry. The CCP carried out land reform and organized village cooperatives, but according to Franz Schurmann, it was not until the Yan'an period (1935–1946), with the formation of anti-Japanese guerrilla bases, that the communists finally achieved what "no state power in Chinese history had been able to do: to create an organization loyal to the state which was also solidly imbedded in the natural village."[62]

Indeed, one of the most profound legacies of the Mao era was effective state penetration of the countryside and the replacement of traditional rural organizations with state-dominated institutions. Through land reform, then later through collectivization and various campaigns, the CCP overturned the old social structure. Peasant associations were established to attack landlords, rich peasants, and other villagers with "bad" class backgrounds. Preexisting organizations based on kinship or religion were generally suppressed, while those related to defense, credit, or production were absorbed by the state. The communists' status as war heroes, combined with the selective application of violence toward perceived enemies, allowed the new regime to consolidate power quickly. By 1955–1956, over 90 percent of administrative villages had functioning party committees, and a comparable share of the rural population had been organized into agricultural cooperatives. Precisely because of the government's strong presence in the villages, the drive to collectivize agriculture, though not without problems, involved much less coercion and resistance than was the case in the Soviet Union.[63]

The cooperatives were enlarged and renamed people's communes during the Great Leap Forward (1958–1960). Following the famine, adjustments were made to the commune system—the average size was reduced, certain functions were eliminated, and power was ceded to lower-level officials—but the basic three-part structure of commune, brigade, and team (corresponding roughly to the township, administrative village, and natural village) remained intact until the reform era. Several scholars have pointed to team leaders who protected villagers from excessive state intrusion as evidence of clientelism or localism.[64] Nevertheless, the ability of villagers to circumvent state power was limited, and virtually all instances of collective action occurred within the state's own organizational framework.

The rural reforms of the 1980s replaced the communes with a "two-layer" system of collective and household-based production. In exchange for the use of collective land, farmers were responsible for selling a share of their output to the state (hence the name household contract responsibility system), but they had more freedom over production and the surplus. Whatever was not consumed could be sold to the state or on the market. After the communes were broken up, cooperatives were promoted as an alternative way of scaling up production and connecting farm households to the larger economy. These took many forms, including rural community cooperatives, supply and marketing cooperatives, rural credit cooperatives, farmers' technical associations, shareholding cooperatives, rural cooperative foundations, and small-scale mutual aid groups.[65] While in principle they were voluntary, community-based organizations, in practice they were controlled by the state. For example, the supply and marketing cooperatives, which were founded in the 1950s, continued to sell inputs and purchase goods on behalf of the state, and the rural credit cooperatives functioned as an appendage of the state-owned Agricultural Bank of China (they were not separated until the mid-1990s). The technical associations, though more independent, were usually linked to the Ministry of Agriculture or the China Association for Science and Technology.[66]

Setting aside for a moment the issue of autonomy, the bigger problem with cooperative development was that decollectivization created an environment that did not support it. The transition to household farming was swift and seemingly irreversible: early experiments generated tremendous momentum for the reforms and, because of their success, propelled sympathetic provincial leaders like Wan Li and Zhao Ziyang into positions of power at the center.[67] Except in a minority of cases where the communes appeared to be working, popular support for household farming was so overwhelming that any mention of collective institutions was met with skepticism. In this context, state control over the cooperatives only fueled farmers' distrust. Many local governments, rather than making a big push to reform (or withdraw from) the cooperatives, decided to provide assistance to a few experimental sites and leave the rest of the countryside alone. The collective institutions of state socialism gradually withered away.

A shift occurred with the decline of agriculture in the late 1990s, and public support for cooperatives grew. Several "New Left" intellectuals argued that capitalism was destroying the countryside, and the only way to save it was by building cooperatives to provide greater social protection. They eventually founded the New Rural Reconstruction Movement (NRRM), a network of mostly nongovernmental organizations committed to reversing the negative effects of marketization and creating sustainable rural communities. As its name suggests, the movement was inspired by the Rural Reconstruction Movement of the 1920s–1930s, a similar, intellectual-led effort to promote community building. In the 2000s, movement volunteers aided the development of agricultural cooperatives, cultural performance troupes, and elderly associations in dozens of locations all over the country, in some cases recruiting rural protest leaders to head these organizations.[68] Their efforts were bolstered by rural policy change at the top. The Agriculture Law of 2002 mentioned the government's responsibility to protect the rights and interests of cooperatives.[69] This position was echoed in numerous central and provincial policy documents, including the eleventh five-year plan, which identified cooperatives as key actors in Building a New Socialist Countryside.

With the rise of Hu Jintao, several rural experts sensed an opportunity to lobby for a national farmers' association along the lines of Nokyo in Japan or the FAs in Taiwan. Wen Tiejun, Yang Tuan, and Li Changping, for example, published essays on the East Asian model, arguing that having a single organization to coordinate production, finance, and marketing would not only promote broad-based development but also strengthen the voice of small farmers in the political system.[70] Du Runsheng, a revolutionary veteran and leading policymaker during the Mao and reform eras, was perhaps the most outspoken advocate for a national association. He first raised the idea with Deng Xiaoping in the mid-1980s, who said that the timing was not right but that he would reconsider it in a few years. When Du brought it up again in the mid-1990s, the center dragged its feet.[71] Even toward the end of his life, Du continued speaking about the importance of farmers' political empowerment.[72]

The weak position of agricultural interests within the National People's Congress (NPC) and other organs of the party-state may explain why various proposals to create a national farmers' association have so far gone nowhere. Since 1983, the share of NPC delegates from a farming background has declined from about 11 percent to 8 percent of the total, despite the passage of laws designed to increase rural citizens' representation. In 2003, for instance, only 251 out of 2,985 delegates were farmers, far fewer than the 815 spots that one source estimates should have been filled by farmers.[73] Proponents of a national association argue that it would benefit the regime by strengthening farmers' ties to the party and crowding out potentially destabilizing forces in the countryside, such as political or religious extremism. They also believe that, just like other social groups (women, youth, workers, and entrepreneurs), farmers should have their own organization on the grounds of equality. The problem, of course, is that a national farmers' association would probably be larger than any of these groups. Even if it functioned as a traditional mass organization, subject to the party's authority, its very existence would alter the balance of power in favor of the peasantry.[74] The government is no doubt aware of Nokyo's outsize influence in

Japanese politics, not to mention China's own experience with what were known as peasant associations. During the Maoist period, these were violent agents of class warfare that the party could not always control.[75]

The Rise of Farmers' Professional Cooperatives

The central government's endorsement of professional or specialized cooperatives was motivated by a genuine desire to strengthen rural institutions that would promote development, without giving farmers too much political power. Their functional and geographic scope was intended to be narrower than the "comprehensive" associations of Japan, Taiwan, and South Korea. The Farmers' Professional Cooperative Law, approved in October 2006, defined them as follows: "Farmers' Professional Cooperatives are voluntarily assembled and democratically managed, mutual aid–based economic organizations, which exist on the foundation of household contract farming, whose members produce the same agricultural goods or use/provide the same agricultural services." Cooperative activities were delineated to include the purchase of production inputs, the sharing of technology and information, as well as the processing, storage, shipment, and sale of agricultural products.

The law also stipulated that FPCs should have at least five members, 80 percent of whom are farmers, and that cooperative affairs be governed by an elected board of directors and board of supervisors. Significantly, legal protections would only be granted to those cooperatives registered with the State Administration for Industry and Commerce (SAIC), and any FPC that was deemed too large or that operated across multiple jurisdictions would be subject to additional regulations.[76] In short, the law was consistent with the CCP's corporatist-like strategy of expanding the number of social organizations, while limiting their activities to specific localities and sectors. China's FPCs would not be corporatist in the same way as the other East Asian cases (which is to say, hierarchically structured, with offices at each level of government, and possessing a monopoly of representation in the farm sector), but the law formalized their status as legitimate economic actors and brought them into the regulatory grasp of the state.

From the central government's perspective, the appeal of cooperatives was primarily economic. First, they would boost rural incomes by lowering production costs and raising the market value of farm goods: they would purchase inputs in bulk at discounted prices, provide access to expensive machinery, develop product brands, and synchronize sales among farmers who might otherwise engage in price cutting. Second, they would increase the volume and efficiency of food production by scaling up agriculture in a way that preserved the smallholder system. Especially in villages where migration had adversely affected the supply and quality of farm labor, cooperatives would provide a formal channel for pooling resources and coordinating production. Third, they would create jobs and encourage entrepreneurship among returned migrant workers, who could use their outside connections to expand cooperative operations.[77]

Scholarly views of cooperatives are mixed, and there is disagreement about whether or not they represent a viable alternative to capitalist agribusiness. Philip C. C. Huang offers a positive assessment, suggesting that cooperatives can achieve vertical integration (combining multiple stages of production) in a way that empowers small farmers economically. He furthermore asserts that family farming is likely to continue because of rising consumer demand for high-value products, which require the intensive use of both capital and labor.[78] For Matthew Hale, the predicament of cooperatives is more complicated. Even for New Rural Reconstruction Movement cooperatives intentionally trying to forge an alternative "social economy" approach to development—wherein the generation of wealth is inclusive, equitable, and sustainable—commercial success has required the adoption of capitalist practices that go against cooperative values.[79] As the following analysis shows, if there was a choice between cooperatives and agribusiness, it has already been made. Local governments are strongly committed to the latter, and the issues Hale identifies with NRRM cooperatives are far worse among FPCs, which have served as instruments for the advancement of capitalist agribusiness.

In the ten years after the new law took effect, the total number of officially registered cooperatives exploded from fewer than one hundred thousand to over 1.9 million.[80] However, according to numerous surveys and reports, it was the government, not farmers, that took the lead in forming cooperatives, and many of them turned out to be fakes. As one Chinese scholar put it, the rapid development of "briefcase cooperatives" after 2008 was a product of intense pressures placed on local officials to scale up and modernize agriculture, at a time when most small farmers felt indifferent about cooperation. In reality, a large number of FPCs (estimates range widely, from 30 to 95 percent) are either controlled by local elites or exist in name only, and the participation of ordinary farmers has been minimal.[81]

The weak organizational capacity of local governments directly contributed to the problem of fake cooperatives. First, decollectivization undermined local officials' ability and willingness to promote them. Next, the decline of TVEs and the hollowing out of the countryside further eroded the organizational resources available to state and societal actors. Then, in the 2000s, fiscal and administrative reforms led to the elimination of team (natural village) leaders in many places, which experts believe stripped villagers of their control over land, weakened their sense of community, and alienated them from the government.[82] These conditions were hardly favorable for cooperative development.

The strong pro-industry bias of local governments added to the problem. They have consistently prioritized agribusiness over cooperatives, treating "dragon head enterprises" as the preferred vehicle for agricultural modernization.[83] Since 1998, when dragon heads first appeared in central policy, these large-scale companies have been working closely with the government to transform China's domestic agriculture and, increasingly, global agriculture. In exchange for status-related benefits and preferential policies (direct subsidies, tax breaks, special loans, etc.), dragon heads are expected to integrate farm households into their operations through contracting, shareholding, or cooperative arrangements. From Beijing's perspective, the precise form of integration is unimportant, so long as farmers benefit from the "radiation" of technology, information, and market opportunities.

In 2011, China reportedly had over 280,000 agro-industrial firms, of which 110,000 were dragon heads. These firms reached 110 million farm households, 60 percent of total crop area, and were responsible for the bulk of livestock and aquaculture products. They accounted for up to two-thirds of the urban food supply and four-fifths of agricultural exports.[84] Because of their profit and growth potential, local governments across the board made them a top priority, part of the mission to "attract business and investment."[85] In theory, dragon heads and cooperatives are complementary institutions, yet the main effect of these policies was to create an unfair playing field for cooperatives, such that FPCs without close ties to agribusiness could be easily pushed out of the market.

The Ministry of Agriculture claims that 46.8 percent of the rural population, or about 100 million farm households, belonged to cooperatives in 2017.[86] This figure represents a huge jump from ten years earlier, when total membership stood at 13.8 percent of farm households (or only 2.2 percent, if the criterion is membership in officially registered cooperatives).[87] Given the circumstances just outlined, however, and the fact that agribusinesses commonly inflate the number of farm households they employ, there is good reason to be skeptical of official statistics.[88]

These numbers are more likely about creating an image of modern agriculture than anything else. As one report from the Development Research Center of the State Council states: "Looking at the situation of the rest of the world, in countries with more developed agricultural sectors, it is more common for farmers to belong to cooperatives." The report compares membership rates in certain OECD countries with others in Latin America, South and Southeast Asia, and Africa, concluding that China (in 2007) was worse off than all these places. Taking the statistics at face value, the membership level of FPCs in China went from being tiny to about the same size as in India, Bangladesh, Sri Lanka, and Thailand (30–60 percent), which still pales in comparison with the nearly universal membership rates of Japan, Taiwan, and South Korea.[89]

Another difference between China and the East Asian cases, with regard to linkage, is that FPCs are decentralized organizations: their membership base, political connections, and economic activities (excluding sales) are usually confined to the boundaries of the county or township where they are registered. In the year 2003, around 84 percent of all cooperatives were operating in a single township.[90] Similarly, a survey from 2007 found that in Zhejiang and Henan, two provinces known for having relatively developed cooperative sectors, the share of FPCs operating within a single township was 84 percent and 70 percent, respectively.[91] It seems that cooperatives with a larger reach were mostly founded by dragon heads, rather than small-scale producers.[92]

Practically speaking, the activities of farmers in Taiwan and South Korea were also limited to the local community, but the federated, government-like structure of cooperatives ensured some degree of access to higher levels of the state, especially in Taiwan's case where each FA unit was made up of representatives from the level below. This institutional design solidified the cooperatives' ties with the agricultural bureaucracy as well as their role in rural policy implementation. In contrast, Chinese FPCs have no formal connections with higher levels of the state, or even necessarily with the local agricultural bureaucracy. The Cooperative Law, by giving jurisdiction over cooperatives to the SAIC, arguably weakened the FPCs' ties to the Ministry of Agriculture, which had previously dealt with cooperative registration.[93] The move also signaled that cooperatives would function primarily as businesses, not as multipurpose organizations engaged in extension work, credit provision, and other services.

On the issue of FPC autonomy, nearly all studies confirm that while local government support is necessary for the development of cooperatives, it also undermines their independence and sustainability. One report from 2002 estimated that over 70 percent of the country's FPCs were set up by the government, either directly or indirectly, through financial support and the recruitment of cooperative leaders.[94] According to a different study of Hubei, in 2006 only 10 percent of the province's cooperatives were "real" (out of 4,375 in total), and more than 95 percent were dominated by large farmers, government agencies, or dragon heads.[95] In still another survey of 140 cooperative directors from across China, 36 percent were government officials, and 16 percent were government-backed candidates.[96]

From my interviews in Ganzhou, a large prefecture in southern Jiangxi, it was evident that elections, if they took place at all, were largely ceremonial, and that cooperative affairs were usually managed by a small group of investors. As one local official explained: "The cooperatives are pretty empty. They don't have a profit-sharing mechanism. The ordinary people don't vote, either. It's typically the big farmers or the government that makes decisions. The people are too dependent, wanting the government to come and handle everything."[97] Of course, the result of officials handling everything—which probably has more to do with administrative pressure than with farmers' attitudes—is a whole bunch of cooperatives that do little more than "hang up signs" and cannot sustain themselves in the long run. Since cadre evaluations stress quantitative measures of progress, local officials have focused on boosting membership numbers, rather than building solid organizations, and have required many cooperatives to waive membership fees.[98] The lack of buy-in from farmers, financially or otherwise, may explain why cooperatives in China tend to have a life span of less than five years,[99] and why several of the cooperatives I visited in 2010 no longer existed when I returned in 2013.

The local government in Ganzhou was promoting a "company + cooperative + households" model for about a dozen specialty products and commodities. The larger cooperatives were usually established by county or township officials, and the smaller ones by village party secretaries. The citrus cooperatives were the most developed and were still operating at the time of my second visit, yet they were obviously dominated by dragon heads. In one case, while on the road to see a cooperative, I was told that the farmers had banded together to block a dragon head executive from making himself cooperative director and covering all of the registration and membership fees. After arriving, however, I discovered that the cooperative shared the exact same office as the executive, who had been recruited by the government from another province to invest in the area and whose company had acquired over 10,000 *mu* (1,647 acres) of orange groves through land transfers. I did not meet a single ordinary farmer at the site, so it was impossible to gauge how much of the cooperative's assets were owned by farmers or to evaluate the effect of the whole arrangement on farm incomes.[100] Most likely, the effect was suboptimal, since dragon heads generally want to purchase goods from farmers as cheaply as possible and can leverage their resources to negotiate prices.[101] Additionally, the company's control over land and production practices made it a de facto employer, instead of a client or partner of the cooperative.

Compared with a more entrepreneurial model of commercial agriculture, in which farmers control their own land, labor, and output, the affected households in this case had become "semi-proletarian farm workers." I borrow this term from Qian Forrest Zhang and John Donaldson, whose work highlights the impact of large-scale agriculture on rural class differentiation. They note that China's system of collective land rights has shielded most farmers from full proletarianization (landlessness), although other scholars have shown how reforms to integrate rural and urban land markets may be undermining those protections.[102] The state of cooperative development in Ganzhou was certainly not what New Left intellectuals envisioned, nor did it align very well with the goals of the Cooperative Law.

The Costs of Institutional Underdevelopment (and the Causes of Policy Change)

In summary, Chinese farmers' organizations have played a minimal role in rural development. By design, the FPCs were cut off from higher levels of the party-state that managed the distribution of developmental resources and the direction of rural policy. At the same time, they were too closely connected with local elites, though not necessarily with agricultural officials, who presumably would have been more invested in their success. The FPCs' strong ties to county and township governments, as well as the agribusiness sector, subverted their autonomy and caused many farmers to look at them warily—something they were already inclined to do, given the history of collectivization in China. The public's "lingering fear" of cooperatives was matched by apprehension on the part of officials about how these institutions might affect local power relations and policy priorities.[103] These attitudinal barriers, combined with legal constraints on the size and scope of FPCs, not to mention real deficits in local government capacity, resulted in shallow organizations that lacked both linkage and autonomy.

Despite the push to expand FPCs, only a minority of farmers joined them, and even fewer benefited from them. Credit services were nonexistent, and extension services were geared toward helping the agribusiness sector. The subordination of small farmers' interests by more powerful actors occurred in the other East Asian cases as well, but to a lesser degree. The FAs in Taiwan were internally controlled by small farmers, and while the NACF in South Korea was dominated by the state, small farmers did not have to contend with agribusiness for access to vital resources. China's transition from small-scale subsistence farming to larger-scale commercial agriculture, which has been under way for at least two decades, is being led by dragon head enterprises, not cooperatives. As the agribusiness sector consolidates, new forms of rural resource extraction and labor exploitation are likely to emerge. This is not to suggest that family farms are destined to vanish from the countryside, just that cooperatives will not be the thing that saves them from disappearing.

The gains in production and incomes achieved in the 2000s likely had more to do with subsidies and the growth of agribusiness than with farmers' organizations.

Increased policy support for FPCs probably made a positive difference in some localities, but the overall effect on the economy was marginal. The prospects for broad-based rural development have always been complicated for China because of its huge population and regional diversity. Still, if there is a lesson to be drawn from the comparison with China's neighbors, it is that encompassing, federated, multifunctional farmers' organizations can go a long way toward achieving that goal. Looking back at Chinese history, it was also during periods of greater institutional regularity across the countryside—after land reform, under the commune system, and following decollectivization—that more extensive gains in production were realized. For all its problems, the commune system facilitated a green revolution in the 1960s–1970s by encouraging collective investments in irrigation and electricity, which in turn led to the spread of new technologies and higher crop yields.[104] The mostly failed effort to replace communes with cooperatives in the reform era partly explains why the gains from decollectivization were so short-lived and, relatedly, why assistance for Chinese farmers has been so limited and uneven.

Lastly, farmers' organizations played no role in the shift from urban to rural bias in China. Of the factors that were important in Taiwan and South Korea, concerns about food security and migration may have been influential, although the precipitating event was the change in leadership from Jiang Zemin to Hu Jintao. Since Hu had worked in Gansu, Guizhou, and Tibet, three of China's poorest provinces, he was perceived as being more sensitive to rural issues. The same was true of Premier Wen Jiabao, who spent over a decade working in Gansu at the beginning of his career. The Hu-Wen administration's decision to prioritize the countryside may have been related to those backgrounds or, more likely, was driven by the sharp rise in rural unrest described earlier. It may have been strategically motivated as well, a way for Hu to distinguish himself from Jiang and other elites belonging to the "Shanghai Gang."[105]

Regardless if it was about addressing farmers' needs or consolidating power (or both), the leadership transition created a political opening for rural advocates to get their message out. They raised the specter of rural crisis, and the term *sannong* started to appear more frequently in the media and official statements. Yet, significantly, the populist turn in Chinese politics was not a product of direct electoral pressure or legislative coalition building as it was in the other cases. Rural protests affected the regime, but only indirectly: they were sporadic, localized, and rarely accompanied by policy demands. The effective absence of elections and other input institutions not only inhibited the articulation of rural interests, but also meant that the pro-rural agenda initiated by Hu could be more easily blocked or manipulated by local governments. It was perhaps for this very reason that the central government put so much muscle behind the policy, marshaling enormous resources to signal the intention of producing change quickly and without resistance.

Building a New Socialist Countryside

We must look after the cities and the countryside. We must do urban work and rural work, so that we can unite the workers and peasants, industry and agriculture. We cannot throw away the countryside and just look after the cities. If we think that way, we would be completely mistaken.

—Mao Zedong, 1949

The expression "building a new socialist countryside" has been in use since the early Maoist period. In the 1950s, it appeared in the Twelve-Year National Program for Agricultural Development, an ambitious document that helped launch the Great Leap Forward. In the 1960s–1970s, millions of urban youth were instructed to build new socialist villages in the Up to the Mountains, Down to the Countryside Movement. The slogan was also used during the Learn from Dazhai in Agriculture Campaign, which stressed self-reliance and the primacy of socialist consciousness over material incentives as the basis for economic activity. Despite the eventual repudiation of Maoist campaigns, the language of rural socialist construction made its way into several policy documents of the reform period.[106] Then, with the eleventh five-year plan (2006–2010), it once again became a prominent feature of rural policy discourse. Hu Jintao and other central leaders avoided calling the New Socialist Countryside a campaign but were nevertheless intentional about linking it to the past. At a meeting with provincial leaders in February 2006, Hu reviewed the historical foundations of the policy and invoked the above quote from Mao as a reminder that the party had yet to fulfill its duty of looking after both the cities and the countryside.[107]

The New Socialist Countryside was more than a rural stimulus package. The resurrection of this slogan, fifty years after it first appeared, imbued the policy with a revolutionary quality. Wen Jiabao described it as a "major historical task of national modernization," requiring "arduous work" and a "long-term struggle mentality."[108] As previously explained, the policy included fiscal reforms, farm subsidies, and substantial investments in infrastructure and social welfare, all typical components of an agricultural adjustment program. But it also went far beyond these measures, employing Maoist rhetoric and tactics to elicit broad support from the bureaucracy and the public. In everything but name, it had all the markings of a state-sponsored campaign. The New Socialist Countryside is therefore significant, empirically and theoretically, for its far-reaching impact on rural development, and for what it illustrates about the evolution of campaign politics in China.

Origins

The use of mobilization to accomplish state goals is an enduring legacy of the Chinese Communist Revolution. During the 1950s–1970s, the CCP's guerrilla warfare strategy, which had been used against the Japanese and Chinese Nationalist armies, inspired literally hundreds of mass mobilization campaigns, launched for a wide variety of economic, social, political, ideological, and strategic purposes.[109] Taking into account the Great Leap Forward and the Cultural Revolution, it goes without saying that many of these campaigns were destructive and that Deng Xiaoping's pledge in 1978 to end mass campaigns was a welcome change. Yet, time and again, the party has leaned on mobilization as an instrument of rule, in spite of its increasingly technocratic character. The emergence of a modified version of campaign politics—whereby mass participation is encouraged but not required, and the main target of mobilization is the bureaucracy—is evident from studies of economic development, policy enforcement, crisis management, anticorruption, and ideological work.[110]

The continuation of campaigns in the reform era is to some extent a product of path dependence and the Maoist imprint on political culture. It furthermore reflects the regime's confidence in mobilization as a check on bureaucratic inertia and as a tool for promoting development. Following this logic, the adaptation of Maoist campaign practices to suit the New Socialist Countryside was a deliberate choice.[111] Even so, a certain wariness of campaigns can be seen in central leaders' admonitions to guard against the pursuit of "overnight success," wasteful exercises in "image engineering," and actions that "violate the wishes of the masses."[112] This tension between the appeal of mobilization and the need to curb its potential excesses is key to understanding why, since 1978, the government has repeatedly conducted campaigns without announcing them as such.

The New Socialist Countryside called for sweeping changes in rural production, livelihoods, culture, the environment, and governance. Implicit in the policy was a negative, stereotypical view of the peasantry as a backward social class. The countryside was "dirty, disorderly, and poor," and modernization would require "cultivating a new kind of farmer."[113] However, unlike the New Village Movement in South Korea, the spiritual transformation of the peasantry was not a major goal of the New Socialist Countryside. Rather, in China's case, agricultural adjustment took the form of a campaign in order to overcome bureaucratic obstacles to change.

More than two decades of growth-first development policies had conditioned local officials to emphasize industry over agriculture and the cities over villages. Urban bias was deeply entrenched, not only at higher levels of the party-state, but also among officials serving in rural townships. There were, of course, some exceptions (Donaldson's research on Guizhou comes to mind), but the majority of officials in the 1980s and 1990s marched to the same drumbeat of GDP growth.[114] The central government knew that reshaping the attitudes and priorities of local officials could not be achieved through normal means alone: issuing directives, passing legislation, increasing spending, and so forth. It therefore raised the banner of rural modernization with the vigor of a Leninist campaign: setting core tasks, ratcheting up propaganda, organizing cadre work teams, and appealing to the masses for support.

In 2004, one year before the central government unveiled its policy, Ganzhou rolled out a local New Socialist Countryside plan, envisioning "new townships and villages, new rural commodities, new economic organizations, new farmers, new culture, and good government leadership."[115] The local party secretary, Pan Yiyang, through articles appearing in the *People's Daily* and *Qiushi* (Seeking Truth), described the "Ganzhou model" as emphasizing village environmental improvement and the active involvement of peasant councils.[116] Similar to the community and village development committees in Taiwan and South Korea, Ganzhou's peasant councils were characterized as democratically elected, village-level organizations in charge of campaign implementation. According to official sources, during the first year of the policy (2004–2005), a total of 4,025 villages in Ganzhou were renovated. About 740,000 people obtained clean water, 67,000 flush toilets were installed, 3,420 kilometers of roads were paved, and more than three million square meters of abandoned housing was demolished, reportedly without a single protest. Additionally, the government spent only 76 million yuan, or 30–40 percent of the cost, with villagers making up the difference.[117] News of Ganzhou's achievements attracted the attention of central leaders, who made several visits to the area and endorsed the model as an innovative solution to China's rural problems.[118]

The interaction of central and local officials leading up to Beijing's adoption of the New Socialist Countryside is an example of "experimentation under hierarchy," a pragmatic approach to policymaking that facilitates bottom-up learning and innovation.[119] Pan Yiyang had previously served as director of the Jiangxi Rural Work Department and published a book on rural modernization titled *A Peasant-Centered Theory* (2002). His appointment as party secretary of Ganzhou was an opportunity to test out his ideas, and he was well positioned to make it a national model. As one Chinese journalist explained, Pan likely had privileged access to the Hu administration through the Communist Youth League, allowing him to anticipate central policy and take early action.[120] This theory is difficult to confirm, however, given the sensitivity surrounding factional politics in China. More often, local officials cite the area's long history of rural policy experimentation to explain its frontrunner status. Ganzhou is where the CCP first carried out land reform and related policies during the Jiangxi Soviet period, and where the KMT conducted the New Life Movement, a campaign to improve rural education and sanitation.[121] In any case, Ganzhou had a significant impact on the rest of the country. Approximately five hundred official delegations, representing twenty central agencies and all provinces, went there to study the model, and many places replicated certain aspects of it.[122]

The New Socialist Countryside was also inspired by South Korea. Soon after diplomatic relations between the two countries were established in 1992, China's Ministry of Agriculture started organizing conferences and study tours with the Korean government. Through these exchanges, Li Shuishan, a Chinese-born ethnic Korean, learned of the New Village Movement and visited the Korea Saemaul Undong Center. Li began collaborating with colleagues from both countries on projects concerning the movement and published several works on the subject.[123] When I met him in 2010, he suggested that Chinese scholars and officials readily identified with the New Village Movement because it was representative of the East Asian experience: a strong central state confronting the problem of how to modernize a densely populated countryside with underdeveloped markets and scarce resources. The campaign approach, he added, was something the Chinese practically invented.[124]

In the 2000s, numerous studies and reports compared the New Village Movement with the New Socialist Countryside, indicating a connection between the policies.[125] But the strongest evidence of South Korea's influence comes from Zheng Xinli, the former deputy director of the Central Policy Research Office, who led a group of high-level officials to Korea in 2005. Their objective was to study the New Village Movement "in order to draft the 11th five-year plan, resolve the three rural issues [peasants, villages, agriculture], and promote rural economic and social development." After the trip, Zheng submitted two reports to the State Council recommending ways that China might emulate Korea, for instance by focusing on village improvement and using selective rewards to generate mass participation.[126] The next year, the Chinese government announced it was sending thirty thousand civil servants to Korea for Saemaul training.[127]

In fact, countless Chinese officials learned about the New Village Movement from workshops, lectures, and officially circulated study materials. Jeong Gyogwan, former director of the Saemaul Undong Central Training Institute, was invited to China to teach thousands of people about the campaign.[128] The memoir of Park Jin-hwan, chief rural policy adviser to President Park, was translated from Korean into Chinese.[129] Cooperative projects were launched in places like Henan, where the North Kyongsang provincial government opened a Saemaul-themed primary school, and Guangdong, where Foshan city officials partnered with Korean experts to exchange insights on a number of agricultural programs. The Korean media covered these types of events favorably, portraying them as proof of South Korea's global leadership and boasting that Hu Jintao himself had studied the campaign.[130] Even more surprising was just how frequently Chinese officials at the time would reference Korea. During fieldwork, several county and township cadres, without any kind of prompt (or knowledge that Korea was part of my study), volunteered that China was following Korea's example. Upon being asked how they learned about the New Village Movement, they replied that everyone was required to read about it when the New Socialist Countryside started.

This analysis suggests, first, that more research is needed on the process, scope, and impact of regional policy learning and, second, that mobilization is not simply a relic of the Mao era. Mobilization is seen as a tried-and-tested strategy that was fundamental to South Korea's rural transformation and, more generally, to the East Asian miracle. The promise of the New Village Movement, and of Ganzhou's local New Socialist Countryside initiative, was that through a nationwide campaign, China could overcome the problem of urban bias, reduce the rural-urban gap, and achieve modernization in a short period of time. Unfortunately, the political-institutional context in which the campaign took place undermined its chances of success.

Goals and Implementation

The mixed outcomes of the New Socialist Countryside can be attributed to ambiguous and shifting goals, weak central controls, and low levels of rural participation. China was different from Taiwan and South Korea in each of these respects and was consequently the least successful of the three cases. While the overriding aim of the policy was to promote rural development, there was a lot of debate about whether or not the campaign might also be used to support urbanization and boost consumption, which opened the door for local officials to advance their own agendas with relative ease. Higher-level authorities were less effective at monitoring the activities of those at the county level and below, and villagers often had no recourse against negligent or overzealous officials. With few exceptions, the government's calls for mass participation amounted to little more than rhetoric.

Addressing these points in turn, the campaign set broad goals for rural development, although production was recognized as paramount. Only through gains in production, central leaders asserted, would the trends of declining grain output and rising income inequality come to a halt.[131] Improved access to health care and education was also considered necessary for raising rural living standards. Progress on these fronts would require significant financial resources, and local governments worried about how their budgets would be impacted, even with increased fiscal transfers coming from the center. Still, it was easier to build consensus around these goals than consumption and infrastructure, which were more controversial.

Consumption was not an explicit goal of the campaign, but it was a motivating factor from the beginning. In the wake of the Asian Financial Crisis of 1997–1998, Justin Yifu Lin (who would become the World Bank chief economist a decade later) proposed the idea of a "new village movement" as a solution to excess industrial capacity and unsatisfied rural demand. In the 2000s, the notion that consumption, rather than exports, was key to China's economic future became mainstream, especially after the global recession of 2008–2009. Thus, for Lin and many others, a crucial part of the New Socialist Countryside was investment in "consumption-related infrastructure," namely better power, water, roads, and telecommunications.[132]

Several prominent scholars were quick to criticize the domestic demand perspective and offer alternative views of the policy. Pan Wei, for example, argued that infrastructure investment was wasteful. The real solution to rural decline was institution building and fast-paced urbanization, bringing the farm population down to under 10 percent so that agriculture could become more specialized and efficient. Flipping Mao's revolutionary dictum on its head, he stated that the "cities should encircle the countryside."[133] Wen Tiejun, while also supportive of putting institutions above hard infrastructure, disagreed that rapid urbanization was the answer, as it would likely result in massive slums, a problem that China had so far managed to avoid. Instead, rebuilding the village community by organizing and empowering farmers represented a more appropriate path forward.[134] He Xuefeng took a similar position and further insisted that fixating on consumption was harmful. Unless the average cost of living fell dramatically, then a push to increase consumption would cause peasant burdens to return. Accordingly, "low consumption, high welfare" was a better guiding principle.[135]

The government refrained from intervening in these debates, partly because it did not regard consumption and welfare, or infrastructure and institutions, as zero-sum choices. It also wanted local governments to have some flexibility in determining what goals to prioritize. A noticeable shift occurred after 2007, however, as rural subsidies were expanded to include household electronics, cars, and materials for new home construction.[136] Along with a greater emphasis on consumption, increased rhetoric about "integrated urban-rural development" blurred the lines between rural policy matters and urbanization.

In the south-central cities of Chongqing and Chengdu, which were designated as national experimental sites for integrated development, massive apartment complexes were built to accommodate hundreds of thousands of villagers, who effectively traded in their rural landholdings for an urban *hukou*. New regulations linking urban and rural construction land quotas created quasi-markets in those cities and inspired elaborate land transfer schemes in many others.[137] Even in the remote countryside, local governments borrowed heavily from urban models of residential life, especially after the Urban and Rural Planning Law took effect in 2008, requiring that plans for cities, counties, townships, and villages be coordinated and implemented hierarchically.[138] In October of that same year, the Third Plenary Session of the Seventeenth Party Congress ushered in changes to the macro-policy environment, such that land transfers and urbanization became more important.[139] And as the global recession deepened, central investment in rural infrastructure skyrocketed in order to protect growth and encourage the employment of tens of millions of migrant workers, who, having lost their factory jobs, were returning to the countryside in droves.[140]

These changes amounted to an endorsement of the domestic demand policy frame. And yet the focus on new housing was actually not something that proponents like Lin advocated: "Unlike infrastructure, a public good, farmers' houses are private property. Asking farmers to live in a concentrated manner means demolishing their old houses, tantamount to encroaching on their private goods. Such a practice should never be allowed. Especially when land prices are surging, some people are tempted to destroy villages to seize the land under the pretext of building a new socialist countryside."[141] Central leaders expressed similar concerns about village modernization going too far, but their own policy statements on urbanization and consumption, as well as the models they championed, conferred legitimacy on local plans to completely transform the rural built environment.[142]

Local government intervention in this area was further justified on the grounds of protecting arable land, rationalizing construction land, and improving service delivery. Additionally, housing was a visible target that could be used to showcase achievements and curry political favor, and as the above quote suggests, local governments' fiscal dependence on land revenue was a big contributing factor. According to one source, in the late 2000s, rural land sales accounted for about 60 percent of local government revenues; meanwhile, affected households received less than 5 percent of profits.[143] Villagers were pressured to move into apartments or multistory homes occupying less land than traditional homes, thereby releasing land for other uses and creating new rent-seeking opportunities for officials.[144]

In short, Beijing's mixed signals gave local governments too much interpretative leeway, causing the policy to drift quite far from its original vision, which was never entirely clear but included a number of goals that ultimately fell by the wayside. The New Socialist Countryside gradually became synonymous with concentrated housing and mass relocations, and the Xi administration's move toward New-Style Urbanization, a sweeping proposal to urbanize hundreds of millions of people, only exacerbated the problem.[145]

On the issue of central control, I explained in chapter 1 that central-local government coherence was hard to achieve and that local officials were able to manipulate the policy because of the high costs of monitoring. Paradoxically, despite the regime's weakness in this regard, its capacity for bureaucratic mobilization was strong. In Ganzhou, for example, one of the government's first actions was to bring the rural programs of various departments under the umbrella of two key organizations at the city and county levels—the Rural Work Department and the New Socialist Countryside Leading Group—both of which were controlled by the local party committee. Cadre evaluation and promotion standards were then revised to reflect campaign objectives. Following these changes, local officials from every agency were spurred into action. Between 2004 and 2009, over nine thousand cadre work teams, or approximately thirty-nine thousand officials, were sent to the villages.[146] These tactics drew praise from central leaders and were more or less adopted throughout the country. Of course, with Ganzhou being a model, it was more inclined to support Beijing's agenda than other places. So, to steer the policy, the central government released a set of recommended program indicators and cadre evaluation standards. It also used earmarked transfers and matching-fund requirements to limit the fiscal autonomy of subnational units.[147]

The increase in transfers was part of a larger process of recentralization, which started in the mid-1990s. Briefly summarized, numerous township and village governments were eliminated or merged; many of their functions were reassigned to county governments; the personnel appointments of certain departments were centralized; and all levels became more reliant on transfers in the wake of legislation that allocated the lion's share of taxes to the central government.[148] The reforms were intended to facilitate monitoring and compliance. However, they did not necessarily reduce the size of government, and in some ways, they undermined bureaucratic accountability.

Previous research shows that while township budgets were being slashed, county payrolls expanded rapidly. Streamlining efforts did little to affect the "shadow state" of secretaries and assistants surrounding the formal bureaucracy, and surplus cadres were often just transferred somewhere else.[149] Moreover, the centralization of personnel appointments gave greater power to the provinces, not the central government, and was limited to those departments with the greatest revenue potential, such as the SAIC. It also meant that horizontal oversight by local officials became more difficult.[150] Particularly at the township level, divisions among "vertical" and "devolved" agency staff weakened bureaucratic cohesiveness.[151] And even with the sharp rise in transfers, the fiscal system remained decentralized. Subnational governments still accounted for the majority of expenditures, and central investment had to pass through each layer of government (province, prefecture, county, township, village) before reaching individual households, making it very hard to track.[152]

The campaign was somewhat successful at overcoming these challenges and altering the priorities of local governments. Nevertheless, the enormous scale of the state placed limits on the effectiveness of centralizing reforms. As Pierre Landry has noted, China is actually one of the most decentralized countries in the world, not only among authoritarian regimes but also among democracies. He asserts that the key institution holding the regime together is the personnel management system, which gives higher-level authorities the power to appoint, remove, or dismiss officials below them.[153] Still, it should not be assumed that this mechanism alone fosters compliance, since study after study has shown huge gaps in policy implementation.[154] In China, compared to Taiwan and South Korea, local officials had much greater discretion over how the campaign was implemented, and while some scholars have stressed the merits of local flexibility, the virtual collapse of the campaign into a housing policy (to name just one failure) points to serious deficits in bureaucratic oversight.[155] It also underscores how easily campaigns can get out of hand. Once set in motion, a kind of "more, faster, better, cheaper" Leap mentality takes over, and there is not much Beijing can do to scale things back.

Another problem was the lack of checks from below. The government tried to induce popular participation through propaganda, subsidies, and pressure tactics. Besides the usual coverage in official media outlets, significant resources were invested in posters, books, magazines, and websites dedicated to the New Socialist Countryside. In Ganzhou, countless images of model homes and villages appeared on billboards, signs, and calendars. Slogans were painted across buildings and fences. The government even made a film about the campaign and hired a cultural troupe to travel around performing musical skits in local Hakka dialects. Similar efforts occurred in other places as well. Elizabeth Perry writes that propaganda and lecture teams were assembled in every province; old revolutionaries and red tourism sites were used to conduct training sessions; and public events like speech competitions and dramas were organized.[156]

As for financial carrots, local governments doled out a range of subsidies, some of which were means-tested, and some of which were tied to villagers' demonstration of enthusiasm. In one county I visited, the government claimed that about 40 percent of renovated villages started out as "autonomous sites," meaning the residents had proactively torn down old structures, widened the roads, and cleaned up the environment in hopes of attracting outside funds. Whether this was true or not, renovation subsidies provided strong motivation for many villagers to go along with the campaign, especially those who already wanted to upgrade their home.[157] To deal with more resistant villagers, cadre work teams engaged in "thought work"—getting friends and relatives on board, threatening to withhold future support, and making frequent if not daily home visits until they gave in.

All these measures helped to mitigate opposition to the campaign, although it would be a stretch to call them participatory. Village plans were usually drawn up by professional planners and then passed down by the government without consulting residents. Farmers' cooperatives were treated as a goal to be achieved instead of partners in the campaign, and rural organizations in general were too weak to make a difference. The dominant position of the village party branch vis-à-vis the elected village committee and village small groups (teams) facilitated top-down implementation, as did the village's fiscal dependence on township and county governments. Attempts to make village affairs more transparent, such as the introduction of participatory budget planning, failed to gain traction because of poor enforcement and strict limits on collective fund-raising.[158] Village mergers and the construction of "new rural communities," an experimental policy to centralize housing and services, also created a more complicated governance structure in which the status of village leaders was uncertain.[159] The quality of village elections and associational life was highly variable, and even under the best of conditions, it was challenging for villagers to assert their interests.

In many developing countries, institutional and attitudinal barriers inhibit participation in the policy process. Interest aggregation structures are weak, and political elites view mass participation as illegitimate and inefficient.[160] The writings of Ganzhou's party secretary suggest that peasant councils were promoted to address those exact problems. Central leaders endorsed the idea as well, reasoning that council members (typically five to fifteen villagers, elected from the ranks of teachers, entrepreneurs, retired officials, etc.) would listen to villagers' demands, foster communication with the government, and mobilize resources for collective action.[161]

Even though support for peasant councils was echoed in local newspapers across the country, it appears that only a few places adopted them.[162] The fact that they lacked formal legal status and were seemingly redundant with the village committee prevented more widespread diffusion.[163] Moreover, in places where the councils were active, their influence was limited. Most local officials

I interviewed espoused the importance of rural participation, provided it did not hinder policy implementation. They recognized peasant councils as representatives of the village, yet ultimately regarded them as instruments for strengthening state power. Chinese survey research likewise reveals that while villagers respected the councils, they also saw them as completely subordinate to the government, subject to the close supervision of work teams.[164] Their main activities were preparing applications for New Socialist Countryside funding and performing tasks that would have been problematic for officials, namely, collecting money and persuading villagers to raze their old homes. In other words, their presence added legitimacy to the campaign and offered a convenient scapegoat if anything went wrong.

Resistance to the campaign mostly took the form of foot-dragging and grumbling about issues such as renovation costs, inadequate subsidies, shoddy construction, low-quality services, and the mishandling of sensitive projects like temple renovations and grave relocations. These types of complaints, while common, rarely went very far. Despite increased interaction between local officials and villagers, there were no regular channels of communication that connected villagers to higher-level authorities, apart from sporadic outside inspections. When grievances arose, the work teams and peasant councils intervened to stop them from escalating, and with the help of certain policy frames, they were surprisingly successful.

In Jiangxi, the New Socialist Countryside was presented in terms of the state's moral obligation to care for revolutionary families and their descendants. In Sichuan, it was intertwined with post-earthquake reconstruction.[165] In Tibet, it was about demonstrating the state's benevolence and capacity for development through the provision of "comfortable housing."[166] Rural families everywhere were expected to profess their gratitude and loyalty. This is not to say that they refrained from expressing discontent, only that petitions, protests, and other disruptive actions were less frequent than one might expect. As Julia Chuang has observed, the campaign muted "rightful resistance" to rural land grabs through economic concessions and the incorporation of some farmers into urban citizenship.[167] While renovation in Ganzhou did not usually lead to eviction or a change in *hukou* status, the government was similarly able to exploit villagers' feelings about housing—a symbol of security and wealth that could determine one's marriage and business prospects—to justify its plans and stifle dissent.[168]

Outcomes and Legacy

The campaign led to moderate gains in production, incomes, and social welfare, but its biggest impact was on the village environment. The decentralized character of China's political system enabled local officials to neglect some goals, while taking others to extremes. On the positive side, the campaign substantially improved rural public infrastructure and sanitation. It brought paved roads, electricity, clean water, flush toilets, and trash collection services to hundreds of millions of villagers. On the negative side, renovation increasingly came to mean "demolishing the old and building anew." Modest proposals to upgrade existing infrastructure were swept aside in favor of ambitious new housing plans. In the provinces of Henan and Shandong, for example, the Xinxiang and Zhucheng municipal governments invested billions in village demolitions and the construction of several hundred centralized housing complexes.[169] For this to have happened in third- and fourth-tier cities raises serious questions not only about local debt financing and land sales revenues, but also about the future of Chinese villages.

An astonishing number of natural and administrative villages have already disappeared as a consequence of urbanization: the *New York Times* reported a decline from 3.7 million in 2000 to 2.6 million in 2010, "a loss of about 300 villages a day."[170] This trend has no doubt continued under Xi Jinping's New-Style Urbanization Plan, which promised to liberalize the *hukou* system in small and medium-size cities in order to attract rural migrants. Village renovation programs carried over into the Xi era as well, although they were altered to reflect the new urbanization agenda. Resources were directed toward larger villages and townships, with the expectation that they would absorb residents from smaller villages. Furthermore, the integration of village renovation with other policies— dilapidated housing renovation, poverty alleviation resettlement, and pastoral sedentarization—led to dramatic changes in remote parts of the countryside.[171] National-level statistics on the extent of renovation and relocation are unavailable, but the direction of change is clear: the New Socialist Countryside accelerated the expansion of existing cities and the in situ urbanization of rural areas, only not in the same way as before.

Unlike the TVE-led model of rural urbanization, which twenty years earlier transformed many communities in coastal and peri-urban China, the campaign imposed an "urban lifestyle" on villagers that was often incongruous with their rural surroundings and economic realities.[172] Most families took on large debts to pay for the new housing and saw an increase in their monthly expenses. Apartment living came with maintenance fees, utilities bills, and higher food costs, as people gave up their animals and gardens. Some families quit farming altogether, citing the inconvenience of traveling back and forth to their fields and the lack of storage space for farm equipment.[173] Households without alternative sources of income had to find ways around these problems or transition out of farming. Many people faced age- and skill-related barriers to employment. Yet, the bigger issue with the new, housing-centered model of rural urbanization is that it occurred without the attendant growth of nonfarm jobs. In this way, it contributed to the return of peasant burdens.

Officials in Ganzhou were reluctant to speak about household debt and instead described the rural housing boom as a success because of its effect on consumption. In 2007, rural consumer spending reached 14.7 billion yuan, up from 8.7 billion in 2003.[174] These figures do not even capture the peak years for new construction, 2012–2015, when nearly seven hundred thousand mud-brick homes were targeted for renovation.[175] Villagers privately admitted to borrowing money from family and unofficial sources, since banks required that loans be repaid within a year, and subsidies covered just a small fraction of expenses. The cost of renovation after subsidies ranged from a few thousand yuan for basic home upgrades to over one hundred thousand yuan for a new home, a sizable sum considering that Ganzhou's rural per capita income was only 3,570 yuan in 2008.

For a village in Ganzhou to become an official New Socialist Countryside site, 85 percent of its residents were required to sign a formal application, in addition to renovation contracts agreeing to cover 60–70 percent of expenses. As the campaign intensified, renovation plans became more uniform and extravagant, and officials demanded 100 percent participation. The government generally paid for impoverished households, but because this designation applied to less than 6 percent of the population, the campaign likely pushed some poorer residents out of the villages. As one woman explained: "They go to the hollow homes and mud-brick homes in villages that have not yet done the New Socialist Countryside."[176]

The point is not to dismiss the campaign's achievements—many people were genuinely pleased with the government's actions—but to suggest that its legacy is complicated. Pan Yiyang left Ganzhou for a senior post in Inner Mongolia in 2010 and was a rising star in the party until he came under investigation for corruption in 2014. The tarnish to his reputation surely raised suspicion about how the campaign had been conducted locally, just as the accumulation of reports about top-down and excessive implementation cast a shadow over the policy nationally.

During the 2010 "two meetings" of the National People's Congress and the Chinese People's Political Consultative Congress, central leaders like Chen Xiwen voiced concerns about housing-related land schemes, warning that the "campaign to make peasants live in storied buildings," if unchecked, would result in "major problems." The Ministry of Land Resources called for stricter regulations on construction land transfers and launched an investigation into local violations: trading low-quality farmland for construction land, transferring quotas outside of designated areas, and failing to compensate or notify villagers. The tightening of control was a stopgap at best. One ministry official, conceding that the audit revealed "only the tip of the iceberg," described actual land transfer payments as an "enigma."[177]

Under Xi Jinping's leadership, the rhetoric about building new socialist villages was toned down, and the goals of agricultural modernization and poverty alleviation were elevated. However, news reports indicate that mass relocations remain central to these efforts and that local implementation has taken on campaign-like qualities.[178] While greater attention to the plight of poor farmers represents a positive development, relocating them promises to be the easiest part of a very difficult process of economic and social integration. In all likelihood, it has made rural land grabs easier and led to increased levels of dependency on the government. Existing patterns of inequality, rather than being erased, have been reproduced at the neighborhood level of receiving cities and towns.

Campaign politics today bears a strong resemblance to past practices, although the popular mobilization element has largely disappeared. Over fifty years ago, James Townsend described how the mass line permeated "virtually every aspect of Party theory and practice." Mao and other leaders shared a "mystical reverence" for the masses, believing that direct and constant communication with the people would determine the success or failure of the revolution. Popular participation in campaigns, whether voluntary or not, was seen as integral to the execution of policy, and cadres who neglected this principle were said to be guilty of "commandism."[179] Gordon Bennett, in his classic study of campaigns, predicted that both the participatory and the commandist impulses of Chinese politics would "continue well into the future."[180] A key finding of this analysis is that while campaigns have indeed survived the post-Mao transition, only the commandist impulse has endured.

In contrast with Taiwan and South Korea, where rural councils were organized in every village, in China local governments made no real effort to include villagers in the policy process. Peasant councils were an exception that just underscored villagers' marginal status: they had no decision-making power, and their participation was limited to a narrow set of tasks that the cadre work teams wanted to avoid. Weak checks on local officials from above and below impeded the formation of a strong implementing coalition, and as village boundaries were redrawn, the village committee, small groups, and other institutions of self-governance were undermined, further enabling local government co-optation of the policy.

Reform-era campaigns have fortunately not been plagued by the same degree of ideological extremism and violence as their Maoist antecedents, yet they have driven local officials to abuse their power and created new tensions between the party and the masses.[181] This conclusion runs somewhat counter to the literature on consultative governance in China, which highlights the party's willingness to accommodate public opinion and the demands of civil society.[182] Certainly, there are arenas where the state has successfully encouraged popular participation, such as volunteer work and nationalist protests, in part because of its confidence in managing how and when such participation occurs.[183] More importantly, even if it becomes necessary and costly to suppress those activities, local officials' careers do not depend on securing particular outcomes from them, which is perhaps the main difference with campaigns.

It is unclear if the party's "mass line education" initiative, launched in 2013, had any effect on the attitudes of local officials, or if mass campaigns will be resurrected as Xi Jinping more fully embraces a populist style of governance.[184] As this case study illustrates, however, a more inclusive, peasant-centered approach to change is unlikely to emerge in the context of a large-scale development campaign. On a related note, so long as the regime is committed to speeding up the process of urbanization, rural policy will continue to be shaped by urban bias, as seen in the application of industrial principles to agriculture and urban planning to villages.

THE RURAL DEVELOPMENTAL STATE

What lessons can be drawn from the East Asian experience? Scholars writing about the developmental state have long struggled with this question. In a 2018 study, Stephen Haggard reflects on the literature's evolution. It was initially motivated as an attempt to explain the high-growth outliers of Japan, Taiwan, South Korea, and, to a lesser extent, Singapore and Hong Kong. It challenged orthodox ideas about development, describing the effective use of industrial policy as markedly different from the socialist or capitalist models. As it was extended to other regions, intermediate cases of success were identified among particular sectors, agencies, and subnational units within countries that otherwise did not conform to the model's expectations. However, the model's broader applicability was limited, and even within the region, it increasingly appeared as a historical relic against the backdrop of democratization and neoliberal economic reform. The Asian Financial Crisis of the late 1990s seemed to confirm the developmental state's shortcomings, namely, its inability to create a responsible financial sector, and the model's appeal waned. That made it all the more surprising when a decade later, after the 2008 global financial crisis, the concept was revived.

Contemporary scholarship has focused on how developmental states can overcome market failures and escape the middle-income trap. It points to the success of countries like China and Vietnam and considers the possibility of "democratic developmental states" emerging in places like India and South Africa. Proponents assert that although the first generation of developmental states grew out of a unique set of historical and international circumstances, these states' commitment to policy learning and their strategic use of industrial policy (as seen in targeted investments, skills promotion, and other sector-based coordination and support measures) are replicable features. Whether or not this renewed interest in industrial policy, or some version of the "Beijing Consensus," becomes accepted practice in a post-neoliberal order remains to be seen, but at the very least, it signals that heterodox theories of growth are here to stay.[1]

Despite the developmental state model's resilience, it still presupposes the existence of a strong state and a Weberian bureaucracy, qualities that are fundamentally lacking in many developing countries. The literature has furthermore remained silent on the issue of agriculture's role in development, indirectly suggesting that the rural sector automatically contributes to and benefits from rapid industrialization.

This book disputes the generalizability of the model and offers a corrective to some of its core assumptions. I argue that while rural development, like industrial development, was a state-led phenomenon in East Asia, it embodied a distinct political logic, melding technocratic with mobilizational approaches to development in order to effect transformative change. It was not just the use of campaigns but the timing of them that was unusual: they occurred at the later stages of industrialization when, theoretically, the benefits of growth had begun to trickle down to the countryside, and after these regimes had settled into a postrevolutionary phase of governance.

The implication is that rural development was not a byproduct of industrialization or the related processes of urbanization and marketization, as many studies have presumed. Even the literature on land reform fits that narrative, insofar as it emphasizes property rights, production incentives, and the transfer of surplus labor and capital to urban-based industries. On the contrary, my analysis reveals that the effects of land reform on the countryside were mixed and, more importantly, that the prospects for rural development improved when it was treated as an intentional policy goal. This finding is in keeping with previous studies of poverty reduction and urban bias, though few Western scholars would prescribe campaigns as a solution to those problems.[2]

That brings me to a second implication, which is that East Asian political development did not progress in a linear fashion toward a rational-legal form of rule. To be sure, these regimes did become more institutionalized over time, yet the mobilization tactics forged decades earlier in the context of war were adapted to the tasks of state building, governance, and development. Political leaders' embrace of campaigns in a technocratic setting demonstrates that different strands of political culture coexisted. Going back to Weber, the transition from one form of rule to another (legal, traditional, charismatic) is a recursive process that usually results in hybrid systems.[3] From that perspective, campaigns were not an aberration but a normal expression of politics.

There are in fact hundreds if not thousands of historical examples of rural sanitation campaigns, collectivization drives, cooperative movements, infrastructure schemes, and green revolutions led by states all over the world. However, besides the inherent difficulty of mobilization, I have shown that the conditions necessary for campaign success are rare. These include a clear commitment to rural development, a strong capacity for bureaucratic oversight, and a meaningful degree of rural participation. Campaigns often fail, and as anyone familiar with the history of Soviet, Chinese, or Tanzanian collectivization can attest, they sometimes fail miserably. Even among cases of relative success, such as the ones discussed in this book, outcomes can vary significantly, depending on the larger political-institutional environment.

On that note, another strength of this study, in addition to its novel focus on campaigns, is the systematic comparison of East Asia's rural institutions. The very idea of an "East Asian model" is predicated on institutional convergence across the region, which gave rise to similar development strategies and outcomes. While this premise is not wrong, a close examination of the rural sector reveals key points of divergence as well—specifically, the status of agriculture in the national economy; the clout of the agricultural bureaucracy; the responsiveness of local governments to rural issues; and the structure, functions, and influence of farmers' organizations. All these things had an impact on the way rural policy was formulated and implemented. Without getting into the details, the analysis of Taiwan, South Korea, and China illustrates that there are effective and ineffective ways of organizing rural society and that institutions with linkage and autonomy are better for development. It also highlights the importance of central-local government coherence, controlled decentralization, and forming an implementing coalition that includes the intended beneficiaries of the policy.

Clearly, the parallels among East Asian countries are sufficient to constitute a regional pattern of development, deriving from Japanese colonialism, US assistance, land reform, and what might be called a common "strong state, smallholder society" structure. My point is only that the developmental state model, as it has traditionally been conceived, needs to be qualified to account for the region's campaigns and variation in rural development outcomes. To put it simply, the rural developmental state is not as rational or as efficacious as the original prototype. Nor is it something that can be easily replicated. Apart from urban bias and the associated political barriers to rural development, there are also formidable institutional barriers, and campaigns without adequate institutions are dangerous. So, how did East Asia manage to overcome (or at least partially overcome) these challenges?

The developmental state's origins have been linked to a security dilemma environment, which facilitated elite consensus around military readiness and economic development as a dual strategy for thwarting communism. Faced with existential threats from China and North Korea, the newly formed governments of Taiwan and South Korea committed themselves to industrialization. And because of preexisting institutional resources and hard budget constraints, they were able to realize their development goals and avoid falling prey to predatory corruption. Unfortunately, while the urban-industrial sector profited, many farmers saw their standard of living level off or even decline as a result of discriminatory policies. It took about two decades before this problem was addressed, and the motivation again had to do with security—just as external pressures led to the creation of developmental rather than predatory states, internal pressures (related to elections, food security, and migration) led to the reversal of urban bias and expanded opportunities for rural participation. Domestic unrest was a factor in China as well, where an escalation of rural protest two decades into the reform era prompted the central government to reevaluate and eventually overhaul its rural policies.

Regional policy learning was also important. Although many governments encourage the study of other countries and send people abroad in search of "best practices," the knowledge they acquire frequently ends up sitting on the shelf. East Asia is different. The diffusion of ideas, culture, and technology has a long history in the region, and active policy learning has been an integral part of the modernization process since the mid-nineteenth century, if not earlier. In the post–World War II period, Taiwan and South Korea regularly copied each other and Japan, a product of their shared colonial history, close physical proximity, and similar geopolitical concerns. As for China, despite periods of relative isolation, the Chinese Communist Party has always valued policy learning, and with the decline of ideology, its pragmatic and experimental orientation has become more pronounced. Early reformers looked to China's neighbors for clues about how to introduce markets and build institutions while maintaining political control, and they promoted countless exchange programs in hopes of attracting outside investment and technical assistance. Policy learning took off because it satisfied a real hunger for practical information and, furthermore, provided an indirect channel for criticizing the regime. The sharing of knowledge about other countries' achievements was simultaneously a way of commenting on China's own policy failures and making suggestions about the future direction of reform.

I am not arguing that learning causes policy change, only that the substance of policy often has a lineage that transcends national boundaries. Moreover, the back-and-forth borrowing of policy among East Asian countries, as reflected in the region's rural modernization campaigns, has shaped what the East Asian model means just as much as the structural conditions that gave rise to it in the first place.

Yet, to be clear, saying that the model is a product of learning is different from saying that other countries should emulate the model. Going back to my initial question about lessons, the fact that similar campaigns produced such a mixed range of outcomes underscores the contingent nature of success. South Korea's New Village Movement did not succeed because of farmers' determination and collective can-do spirit. Rather, it was the combination of centralized bureaucratic control with (a limited degree of) decentralized rural participation that led to success in some areas (but not others). I bring up this example because the Korean government has for decades tried to export the New Village Movement, while hardly mentioning the state's outsize role in the campaign, its authoritarian politics, or its failure to make the rural economy more competitive. Ignoring these issues and endorsing a watered-down version of the campaign is unhelpful for countries wanting to learn from Korea.

An alternative lesson, which is evident in all three cases, is simply that rural development needs state support. Policymakers must recognize that it is not a natural outgrowth of industrialization and that urban bias is a political problem that demands a political solution. Rural development requires public investment and institutions capable of providing tenure security, credit services, extension programs, market access, and other public goods to smallholders. Campaigns can speed up the pace of change, but in the absence of strong and participatory rural institutions, they are unlikely to make a long-term difference and can easily spiral out of control.

STRUCTURAL FEATURES OF THE TAIWAN FARMERS' ASSOCIATION

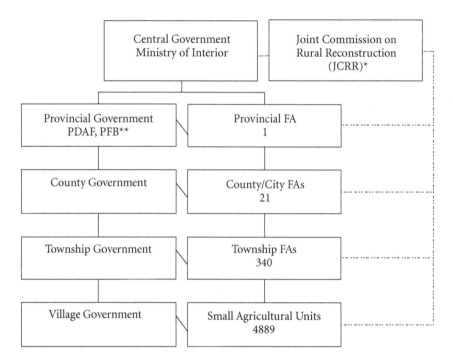

FIGURE 1. The Farmers' Association System in Taiwan

Supervisory relations ———

Collaborative relations --------

*Replaced by the Council for Agricultural Planning and Development in 1979.

**Provincial Department of Agriculture and Forestry, Provincial Food Bureau.

Source: Number of FAs based on 1971 estimates; see Kuo 1984, 167.

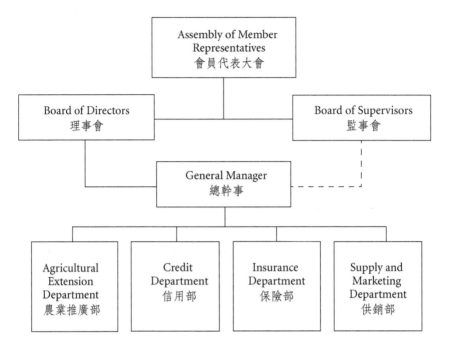

FIGURE 2. Internal Structure of a Township Farmers' Association in Taiwan

Supervisory relations ———

Secondary line of supervision --------

Notes

INTRODUCTION

1. World Bank 2015. Following S. Chen and Ravallion 2010, the World Bank defines poverty as having an income below $1.25 per person per day (the standard was raised in late 2015 to $1.90).

2. Bates 1981. See also Lipton 1976; Schultz 1964, 1978.

3. Bezemer and Headey 2008.

4. Marx 1964, 124.

5. Sharma 2015.

6. Denyer 2011.

7. Petras and Veltmeyer 2001.

8. Boone 2014.

9. Wallace 2014.

10. Figures in constant 2000 dollars; see K. Anderson 2009, 71–72.

11. A Gini coefficient of 0 means complete equality in the distribution of income, while a value of 1.0 suggests complete inequality; see Kuznets 1988, S15–16.

12. Estimates for just Korea and Taiwan are closer to 4 percent; see Ban, Moon, and Perkins 1980, 16.

13. The NRA compares the domestic and international prices of various farm products, while the RRA compares the NRA of farm products with the NRA of nonfarm products; negative values suggest anti-agricultural bias; see K. Anderson 2009, 87–92, 364–73; Francks 1999, 42.

14. Owen 1966.

15. K. Anderson 2009.

16. North 1981.

17. Evans, Rueschemeyer, and Skocpol 1985.

18. This idea was first developed by Chalmers Johnson in 1982. Other notable studies of the developmental state include Amsden 1989, 2001; H. Chang 1994; Cumings 1984; Deyo 1987; Doner, Ritchie, and Slater 2005; Evans 1995; Haggard 1990; Wade 1990; Waldner 1999; G. White 1988; J. Woo 1991; Woo-Cumings 1999.

19. See, for example, Haggard 2018; Singh and Ovadia 2018; Wade 2018.

20. See, most notably, Scott 1998.

21. Weber 1958.

22. See tables 3, 9, and 12.

23. For a good discussion of China and the developmental state model see Kroeber 2011.

24. Illustrative cases, also known as plausibility probes, are intended to provide preliminary support for a theory before it is more rigorously applied to other cases; see Eckstein 1975, 108–13.

25. Again, see tables 3, 9, and 12. The growth rate for China comes from Bramall 2009, 340.

26. de Lasson 1976.

27. The JCRR was a US aid mission that operated in Taiwan during the 1950s–1970s.

28. Fewsmith 1994, 34.

29. For a broad discussion of this methodology see Mahoney and Rueschemeyer 2003; Mahoney and Thelen 2015.

30. Mahoney 2003, 135.

1. THE ROLE OF RURAL INSTITUTIONS AND STATE CAMPAIGNS IN DEVELOPMENT

1. This phrase comes from Kueh 1985.

2. Eckstein 1975, 108–13; quote on 108.

3. Francks 1999, 38.

4. Yager 1988, 51–52.

5. Ban, Moon, and Perkins 1980, 35–39.

6. Ban, Moon, and Perkins 1980, 16.

7. Wik, Pingali, and Broca 2008, 20.

8. Francks 2006, 26–36. By one estimate, 70 percent of irrigation infrastructure used in the 1960s was first built in the Tokugawa period; see Rath 2007, 481.

9. Byres 1986, 43–50.

10. Francks 1999, 66.

11. Francks 1999, 47–72.

12. Ho 1978, 28–35, 99–100.

13. Kohli 2004; quote on 43.

14. Liao, Huang, and Hsiao 1986, 5.

15. Ho 1978, 36–37, 46, 57–64; Yager 1988, 47–51.

16. Kohli 2004, 45.

17. Rice consumption in Korea declined from 111.5 kilograms per person per year in 1912 to 80.2 kilograms in 1944; see Steinberg 1982, 14.

18. Japanese sources report that over 50 percent of the rural population suffered from "spring hunger" before the spring barley harvests, and that more than one million people left Korea because of food shortages in the 1930s; see Keidel 1981, 20.

19. Ho 1978, 70–78.

20. Taiwan's farm size remained stable during the colonial period, about 1.97 hectares (4.87 acres) per household from 1910 to 1940, which suggests that the expansion of cultivated land kept pace with population growth; see Ho 1978, 42. In contrast, Korea's farm size declined from 1.89 hectares (4.67 acres) per household in 1919 to 1.49 hectares (3.68 acres) in 1943; see Y. Chung 2006, 253.

21. On the riots see M. Lewis 1990.

22. Amsden 1985; Wade 1982.

23. Hsiao 1981, 205–7.

24. Ladejinsky was a Russian-born American who worked for the US Department of Agriculture, the Ford Foundation, and the World Bank. He traveled throughout Asia advising governments on agrarian reform and published his first essay on the subject, examining Soviet collectivization, in *Political Science Quarterly* in 1934. For his collected works see Ladejinsky 1977.

25. Ladejinsky 1977, 154.

26. Huntington 1968, 375.

27. The other systems he examines are decentralized sharecropping, migratory labor estate, commercial hacienda, and plantation; see Paige 1976. Hsin-huang Michael Hsiao first alerted me to the points by Huntington and Paige; see Hsiao 1981, 123.

28. For an overview of land reform in each country see Ladejinsky 1977. Figures from Dore 1959, 175–76.

29. *Taiwan Agricultural Statistics* 1966, 8–9; *Taiwan Agricultural Statistics* 1977, 1–2.

30. Shin 1998, 1336–40. See also Cumings 1981.

31. Ban, Moon, and Perkins 1980, 286.

32. Ladejinsky 1977, 80–82; Mulgan 2000, 43–47.

33. Ho 1978, 44–45.

34. Huang C. 2006, 39–41.

35. For these points and a comparison of East Asia with Latin America see Kay 2002.

36. For a positive perspective on land reform see Griffin, Khan, and Ickowitz 2002. For a more critical view see Bramall 2004.

37. Ladejinsky 1977, 356.

38. Lipton 1976, 171.

39. Bramall 2004.

40. For the 1960 statistic see Stavis 1974, 18. For the survey results see M. Yang 1970, 267–70.

41. Ho 1978, 143.

42. Summary derived from C. Johnson 1982 and Wade 1990.

43. Criticisms of the model have centered on its limited applicability to other developing countries, its misrepresentation as free market capitalism, and its apparent failure in the 1997–1998 Asian Financial Crisis; see Pempel 1999; Stiglitz and Yusuf 2001. On China as a developmental state see Knight 2014. On South Africa see Edigheji 2010.

44. On these points see Cumings 1984. Elite cohesion was further bolstered by the exclusion of labor from political coalitions; see Waldner 1999. On the larger question of how war affected East and Southeast Asia's economic success see Stubbs 2005.

45. Doner, Ritchie, and Slater 2005.

46. Dependency theory asserts that resource flows from developing to developed countries sustain economic inequality and that import substitution can help solve this problem; see Cardoso and Faletto 1979; Gunder Frank 1991. For a good discussion of cross-regional differences, the developmental state, and dependency theory see Evans 1987.

47. Minami and Ma 2010.

48. For a broad discussion of the Lewis model and its critics see Ranis 2004. For a similar critique of the developmental state literature and an example of work that stresses land reform see Kay 2002.

49. Rowen 1998, 23.

50. Ho 1978, 144; Mason et al. 1980, 342–78.

51. On the Taiwanese case see Amsden 1985.

52. Hsiao 1981, 244.

53. Figures from Ho 1978, 110–11; Steinberg 1982, 4. For a comparison of US aid to Taiwan and Korea, including P.L. 480, see Hsiao 1981, 165–257.

54. On the JCRR see Yager 1988.

55. On East Asia's "state-rice complex" see Burmeister 2000.

56. Bates 1981.

57. Estimates for how many people died range from fourteen million to forty-five million; see Banister 1987; Dikötter 2010; Kane 1988.

58. Kelliher 1992; D. Yang 1996; Zhou 1996. For a contrasting, elite-centered account see Fewsmith 1994, chap. 1.

59. On the "silent revolution" of the 1940s and the "honeymoon period" of the early 1950s see Friedman, Pickowicz, and Selden 1991.

60. Bramall 2009, chap. 7; Perkins and Yusuf 1984, chaps. 3–4.

61. Gao 1999, chaps. 6–7.

62. Ash 2006. For key monographs on the Leap see Bachman 1991; Becker 1996; Chan 2001; P. Chang 1975; Dikötter 2010; MacFarquhar 1983; Teiwes and Sun 1999; Thaxton 2008; J. Yang 2012.

63. On the Anti-Rightist Movements and the Leap see Bernstein 2006. Dazhai was a model brigade (collectivized village) famous for rewarding farmers based on political attitude rather than labor. On Dazhai and agrarian radicalism during the Cultural Revolution see Zweig 1989.

64. Bramall 2009, 340, 447.

65. On the change in village leadership see Madsen 1984.

66. Oi 1999b, 620; Zhou and White 1995, 462, 474.

67. See, most notably, Oi 1995.

68. For arguments that China is not (or is no longer) a developmental state see Ang 2016; R. Hsueh 2011; Ong 2012a; Pei 2006; Shih 2004.

69. On this debate and challenges to tenure security see Andreas and Zhan 2016.

70. For more on the distinguishing features of campaigns see Bennett 1976; Cell 1977.

71. Tucker 1961.

72. Linz 1975, 191–92.

73. For a diverse examination of state-mobilized movements see Perry, Ekiert, and Yan 2020.

74. T. White 2006, 2.

75. On the cyclical pattern of mobilization see Skinner and Winckler 1969. For the argument that campaigns are institutions see Bennett 1976; Cell 1977; T. White 2006.

76. Cell 1977, 75–76.

77. Cell 1977; F. Yu 1967.

78. In that order see T. White 2006; van Rooij 2006; Dimitrov 2009; Goodman 2004; Shih 2008; Mertha 2017; Z. Wang 2012; Thornton 2009; Tong 2009.

79. For work on earlier anticorruption campaigns see Manion 2004; Wedeman 2012.

80. Brooks 2012, 33.

81. The word for campaign in Chinese, Japanese, and Korean (*yundong, undo, undong*) is the same, deriving from the Chinese characters 運動.

82. The literature on Korea's New Village Movement illustrates this discrepancy between Asian and Western scholarship; see, for example, M. Lee 1981 and Moore 1984–1985.

83. Bennett 1976, 15. See also Cell 1977, 32–34, 153–54, 174–75.

84. North 1990, 3.

85. On path dependence see Pierson 2004.

86. On institutional capacities see Doner 2009.

87. For a thorough account of the Cultural Revolution see MacFarquhar and Schoenhals 2006.

88. Jowitt 1975. For a contrasting view that mobilization disappears in the postrevolutionary phase of governance see Lowenthal 1970.

89. Perry 2011.

90. For a discussion of how problems related to policy "content" and "context" undermine implementation see Grindle 1980. Although Grindle's book does not deal with campaigns specifically, Stephen Quick's chapter on "ideological policies" raises many of the same points made here; see Quick 1980.

91. Grindle 1980, 16–17.

92. Scott 1998, chap. 7.

93. For a positive assessment of decentralization see Montinola, Qian, and Weingast 1995; Shirk 1993. For a more negative view see Bernstein and Lü 2003; L. Tsai 2007.

94. Landry 2008, 3–9.

95. Francks 1999, 16.

96. See, for example, Waswo 2003, 5.
97. Uphoff and Esman 1974, xii.
98. Uphoff and Esman 1974, xvii–xx, 63–96.
99. Evans 1995.
100. For foundational work on corporatism see Schmitter and Lehmbruch 1979.
101. Burmeister, Ranis, and Wang 2002, 130–37.
102. Bernstein and Lü 2003, 224–40.
103. For official data on Taiwan and Korea see Liu J. 1991, 69–72; S. Park 2009, 126. As discussed in chapter 4, the only data I have for China is an aggregate measure of rural sector spending in the 2000s, but in my fieldwork sites, villagers had to sign contracts agreeing to cover 60–70 percent of campaign expenses.
104. Ma X. 2008, 49.
105. Pyle 1973, 57–58.
106. Masao 2003; Pyle 1973; Waswo 1988, 569–76.
107. Waswo 1988, 578–85.
108. Rath 2007, 479–80.
109. K. Smith 2001, 43–44, 80–87, 94–113, 172–88; Waswo 1988, 556, 589–603.
110. K. Smith 2001, 12–13.
111. Waswo 1988, 603.
112. Partner 2001, 497–98; K. Smith 2001, 172, 206–14.
113. K. Smith 2001, 225–34.
114. K. Smith 2001, 17–18.
115. Francks 1999, 78–80.
116. K. Smith 2001, 362–63.
117. Partner 2001.
118. Garon 1997.
119. K. Smith 2001, 363.
120. Mulgan 2000, 645.
121. K. Smith 2003, 153. For a comprehensive account of Nokyo's role in politics see Mulgan 2000, 2006.
122. Bates 1981; Lipton 1976.
123. Scott 1998.
124. For speeches using this slogan see C. Park 1979, 152, 167, 204, 222.
125. Kohli 2004, 22.

2. RURAL DEVELOPMENT IN TAIWAN, 1950s–1970s

1. Lee defines the surplus as the net flow of material resources from the agricultural sector to the industrial and service sectors, including agricultural products, exports, rents, taxes, and savings for the period 1895–1960; see T. Lee 1971, 20–21. The point about his unique background comes from Francks 1999, 160.
2. Wade 1990.
3. See, for example, Scott 1985.
4. On the KMT's Leninist reorganization in Taiwan see Dickson 1993.
5. Local elections occurred at the village, township, county, city, and provincial levels. "Parliament" refers to the National Assembly, the Legislative Yuan, and the Control Yuan; see Chao and Myers 2000.
6. Lenin believed that mass organizations such as trade unions could carry power from the party to the masses, similar to the way that transmission belts carry power from an engine to the parts of a machine. For comparative work on administered mass organizations see Kasza 1995.

7. On the rise of these regimes in the post–Cold War period see Levitsky and Way 2002.

8. Central Committee of the Kuomintang 1972, 5.

9. Ho 1978, 104.

10. On the uprising see Lai, Myers, and Wou 1991. The refugee statistic comes from the US Mutual Security Agency Mission to China 1952a, 2.

11. The population figures represent an average for the decade; see *Taiwan Agricultural Statistics* 1966, 7.

12. In 1952, agricultural products accounted for over 90 percent of total exports, of which rice and sugar accounted for 78 percent; see Ho 1978, 134.

13. All percentages come from Yager 1988, 2–3, 51–52, 61–62. For data on Taiwan's export structure, I consulted the *Taiwan Statistical Data Book* 1982, 189.

14. T. Lee 1971, 29; Yager 1988, 254–55.

15. In total, 824,000 farm laborers entered the nonagricultural sector between 1952 and 1970; see Hsiao 1981, 60.

16. *Taiwan Agricultural Statistics* 1966, 7, 11; *Taiwan Agricultural Statistics* 1977, 1, 3.

17. Ho 1978, 150–55.

18. Amsden 1985, 86; Francks 1999, 173.

19. Stavis 1974, 11–14.

20. Hsiao 1981, 61.

21. Francks 1999, 29; Stavis 1974, 18.

22. For a comparison of industrialization in Taiwan and South Korea see Ho 1979a.

23. For the sections on survey design, perceptions of change, and consumption patterns see M. Yang 1970, 92–128, 261–335.

24. For the 1950s see T. Lee 1971, 20–21, 92; *Taiwan Agricultural Statistics* 1966, 239. For the period 1959–1981 see *Statistical Yearbook of the Republic of China* 1982, 528–29.

25. K. Anderson 2009, 11–12, 33–35, 92; Francks 1999, 42.

26. Gross fixed capital formation also captures private investment, but in Taiwan's case the government was a more important actor. It was directly responsible for 54 percent of the total in 1955–1960 and for 40 percent of the total in 1961–1973. It was also capable of influencing the size and direction of private investment; see Ho 1978, 234–35.

27. Hsiao 1981, 63.

28. Leaving the countryside became a noticeable trend after 1965, with the rate of net migration averaging 5.7 percent per year for the 1965–1981 period; see Liao, Huang, and Hsiao 1986, 346.

29. Francks 1999, 42.

30. Liao, Huang, and Hsiao 1986, 36.

31. Between 1970 and 1980, the share of farm households who owned televisions increased from 16.5 to 60.1 percent; washing machines 0.9 to 37.6 percent; refrigerators 4.3 to 89.4 percent; and telephones 1.4 to 24.1 percent; see *Statistical Yearbook of the Republic of China* 1982, 133.

32. T. Cheng 2001, 20.

33. Lin H. 2004, 1–4, 40–45, 101–2.

34. Ho 1978, 63–64; US Mutual Security Agency Mission to China 1952b, 4–5.

35. Gallin 1966, 15–17. The total area under irrigation increased from 200,000 to 545,000 hectares (from about 495,000 to 1.35 million acres); see Ho 1978, 36.

36. Gold 1986, 37.

37. Yager 1988, 49.

38. Ho 1978, 46.

39. Francks 1999, 53.

40. This estimate is for the entire colonial period; see T. Lee 1971, 173.

41. Amsden 1985, 81–82.

42. Ladejinsky 1977, 106.

43. Ho 1978, 70–72, 90.

44. Gallin and Gallin 1982, 215.

45. Ho 1978, 110–11; *Taiwan Statistical Data Book* 1982, 223. The statistic on Korea comes from Hsiao 1981, 195.

46. Hsiao 1981, 177, 180–83, 245–46. The $366 million figure comes from Yager 1988, 63–64.

47. While the number of commissioners was always small, the general staff ranged from about 200 to 240; see Yager 1988, 11, 62–63.

48. See, for example, the recollections of JCRR commissioner Hsun-shun Chang in Huang C. 1991, 130–32.

49. Ladejinsky 1977, 96–98; quote on 98.

50. On the Sichuan case see Ladejinsky 1977, 113–29.

51. For reprints of letters exchanged between Truman and Chiang on this matter in 1946 see Huang C. 1991, 16–20.

52. As discussed in chapter 1, in the 1970s, the bottom 40 percent of the population received 20 percent of national income, and the Gini coefficient was only .28; see Ho 1978, 143; Kuznets 1988, S15–16.

53. Ho 1978, 166–67.

54. Gallin 1966, 96–97, 108–11; quote on 108.

55. The ROC government used the name Taiwan Provincial Farmers' Association in place of Taiwan Agricultural Association, as it was called under the Japanese. It was later renamed the ROC Farmers' Association. For the sake of convenience, I refer to all these organizations as the FA or FAs.

56. US Mutual Security Agency Mission to China 1953, 59–64. For statistics on FA debts during this period see Kuo 1984, 3–11, 128–29.

57. W. Anderson 1950, 27–29; Central Committee of the Kuomintang 1954, 30.

58. One slight difference between the 1952 law and what Anderson recommended is that he defined active members as those deriving 70 percent or more of their income from farming; see W. Anderson 1950, 29. For the full text of the law in Chinese see Central Committee of the Kuomintang 1954, 110–24. For an English translation see Kuo 1964, 93–117.

59. Central Committee of the Kuomintang 1955, 4–5; US Mutual Security Agency Mission to China 1953, 59–64;

60. Interviews with FA leaders recorded in Huang T. 1981, 17–41.

61. The points about marketing boards and large farmers come from Bates 1981, 11–29, 54–60.

62. Gallin 1966, 44–45; Joint Commission on Rural Reconstruction 1978, 169–75.

63. Ho 1978, 178.

64. *Taiwan Agricultural Statistics* 1977, 13, 198.

65. T. Lee 1971, 45.

66. Ho 1978, 179–80.

67. Gallin 1966, 70–71.

68. de Lasson 1976, 243; Stavis 1974, 118.

69. For comparison with Korea see Burmeister, Ranis, and Wang 2002. On the composition of FA revenue see Kuo 1984, 36.

70. Bosco 1992, 158.

71. I was unable to locate comparable statistics for later years, but most sources suggest that KMT representation remained strong.

72. W. Anderson 1950, 10–11; Stavis 1974, 55–61, 95–103.

73. It should also not be assumed that clan involvement breeds corruption. Research on lineage-based solidary groups shows how, under certain conditions, they can increase government accountability; see L. Tsai 2007.

74. Data available in Kuo 1984, 146–69.

75. M. Yang 1970, 367–70, 490.

76. Burmeister, Ranis, and Wang 2002, 137.

77. Gold 1986, 91–92, 114.

78. Bosco 1992.

79. Huang T. 1981. For Mr. Fan-Chiang's biography see 287–91.

80. See Liao, Huang, and Hsiao 1986, 93–249; quote on 154.

81. K. Li 1988, 296; Moore 1988, 139–41.

82. Specifically, the ARDP consisted of "Nine Measures for Accelerating Rural Construction": abolish the barter system; eliminate the educational surtax on rural land; ease the terms of rural credit; improve agricultural marketing services; strengthen rural infrastructure; integrate production techniques; create specialized production zones (i.e., large farms); strengthen research and extension work; and encourage new rural industries; see Yager 1988, 95–98. Government spending figures come from Joint Commission on Rural Reconstruction 1978, 33; *Statistical Yearbook of the Republic of China* 1982, 467.

83. On these campaigns see Merkel-Hess 2016.

84. On the New Life Movement's fascist qualities see Dirlik 1975. For the state-building perspective see Ferlanti 2010.

85. For a detailed account of the campaign see Central Committee of the Kuomintang 1961; Lee S. 1965. For English see Joint Commission on Rural Reconstruction 1960.

86. On the evolution of community development policies and UN involvement see Hung 1978; Tan Y. 1969.

87. Lee C. 1979.

88. Dickson 1993; Strauss 2017.

89. On the government's concern about rural discontent and factions see Francks 1999, 193–94, 220. On Chiang Ching-kuo's rural populism see Moore 1988, 139–41.

90. For a negative assessment see Hsueh W. 1987.

91. For a thorough elaboration of government policy see Republic of China Community Development Research and Training Center 1972; Tan C. 1972; Wu 1986. For English see Taiwan Provincial Government 1970.

92. In 1972 government support amounted to 330,000 yuan for regular sites and 530,000 yuan for poverty sites; see Hung 1978, 106–8.

93. See, for example, Chen W. 1973; Chuang C. 1972; Hsueh W. 1987.

94. Huang T. 1978, 1979.

95. M. Yang 1970.

96. See, for example, Hsiung 1973; Wang P. 1974.

97. I found one English-language article that mentioned the campaign; see Knapp 1996, 785–87.

98. S. Huang 1993, 50, 60.

99. Taiwan's Second Stage Land Reform of 1980 tried to resolve this problem but was only moderately successful. On this policy and similar ones in East Asia see Bramall 2004.

100. I found only one source that mentioned construction companies taking advantage of the campaign in order to build large housing complexes; see Hung 1978, 115–16.

101. Read 2012.

102. For example, in Taiwan's 2018 midterm elections, many farmers supported the KMT; see Luo and Chen 2018.

103. Bain 1993; Burmeister, Ranis, and Wang 2002.

104. de Lasson 1976.

3. RURAL DEVELOPMENT IN SOUTH KOREA, 1950s–1970s

1. *Major Statistics of the Korean Economy* 1982, 3.

2. See, for example, Amsden 1989; Doner, Ritchie, and Slater 2005; Kohli 2004.

3. Y. Lee 2011, 356–57.

4. Sigurdson and Kim 1981, 222.

5. Since migration data are spotty and inconsistent, the decline of the rural population is being used as a proxy measure; see J. Park 1998, 212.

6. W. Lewis 1954.

7. See, for example, Ban, Moon, and Perkins 1980.

8. See, for example, B. Kim and Vogel 2011.

9. On varieties of corporatism see Schmitter and Lehmbruch 1979.

10. Eberstadt 2010, 94.

11. J. Park 1998, 15–20.

12. Except for the average annual growth rates presented in table 9, all other figures come from Ban, Moon, and Perkins 1980, 12–24, 35–39.

13. Hsiao 1981, 82.

14. Y. Lee 2011. The detail about his family comes from J. Park 1998, 3–4.

15. Hsiao 1981, 82–93, 195–96, 237–45.

16. Brandt 1971, 50–51.

17. Ho 1979b, 648. Ban and colleagues report much higher levels, around 20 to 25 percent, although it was still significantly less than investment in industry and services; see Ban, Moon, and Perkins 1980, 171–73, 178–80.

18. Ban, Moon, and Perkins 1980, 240.

19. *Major Statistics of the Korean Economy* 1982, 205.

20. K. Anderson 2009, 91; Francks 1999, 42.

21. Ban, Moon, and Perkins 1980, 45, 291.

22. K. Anderson 2009, 75; Francks 1999, 29; *Major Statistics of the Korean Economy* 1982, 64.

23. The incidence of absolute and relative poverty in rural areas increased between 1961 and 1965, then declined between 1965 and 1970. After 1970, the rate of absolute poverty continued to decline, while the rate of relative poverty increased and even surpassed previous levels; see Adelman 1997, 540.

24. Hsiao 1981, 91.

25. Ho 1979b, 648.

26. Ban, Moon, and Perkins 1980, 5.

27. For comparative estimates of urban bias see K. Anderson 2009; Bezemer and Headey 2008.

28. Douglass 2014, 145, 148.

29. Y. Lee 2011, 359–60.

30. Y. Lee 2011, 346.

31. Ho 1979b, 651.

32. *Major Statistics of the Korean Economy* 1982, 205.

33. On consumption see Ho 1979b, 648. On incomes see Sigurdson and Kim 1981, 222.

34. Francks 1999, 42.

35. Francks 1999, 109.

36. Burmeister 1988, 60–65.

37. Average household debt increased more than tenfold, from about 110,000 won in 1978 to 1.29 million won in 1983. Tenant farming increased from 33.5 percent in 1970 to 63.2 percent in 1984; see Boyer and Ahn 1991, 76–79. The relative poverty rate among rural households increased from 3.4 percent in 1970 to 11.2 percent in 1980; see Adelman 1997, 540.

38. Beghin, Bureau, and Park 2003.

39. J. Park 1998, 1; Rossmiller 1972, 28.

40. C. Park 1979, 3–6 (introduction by J. Park).

41. For a critical view of renovations see Steinberg 1982, 17–18.

42. van Gevelt 2014, 182–85.

43. Statistics from S. Park 2009, 120.

44. The top ten achievements were (1) the New Village Movement, (2) the Olympics, (3) the five-year economic plans, especially the 1970s heavy and chemical industrialization drive, (4) completion of the Seoul-Pusan highway, (5) the World Cup, (6) the Gwangju pro-democracy movement, (7) development of the semiconductor industry, (8) per capita gross income surpassing $20,000, (9) the South-North (inter-Korean) summits, (10) the 1987 democracy movement; see Hong 2008. The New Village Movement was also ranked first in a survey conducted ten years earlier for the fiftieth anniversary; see National Council of Saemaul Undong 1999, 50.

45. Kohli 2004, 42–43.

46. On industrialization see Eckert 1991, chap. 2.

47. Francks 1999, 74–75.

48. Keidel 1982, 89–90.

49. Kohli 2004, 45–46; Wade 1982, 24–25.

50. Burmeister 1988, 34; J. Park 1998, 9–10. Estimates of how much land was controlled by Japan vary; the 40 percent figure comes from Steinberg 1982, 13.

51. Keidel 1981, 20.

52. Ho 1979a; Ho 1979b.

53. Steinberg 1982, 4.

54. Hsiao 1981, 195, 200, 237–45.

55. Total aid to Taiwan was $4.2 billion, of which $1.8 billion was allocated to economic assistance. The JCRR's budget was $366 million. P.L. 480 imports were worth $387 million. Figures taken from Ho 1978, 110–11; *Taiwan Statistical Data Book* 1982, 223; Yager 1988, 63–64.

56. I do not have comparative international statistics for 1949, but data on the 1968–1973 period show Korea's rural population density to be higher than in Japan, Taiwan, China, India, Indonesia, and Thailand; see Ban, Moon, and Perkins 1980, 136; Keidel 1982, 33. Estimates of the rural population vary; the 16.7 million figure comes from Boyer and Ahn 1991, 53.

57. Hsiao 1981, 51, 80.

58. Ladejinsky 1977, 54; You 1986, 13.

59. Shin 1998, 1320–43; quote on 1324.

60. Ban, Moon, and Perkins 1980, 284–85; Shin 1998, 1340–41.

61. Jager 2003, 32.

62. Ladejinsky 1977, 152.

63. Hsiao 1981, 118.

64. Shin 1998, 1339–41. See also Cumings 1981.

65. Shin 1998, 1340–42.

66. Ho 1978, 143; Kada 1981, 250; Ranis 1995, 515–16.

67. For more on this point see Bramall 2004.

68. Ban, Moon, and Perkins 1980, 291–92.

69. In 1955, 74 percent of farms were still smaller than 1 hectare, and 43 percent were smaller than 0.5 hectares; see Hsiao 1981, 80.

70. Moon and Sul 1997, 481.

71. Abelmann 1996, 213–16; Boyer and Ahn 1991, 77–79.

72. Its full name was changed in 1973 from the Ministry of Agriculture and Forestry to the Ministry of Agriculture and Fisheries.

73. Ban, Moon, and Perkins 1980, 269–75; quotes on 269.

74. Y. Lee 2011, 352, 356–59.

75. Ban, Moon, and Perkins 1980, 262–68, 280.

76. Ban, Moon, and Perkins 1980, 270–72; Rossmiller 1972, 27.

77. Ban, Moon, and Perkins 1980, 272.

78. Burmeister 2006, 67–68; quote on 68. See also Ban, Moon, and Perkins 1980, 272–75.

79. Burmeister, Ranis, and Wang 2002, 136.

80. Burmeister 2006, 68–69.

81. Ban, Moon, and Perkins 1980, 269; Burmeister, Ranis, and Wang 2002, 141–42.

82. Burmeister 1988, 111–17.

83. Hough 1969, 183.

84. In Burmeister's study of the ORD and Tong'il, he uses the phrase "directed innovation" to describe the Korean case. On the differences between induced and directed innovation see Burmeister 1988, chap. 2.

85. Burmeister, Ranis, and Wang 2002, 130, 134–40.

86. Burmeister, Ranis, and Wang 2002, 133–34.

87. Rossmiller 1972, 18, 24–28.

88. For more on the Yushin regime see Im 2011.

89. Y. Lee 2011, 353–68.

90. Hsiao 1981, 162.

91. Burmeister 1988, 65–73; Steinberg 1982, 16.

92. Wallace 2014.

93. Y. Lee 2011, 354.

94. See, for example, K. Anderson and Hayami 1986; Bates 1981.

95. Moore 1993. As an aside, I disagree with Moore's analysis of Taiwan. He argues that the FAs did not lobby for change, and he uses the 1974 FA reforms as evidence that they lacked autonomy. I agree that the new FA law was a setback for autonomy (it required the board of directors to select a general manager nominated by the government, called for smaller FAs to merge with larger units, banned associate members from serving on the board of supervisors, and changed how members' stocks were invested). Yet, by that point, the FAs had already succeeded in bringing about sectoral change, and the new law's intention was good. It aimed to professionalize the FAs and reduce factional meddling into how new streams of resources were being distributed. On the reforms and related political debates see Tsai H. 2006.

96. On the campaign as "state populism" see S. Han 2004.

97. See, for example, Aqua 1974; Boyer and Ahn 1991; Brandt 1978; Moore 1984–1985.

98. See, for example, Han D. 2010; Kim Young-mi 2008; Wang Y. 2014; Yoon 2011.

99. C. Park 1979, 75.

100. C. Park 1979, 159–60.

101. Jager 2003, 81–83.

102. Quoted in Jager 2003, 81.

103. Weber 1930.
104. J. Park 1998, 41–48, 146–53.
105. J. J. H. Han 2011.
106. C. Kim 1994, 90.
107. On Park's "Japanese identity" see Moon and Jun 2011, 117–22. See also Kohli 2004, 87–88.
108. Shin and Han 1999; quote on 96. The authors are careful to note that Korea's Rural Revitalization Campaign was not just an extension of Japanese policy, since it borrowed a lot from Korean agrarianism and other rural social movements. Clark Sorensen takes this argument further, suggesting that the direction of influence may have been reversed, with Korea serving as a model for Japan; see Sorensen 2011, 159–61.
109. Cumings 1984, 1.
110. For speeches using this slogan see C. Park 1979, 152, 167, 204, 222.
111. The central government published dozens of pictorials about the New Village Movement. In the bibliography see *Saemaul* 1975, 1976. For an English translation of the song see J. Park 1998, 179–80.
112. See, for example, Kohli 2004, 92–93. For more comparisons with Chollima and the Great Leap Forward see Woo S. 2013.
113. For details see Yoo-hyuk Kim 1981, 48–53.
114. Y. Lee 2011, 349–57.
115. Sources vary on the total number of villages in Korea; estimates range from about thirty-three thousand to thirty-six thousand.
116. For an overview of the campaign's phases see Boyer and Ahn 1991, 29–42. On training see J. Park 1998, 182–96. The New Spirit Movement promoted Confucian cultural values like loyalty, filial piety, and respecting nature. It was led by Park's eldest daughter; see K. Park 1979.
117. Quick 1980, 58.
118. Burmeister 1988, chap. 4.
119. K. Chung 2009, 39–49.
120. Brandt and Cheong 1979, 17.
121. The 84 percent figure comes from a 1973 government survey of three thousand leaders, cited by Y. Yang 2017, 1001. The 48 percent figure comes from an academic survey of eighty-eight leaders published in 1980; see Eom 2011, 605–6.
122. Han D. 2010, 271; Ministry of Strategy and Finance 2013, 101.
123. J. Park 1998, 111–17; quote on 111. On birth control see Meier 1982.
124. S. Han 2004; quote on 82.
125. For English translations of success cases see Yoo-hyuk Kim 1981; quote on 400.
126. Douglass 1983, 201. For a list of criteria see Brandt and Lee 1981, 72.
127. C. Park 1979, 245.
128. Sonn and Gimm 2013.
129. Aqua 1974, 45.
130. Burmeister 1988, 45–46.
131. See, for example, *Saemaul* 1975, 1976. On the guidelines see Boyer and Ahn 1991, 33; Jang 1983, 2.29–2.31.
132. The Ministry of Home Affairs defined dilapidated housing as construction older than thirty years, smaller than 23 square meters, or just poorly located; see Jang 1983, 1.3.
133. Jang 1983, chaps. 1 and 2, quotes on 1.2–1.3.
134. S. Park 2009, 126.
135. Ho 1979b, 652; Hsiao 1981, 95.
136. Brandt and Lee 1981, 107–8.
137. Jang 1983, 12.37–12.39.

138. Brandt and Lee 1981, 100–106.

139. Burmeister 1988, chap. 4; quote on 59.

140. Ho 1979b, 653–57. In urban areas, Factory Saemaul had a strong ideological bent and was focused on trying to prevent labor unrest; see Yim 2010.

141. Moon and Sul 1997, 476.

142. Wade 1982, 99–100.

143. Francks 1999, 139–40.

144. S. Han 2004, 75–76, 89. On farmers' mobilization in the 1960s–1990s see Abelmann 1996, chap. 8.

145. Boyer and Ahn 1991, 48–52; Chira 1988. Increased government transparency and data dissemination in the early 1980s likely added fuel to the protests; see Hollyer, Rosendorff, and Vreeland 2018, 150–53.

146. Interview with staff at the Saemaul Undong Central Training Institute (the successor organization to SLTI), October 2009. The institute is part of a larger organization called the National Council of Saemaul Undong, or the Korea Saemaul Undong Center.

147. Sorenson 2011, 147–48.

148. As an example see Ministry of Strategy and Finance 2013.

149. In English: https://www.saemaul.or.kr/eng/; accessed December 9, 2017.

150. See, for example, Moore 1984–1985.

151. For a critical take on the export of Saemaul see Doucette and Müller 2016.

152. These terms refer to different types of officials in Maoist China. Experts were more educated and technocratic, while reds were more ideological and radical.

153. Douglass 2014, 168–69.

4. RURAL DEVELOPMENT IN CHINA, 1980s–2000s

1. Naughton 1995.

2. Bramall 2009, 340, 447.

3. For the 2004–2016 Number One Documents see the Ministry of Agriculture, http://www.moa.gov.cn/ztzl/yhwj2017/wjhg_1/; accessed July 10, 2018. The last time agriculture received such attention was 1986. The quote about industry nurturing agriculture first appeared in the 2005 document.

4. Translation from Perry 2011, 39. For the full text of the eleventh five-year plan see http://www.gov.cn/ztzl/2006-03/16/content_228841_2.htm; accessed July 10, 2018.

5. McGregor 2006.

6. For books in English see Ahlers 2014; Harwood 2014; Su 2009.

7. For a Chinese perspective on the East Asian model see Wen T. 2011, 118–60.

8. Xi Chen 2012.

9. O'Brien and Li 1999.

10. Percentages represent the national median; see Bramall 2000, 59–67.

11. Figures from Bramall 2009, 340. When Mao died in 1976, grain accounted for about 80 percent of total sown area. On the diversification of farming see Bramall 2000, 23.

12. Kelliher 1992.

13. Bramall 2009, 220–26, 250–54. See also Perkins and Yusuf 1984.

14. Bramall 2006.

15. Despite all the problems with government land grabs, previous research also suggests that land tenure is not the main problem facing Chinese agriculture and that privatization would likely increase the incidence of landlessness; see Kung 1995; Q. Zhang and Donaldson 2008.

16. Figures represent rural capital construction, a subset of fixed assets related to production capacity and efficiency; see *Zhongguo nongcun tongji nianjian* [China Rural Statistical Yearbook] 2013, 77–78.

17. Oi 1993, 132–40. Terms of trade data are available in *Zhongguo nongcun tongji nianjian* [China Rural Statistical Yearbook] 2013, 207.

18. K. Anderson 2009, 373.

19. Oi 1999b, 620; Zhou and White 1995, 462, 474.

20. Y. Huang 2008.

21. Oi 1999a; quote on 97.

22. Bernstein and Lü 2003.

23. Bernstein and Lü 2003. On urban bias see Knight and Song 1999; Oi 1993; Wallace 2014. The 30 percent figure comes from Chen X., Zhao, and Luo 2008, 234–35.

24. Brown 2012. On social cellularization see Shue 1988.

25. For estimates covering the period 1978–2004 see Cheng Y. 2007, 51–52. See also Naughton 2007, 217–18.

26. For the period 1952–1995 see Knight and Song 1999, 28–29. For 1995–2012 see *Zhongguo nongye fazhan baogao* [China Agricultural Development Report] 2013, 179–80.

27. Bramall 2009, 473, 478.

28. Solinger 1999.

29. Looney and Rithmire 2017.

30. Deng never held the position of general secretary but was recognized as China's paramount leader from 1978 until his death in 1997.

31. On support in the 1990s see Bramall 2000, 345–47.

32. Y. Huang 2008, chap. 3; Naughton 2007, 285–93. As an aside, these authors disagree on whether TVEs were private or public and offer different accounts of their rise and fall.

33. Li J. 2009, 27.

34. The example of the one-child policy illustrates this point; see T. White 2006, chap. 5.

35. L. Tsai 2007.

36. A. Chen 2015; J. Kennedy 2007; G. Smith 2010.

37. Two types of villagers gave me this impression. The first had purchased or were saving for a new home outside the village, usually in the nearby township or county seat, and cited better infrastructure and services as the reason. The second were investing in the village because they felt that conditions had finally improved under Hu Jintao.

38. Cai 2010, chap. 2; figures on 30. See also Xi Chen 2012; O'Brien and Li 2006; Yu J. 2007.

39. Bernstein and Lü 2003, chap. 5; quote from Zhu on 120.

40. Data on farmland and grain production come from Zhang P. 2009, 174–75, 200, 269. The statistic on landlessness comes from Sargeson 2013. On development zones and new cities see Cartier 2001; Hsing 2010.

41. Wen Tiejun first coined the term *sannong* in the 1990s. For a discussion of this literature and intellectual debates about the peasantry see Day 2013. Full citations for these books can be found in the bibliography; see Cao 2005 (English translation); Li Changping 2002; G. Chen and Wu 2006 (English translation).

42. Lin J. 2005.

43. Quoted in Sun 2008, 42.

44. Bernstein and Lü 2003, chap. 6. For more recent books see A. Chen 2015; Göbel 2010; L. C. Li 2012; Takeuchi 2014.

45. The government announced "four cuts" (taxes on agriculture, specialty products, slaughter, and livestock) and "four subsidies" (grain production, seeds, machinery, and

other inputs), in addition to "three increases" (budgetary spending, bond and fixed asset investments, and land transfer revenues) and "three primary allocations" (social welfare, basic infrastructure, and land improvement); see Xie 2009, 105–9.

46. *Zhongguo nongcun tongji nianjian* [China Rural Statistical Yearbook] 2013, 77.

47. Fock and Wong 2008; W. Lin and Wong 2012; M. Liu et al. 2009; Oi et al. 2012.

48. Growth rates for agriculture collected from World Bank 2017. Grain output data for 1978–2012 are available in *Zhongguo liangshi nianjian* [China Grain Yearbook] 2013, 553. The main protection was to set a "red line" of 1.8 billion *mu* (297 million acres) to be used exclusively for farming.

49. NCMS participation likely exceeded the rural population because migrant workers, who were not all counted as rural in the latest census surveys, enrolled in their hometowns.

50. W. Lin and Wong 2012, 27–31.

51. Income data for 1990–2012 available in *Zhongguo nongcun tongji nianjian* [China Rural Statistical Yearbook] 2013, 267. For the government's own assessment of its accomplishments see J. Wen 2012.

52. For a good overview of rural-urban inequality see Whyte 2010.

53. *Zhongguo nongye fazhan baogao* [China Agricultural Development Report] 2013, 179.

54. To be specific, domestic production increased from 4.6 to 5.9 trillion tons, and imports increased from 16.1 to 80.3 million tons; see *Zhongguo liangshi nianjian* [China Grain Yearbook] 2013, 553, 589.

55. The statistic on farm size comes from Zhang L. 2009.

56. *Zhongguo nongcun tongji nianjian* [China Rural Statistical Yearbook] 2013, 79.

57. C. Liu et al. 2009.

58. Michelson 2012.

59. Looney 2015.

60. For major works on rural reform see J. Chung 2000; Kelliher 1992; Lardy 1983; Parish 1985; Unger 2002; D. Yang 1996; Zhou 1996; Zweig 1997. On the related topic of rural industrialization see Y. Huang 2008; Oi 1999a; Whiting 2001.

61. For an English translation see Mao 1965, 23–59.

62. Schurmann 1966, 416.

63. Bernstein 1967.

64. Burns 1988; Oi 1985; Shue 1988; Zweig 1989.

65. For a description of each type see Clegg 2006. On credit cooperatives see Ong 2012b.

66. For an overview of reform-era cooperative policies see Han J. 2007, 3–10; Li X., Zuo, and Ye 2009, 9–11.

67. On the leaders who supported reform see Fewsmith 1994, chap. 1.

68. Day 2013; Hale 2013; Thøgersen 2009; Yan and Chen 2013. For a collection of essays on the movement in Chinese see Liu L. 2008.

69. Full text available in Yu J., He, and Yuan 2007, 1714–30; see section 1, article 7.

70. See references in Yan and Chen 2013, 967. See also Yang T. and Sun 2013.

71. Du 2008, 158–60, 163–65.

72. Du passed away in 2015. For one of his last interviews see Ma G. 2011.

73. Li Changping 2012, 12.

74. Bernstein and Lü 2003, 224–40.

75. Yu J., Weng, and Lu 2007, 143–56, 191–205.

76. Full text of the law and registration regulations available in Yu J., He, and Yuan 2007, 1829–43; definition on 1830.

77. Interview with Ministry of Agriculture official, Beijing, April 2010.

78. P. Huang 2011.

79. Hale 2013.

80. In 2008, China had approximately 150,000 FPCs, of which only 58,072 were registered with the SAIC; see Sun 2008, 221. The 1.9 million figure comes from Xinhua News 2017.

81. Zhang D. 2011. Percentages from Yan and Chen 2013, 969–72. See also Hu, Zhang, and Donaldson 2017.

82. Pan W. and He 2006, 15–20.

83. The name comes from the traditional dragon dance and is a metaphor for leading others toward prosperity.

84. Schneider 2017; statistics on 9. See also the China Association of Agricultural Leading Enterprises, http://www.caale.org.cn/newshtml/13.html; accessed July 10, 2018.

85. P. Huang 2011, 120.

86. Xinhua News 2017.

87. Sun 2008, 221.

88. Schneider 2017, 18.

89. Han J. 2007, 191–92.

90. Li R. 2004, 107.

91. Lü X. and Lu 2008, 68.

92. The same DRC report just mentioned contained a survey revealing greater cross-township and cross-county development, but the majority of FPCs were still local. In many cases, dragon heads either directly founded the cooperative (30 percent) or were formal members of the cooperative (41 percent, n=140); see Han J. 2007, 25–27, 196.

93. Chinese sources more often complain that too many agencies are involved in cooperative affairs, including the SAIC, the Ministry of Agriculture, the Ministry of Civil Affairs, the China Association for Science and Technology, and the All-China Federation of Supply and Marketing Cooperatives; see Li J. 2009, 334–35.

94. Cited in Ma X. 2008, 52.

95. Zhang K. and Zhang 2007, 62–63. See also Yan and Chen 2013, 969–70.

96. Han J. 2007, 194.

97. Interview with Rural Work Department official, Ganzhou, July 2013.

98. For a discussion of this problem in Jingyan County, Sichuan, see Han J. 2007, 125–27.

99. Ma X. 2008, 49. See also Li X., Zuo, and Ye 2009, 15.

100. Site visit to cooperative in Xingguo County, June 2010.

101. Sun 2008, 222–23.

102. Q. Zhang and Donaldson 2008. On reforms see Andreas and Zhan 2016. For a thorough account of farmland commodification and the problems facing smallholders see Trappel 2016.

103. Li J. 2009, 333.

104. Perkins and Yusuf 1984.

105. For a discussion of elite divisions on the eve of the transition see Cheng Li 2003.

106. These include the 1984 Number One Document, the Proceedings on Constructing Civilized Villages (1984), two separate Decisions on Rural Work (1991, 1998), the Circular on Rural Grassroots Organization Building (1994), and the Agriculture Law (2002); see Perry 2011, 35–38; Wang S. 2009, 233–36; Wen T. 2006, 62–65. It is also worth noting that Hui Liangyu, Hu Jintao's vice premier in charge of agriculture, coauthored a book titled *Building a New Socialist Countryside with Chinese Characteristics* years before taking office; see Hui and Liu 1993.

107. Speech available in Zhang H. 2007, 43–58; quote from Mao on 45.

108. Quoted in Zhang H. 2007, 60.

109. For classic works on campaigns see Bennett 1976; Cell 1977; F. Yu 1967.

110. In that order, see Goodman 2004; T. White 2006; Thornton 2009; Wedeman 2012; Shih 2008; Mertha 2017.

111. Perry 2011.

112. Wen Jiabao, quoted in Zhang H. 2007, 60–61.

113. These are commonly used phrases; see, for example, Li P. et al. 2006.

114. Guizhou prioritized poverty reduction over GDP growth, whereas neighboring Yunnan Province did the opposite; see Donaldson 2011.

115. Ganzhou City Government 2004.

116. Pan Y. 2005a, 2005b. I am translating *cunmin lishihui* (also called *nongmin lishihui* or *xin nongcun jianshe lishihui*) as "peasant council" to distinguish it from the village committee, which is part of the government and the farmers' cooperatives. Ahlers and Schubert 2013 use the term "village administration council."

117. Technically, the word used is "petition," not "protest;" see Fang and Liu 2006, 58, 178; Li Z. 2008, 136.

118. Gannan Daily News Group 2009, 2–5, 71–72.

119. Heilmann 2008. See also J. Chung 2000.

120. Interview with *People's Daily* reporter, Nanchang, June 2010. In the mid-1990s, Pan became party secretary of the Guangdong Provincial Communist Youth League and a member of the Central Communist Youth League Standing Committee; see Li Y. and Ling 2006, 509–10.

121. Ferlanti 2010; I. Kim 1973.

122. Liu M. 2006, 165–66; Liu T. 2010, 143.

123. Key references are listed in his book; see Li S. 2006.

124. Interview with Li Shuishan, Beijing, April 2010.

125. Using China National Knowledge Infrastructure (CNKI) databases, a simple keyword search for "South Korea New Village Movement" (*Hanguo xincun yundong*) yields thousands of academic articles in Chinese. See also Ma X. 2008.

126. The group included officials from the Central Leading Group on Rural Work, the Ministry of Finance, the Ministry of Construction, the People's Bank of China, and the Guizhou provincial government; see Zheng's essay in Fang and Liu 2006, 51–55; quote on 51.

127. Do 2009.

128. Choi 2006.

129. J. Park (Piao Zhenhuan) 2005.

130. Do 2009. The point about Foshan comes from the Guangdong Provincial Association for Science and Technology: http://gdsta.cn/Item/2610.aspx; accessed December 9, 2017.

131. See Wen Jiabao's speech in Zhang H. 2007, 60.

132. Despite the similar language, it is unclear if the idea was inspired by South Korea, as there is no mention of the campaign in his writings; see Lin J. 2005, 2012.

133. Pan W. and He 2006, 1–19 (of the preface); quote on 19.

134. See Wen's essay in Liu L. 2008, 3–13.

135. Pan W. and He 2006, 3–22.

136. These were all mentioned in the 2010 Number One Document (see item 5): http://www.moa.gov.cn/ztzl/yhwj2017/wjhg_1/201301/t20130129_3209962.htm; accessed July 10, 2018. On housing see Lü T. and Wen 2010.

137. On Chongqing and Chengdu see L. Li 2012; Zhong 2011. On land schemes see Jiang 2011.

138. Bray 2013.

139. The full text of the meeting's "Decision on Rural Reform and Development" is at http://cpc.people.com.cn/GB/64093/64094/8194418.html; accessed July 10, 2018. For a policy analysis in English see Cheng Li 2009.

140. The stimulus package of November 2008 totaled 4 trillion yuan, or about US$600 billion; see discussion in Wallace 2014, chap. 6.

141. Lin J. 2012, 239–40.

142. For a critical take on village renovation see Chen Xiwen 2008, 137–47. For a more ambiguous perspective see the speech by the former minister of construction Wang Guangdao in Fang and Liu 2006, 28–34.

143. Media interview with DRC official Han Jun; see Jiang 2011.

144. There is a large literature on land expropriation in China. For key works see Cai 2003; Guo 2001; Heurlin 2016; Hsing 2010; Mattingly 2016; Rithmire 2015; Sargeson 2012, 2013; Whiting 2011. On housing in particular see Looney 2015; Ong 2014.

145. On New-Style Urbanization see Looney and Rithmire 2017.

146. Gannan Daily News Group 2009, 59–64; figures on 63.

147. For more on these mechanisms see Ahlers and Schubert 2009. Full text of the 2006 indicators and standards available in Chinese Society for Urban Studies 2009, 196–69.

148. On Hu-era centralization policies see Q. Tan 2007. Between 1994 and 2008 the value of all transfers rose from 59 billion yuan to over 1.8 trillion; see Xie 2009, 590. From 2002 to 2012, the number of townships declined from 39,054 to 33,162, while the number of administrative villages declined from 694,515 to 588,407. Data from the National Bureau of Statistics, http://data.stats.gov.cn/index.htm (search for *nongcun jiceng zuzhi qingkuang*); accessed July 10, 2018.

149. G. Smith 2009.

150. Mertha 2005.

151. G. Smith 2010.

152. Fock and Wong 2008.

153. Landry 2008.

154. On rural policy in particular see J. Chung 2000; Göbel 2011; O'Brien and Li 1999.

155. For a positive take on local implementation see Ahlers and Schubert 2013, 2015; Heberer and Schubert 2012; Schubert and Ahlers 2012.

156. Perry 2011, 39–40.

157. Renovation subsidies were worth about 10,000 yuan per household, or one-tenth the cost of a new home; interviews with officials and villagers in Shicheng and Anyuan Counties, July 2010. The 40 percent estimate comes from "Shicheng County Building a New Socialist Countryside Five-year Summary" (on file with the author).

158. After tax reform, village governments were prohibited from soliciting more than a fixed amount of cash and corvée labor per year, subject to the approval of all residents and county-level "burden monitoring" departments. This policy was called "one issue, one discussion"; see Xie 2008, 201–9; Ye 2006, 127–42; Li Changping's essay in Yu J., Weng, and Lu 2007, 184–90.

159. On communities see Rosenberg 2013.

160. Grindle 1980, 16–17.

161. Ma X. 2008, 16; Ministry of Construction 2005.

162. A list of localities that published articles about the Ganzhou model and peasant councils (2004–2013), compiled from CNKI, is on file with the author. National statistics are unavailable, but it seems they were common in Anhui, Hubei, and Jiangxi; see Chen J., Chen, and Liu 2012.

163. Interviews with township and village officials in Qing County, Hebei, August 2010.

164. According to a 2006 survey of 316 households across Jiangxi, when asked who directed the campaign, only 1.9 percent said peasant councils; see Wen R. and Chen 2007, 8.

165. The Wenchuan earthquake of 2008 killed over seventy thousand people. On reconstruction see Abramson and Qi 2011; Sorace 2014, 2017.

166. Yeh 2013, chap. 7.

167. J. Chuang 2014. On rightful resistance see O'Brien and Li 2006.

168. On the value of housing to rural families see Sargeson 2002.

169. Pan G. and Yao 2010.

170. I. Johnson 2014.

171. On poverty alleviation resettlement see Xue, Wang, and Xue 2013.

172. For previous work on rural urbanization see Guldin 1997, 2001.

173. On these points see Li J. 2009, 28; Ong 2014, 6–9.

174. Gannan Daily News Group 2009, 77.

175. Liu S. and Wu 2013. This initiative was backed by heavy central investment in the name of "Soviet base area revitalization," which practically meant larger subsidies (about 40,000 yuan) for families with revolutionary credentials. The policy can be found at http://www.gov.cn/zwgk/2012-07/02/content_2174947.htm; accessed July 10, 2018.

176. Interviews with villagers in Shicheng County, July 2010. Figures on income and poverty households come from *Ganzhou nianjian* [Ganzhou Yearbook] 2009, 50, 56, 422.

177. Jiang 2011.

178. Hernández 2017; Phillips 2018.

179. Townsend 1967; quotes on 72.

180. Bennett 1976, 98.

181. That being said, the one-child policy, the crackdown on Falungong, and migrant eviction campaigns have all used violence.

182. For key works see Heurlin 2016; Teets 2014; Tsang 2009; Weller 2008.

183. Perry 2014; Weiss 2014.

184. Heath 2013. For more on mass line politics and populism in contemporary China see Tang 2016.

CONCLUSION

1. Haggard 2018. On the Beijing Consensus see Ramo 2004. For a critique see S. Kennedy 2010.

2. See, for example, Donaldson 2011 and Kohli 1987 on subnational variation in poverty reduction in China and India.

3. Weber 1958.

Works Cited

Abelmann, Nancy. 1996. *Echoes of the Past, Epics of Dissent: A South Korean Social Movement*. Berkeley: University of California Press.

Abramson, Daniel B., and Yu Qi. 2011. "'Urban-Rural Integration' in the Earthquake Zone: Sichuan's Post-disaster Reconstruction and the Expansion of the Chengdu Metropole." *Pacific Affairs* 84 (3): 495–523.

Adelman, Irma. 1997. "Social Development in Korea, 1953–1993." In *The Korean Economy 1945–1995: Performance and Vision for the 21st Century*, edited by Dong-Se Cha, Kwang Suk Kim, and Dwight H. Perkins, 509–40. Seoul: Korea Development Institute.

Ahlers, Anna L. 2014. *Rural Policy Implementation in Contemporary China: New Socialist Countryside*. New York: Routledge.

Ahlers, Anna L., and Gunter Schubert. 2009. "'Building a New Socialist Countryside'— Only a Political Slogan?" *Journal of Current Chinese Affairs* 38 (4): 35–62.

——. 2013. "Strategic Modelling: 'Building a New Socialist Countryside' in Three Chinese Counties." *China Quarterly* 216: 831–49.

——. 2015. "Effective Implementation in China's Local State." *Modern China* 41 (4): 372–405.

Amsden, Alice H. 1985. "The State and Taiwan's Economic Development." In *Bringing the State Back In*, edited by Peter B. Evans, Dietrich Rueschemeyer, and Theda Skocpol, 78–106. New York: Cambridge University Press.

——. 1989. *Asia's Next Giant: South Korea and Late Industrialization*. New York: Oxford University Press.

——. 2001. *The Rise of "The Rest": Challenges to the West from Late-Industrializing Economies*. New York: Oxford University Press.

Anderson, Kym, ed. 2009. *Distortions to Agricultural Incentives: A Global Perspective, 1955–2007*. Washington, DC: Palgrave Macmillan and the World Bank.

Anderson, Kym, and Yujiro Hayami, eds. 1986. *The Political Economy of Agricultural Protection: East Asia in International Perspective*. Sydney: Allen & Unwin.

Anderson, Walfred A. 1950. *Farmers' Associations in Taiwan: A Report to the Joint Commission on Rural Reconstruction, Economic Cooperation Administration Mission to China*. Taipei: Joint Commission on Rural Reconstruction.

Andreas, Joel, and Shaohua Zhan. 2016. "*Hukou* and Land: Market Reform and Rural Displacement in China." *Journal of Peasant Studies* 43 (4): 798–827.

Ang, Yuen Yuen. 2016. *How China Escaped the Poverty Trap*. Ithaca, NY: Cornell University Press.

Aqua, Ronald. 1974. *Local Government and Rural Development in South Korea*. Ithaca, NY: Rural Development Committee, Center for International Studies, Cornell University.

Ash, Robert. 2006. "Squeezing the Peasants: Grain Extraction, Food Consumption and Rural Living Standards in Mao's China." *China Quarterly* 188: 959–98.

Bachman, David M. 1991. *Bureaucracy, Economy, and Leadership in China: The Institutional Origins of the Great Leap Forward*. New York: Cambridge University Press.

Bain, Irene. 1993. *Agricultural Reform in Taiwan: From Here to Modernity?* Hong Kong: Chinese University Press.

Ban, Sung Hwan, Pal Yong Moon, and Dwight H. Perkins. 1980. *Rural Development. Studies in the Modernization of the Republic of Korea: 1945–1975.* Cambridge, MA: Harvard University Press.

Banister, Judith. 1987. *China's Changing Population.* Stanford, CA: Stanford University Press.

Bates, Robert H. 1981. *Markets and States in Tropical Africa: The Political Basis of Agricultural Policies.* Berkeley: University of California Press.

Becker, Jasper. 1996. *Hungry Ghosts: Mao's Secret Famine.* New York: Free Press.

Beghin, John C., Jean-Christophe Bureau, and Sung Joon Park. 2003. "Food Security and Agricultural Protection in South Korea." *American Journal of Agricultural Economics* 85 (3): 618–32.

Bennett, Gordon A. 1976. *Yundong: Mass Campaigns in Chinese Communist Leadership.* Berkeley: University of California, Berkeley, Center for Chinese Studies.

Bernstein, Thomas P. 1967. "Leadership and Mass Mobilisation in the Soviet and Chinese Collectivisation Campaigns of 1929–30 and 1955–56: A Comparison." *China Quarterly* 31: 1–47.

——. 2006. "Mao Zedong and the Famine of 1959–1960: A Study in Willfulness." *China Quarterly* 186: 421–45.

Bernstein, Thomas P., and Xiaobo Lü. 2003. *Taxation without Representation in Contemporary Rural China.* New York: Cambridge University Press.

Bezemer, Dirk, and Derek Headey. 2008. "Agriculture, Development, and Urban Bias." *World Development* 36 (8): 1342–64.

Boone, Catherine. 2014. *Property and Political Order in Africa: Land Rights and the Structure of Politics.* New York: Cambridge University Press.

Bosco, Joseph. 1992. "Taiwan Factions: Guanxi, Patronage, and the State in Local Politics." *Ethnology* 31 (2): 157–83.

Boyer, William W., and Byong Man Ahn. 1991. *Rural Development in South Korea: A Sociopolitical Analysis.* Newark: University of Delaware Press.

Bramall, Chris. 2000. *Sources of Chinese Economic Growth, 1978–1996.* New York: Oxford University Press.

——. 2004. "Chinese Land Reform in Long-Run Perspective and in the Wider East Asian Context." *Journal of Agrarian Change* 4 (1–2): 107–41.

——. 2009. *Chinese Economic Development.* New York: Routledge.

Brandt, Vincent S. R. 1971. *A Korean Village: Between Farm and Sea.* Cambridge, MA: Harvard University Press.

——. 1978. "The New Community Movement: Planned and Unplanned Change in Rural Korea." *Journal of Asian and African Studies* 13 (3–4): 196–211.

Brandt, Vincent S. R., and Ji Woong Cheong. 1979. *Planning from the Bottom Up: Community-Based Integrated Rural Development in South Korea.* Essex, CT: International Council for Educational Development.

Brandt, Vincent S. R., and Man-Gap Lee. 1981. "Community Development in the Republic of Korea." In *Community Development: Comparative Case Studies in India, the Republic of Korea, Mexico and Tanzania,* edited by Ronald Dore and Zoe Mars, 49–136. London: Croom Helm.

Bray, David. 2013. "Urban Planning Goes Rural: Conceptualising the 'New Village.'" *China Perspectives* 3: 53–62.

Brooks, Jonathan, ed. 2012. *Agricultural Policies for Poverty Reduction.* Paris: OECD.

Brown, Jeremy. 2012. *City versus Countryside in Mao's China: Negotiating the Divide.* New York: Cambridge University Press.

Burmeister, Larry L. 1988. *Research, Realpolitik, and Development in Korea: The State and the Green Revolution*. Boulder, CO: Westview.

——. 2000. "Dismantling Statist East Asian Agricultures? Global Pressures and National Responses." *World Development* 28 (3): 443–55.

——. 2006. "Agricultural Cooperative Development and Change: A Window on South Korea's Agrarian Transformation." In *Transformations in Twentieth Century Korea*, edited by Yun-Shik Chang and Steven Hugh Lee, 64–86. New York: Routledge.

Burmeister, Larry L., Gustav Ranis, and Michael Wang. 2002. "Group Behaviour and Development: A Comparison of Farmers' Organizations in South Korea and Taiwan." In *Group Behaviour and Development: Is the Market Destroying Coopera-tion?*, edited by Judith Heyer, Frances Stewart, and Rosemary Thorp, 125–45. New York: Oxford University Press.

Burns, John. 1988. *Political Participation in Rural China*. Berkeley: University of California, Berkeley, Center for Chinese Studies.

Byres, Terence J. 1986. "The Agrarian Question, Forms of Capitalist Agrarian Transition and the State: An Essay with Reference to Asia." *Social Scientist* 14 (11–12): 3–67.

Cai, Yongshun. 2003. "Collective Ownership or Cadres' Ownership? The Non-agricultural Use of Farmland in China." *China Quarterly* 175: 662–80.

——. 2010. *Collective Resistance in China: Why Popular Protests Succeed or Fail*. Stanford, CA: Stanford University Press.

Cao, Jingqing. 2005. *China along the Yellow River: Reflections on Rural Society*. Translated by Nicky Harman and Huang Ruhua. New York: RoutledgeCurzon.

Cardoso, Fernando Henrique, and Enzo Faletto. 1979. *Dependency and Development in Latin America*. Translated by Marjory Mattingly Urquidi. Berkeley: University of California Press.

Cartier, Carolyn. 2001. "'Zone Fever,' the Arable Land Debate, and Real Estate Specula-tion: China's Evolving Land Use Regime and Its Geographical Contradictions." *Journal of Contemporary China* 10 (28): 445–69.

Cell, Charles P. 1977. *Revolution at Work: Mobilization Campaigns in China*. New York: Academic Press.

Central Committee of the Kuomintang. 1954. *Zhongguo Guomindang nongmin yundong yu Taiwan sheng geji nonghui gaijin* [The Chinese Nationalist Party's peasant movement and the improvement of farmers' associations in Taiwan Province]. Taipei: Fifth Division, Central Committee of the Kuomintang.

——. 1955. *Zhongguo Guomindang nongmin zhengce yu Taiwan nongcun xianzhuang* [The Chinese Nationalist Party's policy toward the peasants and Taiwan's rural situation]. Taipei: Fifth Division, Central Committee of the Kuomintang.

——. 1961. *Jiceng minsheng jianshe shiyan yundong zhuanji (zai ban)* [The People's Live-lihood Construction Experimental Campaign (2nd ed.)]. Taipei: Fifth Division, Central Committee of the Kuomintang.

——. 1972. *Taiwan nongcun jianshe de xin cuoshi* [New measures for rural construc-tion in Taiwan]. Taipei: Division of Cultural Affairs, Central Committee of the Kuomintang.

Chan, Alfred L. 2001. *Mao's Crusade: Politics and Policy Implementation in China's Great Leap Forward*. New York: Oxford University Press.

Chang, Ha-Joon. 1994. *The Political Economy of Industrial Policy*. New York: St. Martin's Press.

Chang, Parris H. 1975. *Power and Policy in China*. University Park: Pennsylvania State University Press.

Chao, Linda, and Ramon H. Myers. 2000. "How Elections Promoted Democracy in Taiwan under Martial Law." *China Quarterly* 162: 387–409.

Chen, An. 2015. *The Transformation of Governance in Rural China: Market, Finance, and Political Authority*. Cambridge: Cambridge University Press.

Chen, Guidi, and Chuntao Wu. 2006. *Will the Boat Sink the Water? The Life of China's Peasants*. Translated by Hong Zhu. New York: PublicAffairs.

Chen Jun, Chen Yisheng, and Liu Shaoyun. 2012. "Guanyu cunmin lishihui de diaocha yu sikao" [Investigation and reflection on villager councils]. *Jianghuai fazhi* [Jianghuai Rule of Law] 17: 55–57.

Chen, Shaohua, and Martin Ravallion. 2010. "The Developing World Is Poorer Than We Thought, but No Less Successful in the Fight against Poverty." *Quarterly Journal of Economics* 125 (4): 1577–1625.

Chen Wen-huang (Chen Wenhuang). 1973. "Taiwan sheng zhengfu tuixing shequ fazhan gongzuo zhi jiantao yanjiu" [Assessment of the Taiwan provincial government's implementation of community development work]. Master's thesis, National Chengchi University.

Chen, Xi. 2012. *Social Protest and Contentious Authoritarianism in China*. New York: Cambridge University Press.

Chen Xiwen. 2008. *Chen Xiwen gaige lunji* [A collection of Chen Xiwen's works on economic reform]. Beijing: Zhongguo fazhan chubanshe [China Development Press].

Chen Xiwen, Zhao Yang, and Luo Dan. 2008. *Zhongguo nongcun gaige 30 nian huigu yu zhanwang* [30 years of rural reform in China, reflections and future prospects]. Beijing: Renmin chubanshe [People's Press].

Cheng, Tun-jen. 2001. "Transforming Taiwan's Economic Structure in the 20th Century." *China Quarterly* 165: 19–36.

Cheng Yonghong. 2007. "Gaige yilai quanguo zongti jini xi de yanbian ji qi chengxiang fenjie" [China's overall Gini coefficient and its decomposition by rural and urban areas since reform and opening up]. *Zhongguo shehui kexue* [Social Sciences in China] 4: 45–60.

Chinese Society for Urban Studies (and the Ministry of Housing and Urban-Rural Construction). 2009. *Zhongguo xiao chengzhen he cunzhuang jianshe fazhan baogao 2008* [China small towns and villages construction and development report 2008]. Beijing: Zhongguo chengshi chubanshe [China City Press].

Chira, Susan. 1988. "Corruption Scandal Widens in Seoul." *New York Times*, March 25.

Choi, Joon-ho. 2006. "Saemaul Gets New Life in China." *Korea JoongAng Daily*, March 16.

Chuang Chao-ming (Zhuang Zhaoming). 1972. "Yilan xian shequ fazhan zhi yanjiu" [Research on community development in Yilan County]. Master's thesis, National Chengchi University.

Chuang, Julia. 2014. "China's Rural Land Politics: Bureaucratic Absorption and the Muting of Rightful Resistance." *China Quarterly* 219: 649–69.

Chung, Jae Ho. 2000. *Central Control and Local Discretion in China: Leadership and Implementation during Post-Mao Decollectivization*. New York: Oxford University Press.

Chung, Kap Jin. 2009. *Research Report on Saemaul Undong: Experiences and Lessons from Korea's Saemaul Undong in the 1970s*. Seoul: Korea Development Institute.

Chung, Young-Iob. 2006. *Korea under Siege, 1876–1945: Capital Formation and Economic Transformation*. New York: Oxford University Press.

Clegg, Jenny. 2006. "Rural Cooperatives in China: Policy and Practice." *Journal of Small Business and Enterprise Development* 13 (2): 219–34.

Cumings, Bruce. 1981. *The Origins of the Korean War*. Vol. 1, *Liberation and the Emergence of Separate Regimes, 1945–1947*. Princeton, NJ: Princeton University Press.

———. 1984. "The Origins and Development of the Northeast Asian Political Economy: Industrial Sectors, Product Cycles, and Political Consequences." *International Organization* 38 (1): 1–40.

Day, Alexander F. 2013. *The Peasant in Postsocialist China: History, Politics, and Capitalism.* New York: Cambridge University Press.

de Lasson, Aksel. 1976. *The Farmers' Association Approach to Rural Development: The Taiwan Case.* Saarbrücken, Germany: Verlag der SSIP-Schriften Breitenbach.

Denyer, Simon. 2011. "In India, Fresh Clashes over Rural Land as Farmers Stand Up to Government." *Washington Post,* May 21.

Deyo, Frederic C., ed. 1987. *The Political Economy of the New Asian Industrialism.* Ithaca, NY: Cornell University Press.

Dickson, Bruce J. 1993. "The Lessons of Defeat: The Reorganization of the Kuomintang on Taiwan, 1950–52." *China Quarterly* 133: 56–84.

Dikötter, Frank. 2010. *Mao's Great Famine: The History of China's Most Devastating Catastrophe, 1958–1962.* New York: Walker & Co.

Dimitrov, Martin K. 2009. *Piracy and the State: The Politics of Intellectual Property Rights in China.* New York: Cambridge University Press.

Dirlik, Arif. 1975. "The Ideological Foundations of the New Life Movement: A Study in Counterrevolution." *Journal of Asian Studies* 34 (4): 945–80.

Do, Je-hae. 2009. "New Community Movement Inspires 72 Countries." *Korea Times,* August 30.

Donaldson, John A. 2011. *Small Works: Poverty and Economic Development in Southwestern China.* Ithaca, NY: Cornell University Press.

Doner, Richard F. 2009. *The Politics of Uneven Development: Thailand's Economic Growth in Comparative Perspective.* New York: Cambridge University Press.

Doner, Richard F., Bryan K. Ritchie, and Dan Slater. 2005. "Systemic Vulnerability and the Origins of Developmental States: Northeast and Southeast Asia in Comparative Perspective." *International Organization* 59 (2): 327–61.

Dore, Ronald. 1959. *Land Reform in Japan.* London: Oxford University Press.

Doucette, Jamie, and Anders Riel Müller. 2016. "Exporting the Saemaul Spirit: South Korea's Knowledge Sharing Program and the 'Rendering Technical' of Korean Development." *Geoforum* 75: 29–39.

Douglass, Mike. 1983. "The Korean Saemaul Undong: Accelerated Rural Development in an Open Economy." In *Rural Development and the State: Contradictions and Dilemmas in Developing Countries,* edited by David A. M. Lea and D. P. Chaudhri, 186–214. New York: Methuen.

———. 2014. "The Saemaul Undong in Historical Perspective and in the Contemporary World." In *Learning from the South Korean Developmental Success: Effective Developmental Cooperation and Synergistic Institutions and Policies,* edited by Ilcheong Yi and Thandika Mkandawire, 136–71. New York: Palgrave Macmillan.

Du Runsheng. 2008. *Du Runsheng gaige lunji* [A collection of Du Runsheng's works on economic reform]. Beijing: Zhongguo fazhan chubanshe [China Development Press].

Eberstadt, Nicholas. 2010. *Policy and Economic Performance in Divided Korea during the Cold War Era: 1945–91.* Washington, DC: American Enterprise Institute.

Eckert, Carter J. 1991. *Offspring of Empire: The Koch'ang Kims and the Colonial Origins of Korean Capitalism, 1876–1945.* Seattle: University of Washington Press.

Eckstein, Harry. 1975. "Case Study and Theory in Political Science." In *Handbook of Political Science,* vol. 7, *Political Science: Scope and Theory,* edited by Fred I. Greenstein and Nelson W. Polsby, 79–138. Reading, MA: Addison-Wesley.

Edigheji, Omano, ed. 2010. *Constructing a Democratic Developmental State in South Africa: Potentials and Challenges.* Cape Town: Human Science Research Council.

Eom, Seok-Jin. 2011. "Synergy between State and Rural Society for Development: An Analysis of the Governance System of the Rural Saemaul Undong in Korea." *Korea Observer* 42 (4): 583–620.

Evans, Peter B. 1987. "Class, State, and Dependence in East Asia: Lessons for Latin Americanists." In *The Political Economy of the New Asian Industrialism*, edited by Frederic C. Deyo, 203–26. Ithaca, NY: Cornell University Press.

——. 1995. *Embedded Autonomy: States and Industrial Transformation.* Princeton, NJ: Princeton University Press.

Evans, Peter B., Dietrich Rueschemeyer, and Theda Skocpol, eds. 1985. *Bringing the State Back In.* New York: Cambridge University Press.

Fang Ming and Liu Jun, eds. 2006. *Xin nongcun jianshe zhengce lilun wenji* [Essays on building a new countryside, policy and theory]. Beijing: Zhongguo jianzhu gongye chubanshe [China Architecture and Building Press].

Ferlanti, Federica. 2010. "The New Life Movement in Jiangxi Province, 1934–1938." *Modern Asian Studies* 44 (5): 961–1000.

Fewsmith, Joseph. 1994. *Dilemmas of Reform in China: Political Conflict and Economic Debate.* Armonk, NY: M. E. Sharpe.

Fock, Achim, and Christine Wong. 2008. *Financing Rural Development for a Harmonious Society in China: Recent Reforms in Public Finance and Their Prospects.* Washington, DC: World Bank.

Francks, Penelope. 2006. *Rural Economic Development in Japan: From the Nineteenth Century to the Pacific War.* New York: Routledge.

Francks, Penelope, with Johanna Boestel and Choo Hyop Kim. 1999. *Agriculture and Economic Development in East Asia: From Growth to Protectionism in Japan, Korea, and Taiwan.* New York: Routledge.

Friedman, Edward, Paul G. Pickowicz, and Mark Selden, with Kay Ann Johnson. 1991. *Chinese Village, Socialist State.* New Haven, CT: Yale University Press.

Gallin, Bernard. 1966. *Hsin Hsing, Taiwan: A Chinese Village in Change.* Berkeley: University of California Press.

Gallin, Bernard, and Rita S. Gallin. 1982. "Socioeconomic Life in Rural Taiwan: Twenty Years of Development and Change." *Modern China* 8 (2): 205–46.

Gannan Daily News Group. 2009. "Xin nongcun jianshe wu zhou nian te kan" [Special issue on the five-year anniversary of Building a New Countryside]. *Xin Ganzhou* [New Ganzhou], November 25.

Ganzhou City Government. 2004. *Guanyu jiaqiang shehuizhuyi xin nongcun jianshe gongzuo de jueding* [Decision on strengthening efforts to build a New Socialist Countryside]. Ganzhou: Ganzhou City Government (on file with the author).

Ganzhou nianjian [Ganzhou Yearbook]. 2009. Ganzhou: Ganzhou City Government.

Gao, Mobo C. F. 1999. *Gao Village: A Portrait of Rural Life in Modern China.* Honolulu: University of Hawai'i Press.

Garon, Sheldon. 1997. *Molding Japanese Minds: The State in Everyday Life.* Princeton, NJ: Princeton University Press.

Göbel, Christian. 2010. *The Politics of Rural Reform in China: State Policy and Village Predicament in the Early 2000s.* New York: Routledge.

Gold, Thomas B. 1986. *State and Society in the Taiwan Miracle.* Armonk, NY: M. E. Sharpe.

Goodman, David S. G., ed. 2004. *China's Campaign to "Open Up the West": National, Provincial, and Local Perspectives.* New York: Cambridge University Press.

Griffin, Keith, Azizur Rahman Khan, and Amy Ickowitz. 2002. "Poverty and the Distribution of Land." *Journal of Agrarian Change* 2 (3): 279–330.

Grindle, Merilee S. 1980. *Politics and Policy Implementation in the Third World*. Princeton, NJ: Princeton University Press.

Guldin, Gregory E., ed. 1997. *Farewell to Peasant China: Rural Urbanization and Social Change in the Late Twentieth Century*. Armonk, NY: M. E. Sharpe.

———. 2001. *What's a Peasant to Do? Village Becoming Town in Southern China*. Boulder, CO: Westview.

Gunder Frank, Andre. 1991. *The Underdevelopment of Development*. Stockholm: Bethany Books.

Guo, Xiaolin. 2001. "Land Expropriation and Rural Conflicts in China." *China Quarterly* 166: 422–39.

Haggard, Stephen. 1990. *Pathways from the Periphery: The Politics of Growth in the Newly Industrializing Countries*. Ithaca, NY: Cornell University Press.

———. 2018. *Developmental States*. Elements in the Politics of Development. New York: Cambridge University Press.

Hale, Matthew A. 2013. "Tilling Sand: Contradictions of 'Social Economy' in a Chinese Movement for Alternative Rural Development." *Dialectical Anthropology* 37 (1): 51–82.

Han Do-hyun (Han Tohyŏn). 2010. "1970 nyŏndae saemaŭl undong esŏ maŭl chidojadŭl ŭi kyŏnghŏm segye" [Life world of village leaders during the Saemaul movement in the 1970s: Focusing on male leaders]. *Sahoe wa yŏksa* [Society and History] 88: 267–305.

Han, Ju Hui Judy. 2011. "'If You Don't Work, You Don't Eat': Evangelizing Development in Africa." In *New Millennium South Korea: Neoliberal Capitalism and Transnational Movements*, edited by In Jesook Song, 142–58. New York: Routledge.

Han Jun. 2007. *Zhongguo nongmin zhuanye hezuoshe diaocha* [Survey on China's Farmers' Professional Cooperatives]. Shanghai: Shanghai yuandong chubanshe [Shanghai Far East Publishers].

Han, Seung-Mi. 2004. "The New Community Movement: Park Chung Hee and the Making of State Populism in Korea." *Pacific Affairs* 77 (1): 69–93.

Harwood, Russell. 2014. *China's New Socialist Countryside: Modernity Arrives in the Nu River Valley*. Seattle: University of Washington Press.

Heath, Timothy. 2013. "Xi's Mass Line Campaign: Realigning Party Politics to New Realities." *China Brief* 13 (16): 3–6.

Heberer, Thomas, and Gunter Schubert. 2012. "County and Township Cadres as a Strategic Group. A New Approach to Political Agency in China's Local State." *Journal of Chinese Political Science* 17 (3): 221–49.

Heilmann, Sebastian. 2008. "From Local Experiments to National Policy: The Origins of China's Distinctive Policy Process." *China Journal* 59: 1–30.

Hernández, Javier C. 2017. "Xi Jinping Vows No Poverty in China by 2020. That Could Be Hard." *New York Times*, October 31.

Heurlin, Christopher. 2016. *Responsive Authoritarianism in China: Land, Protests, and Policy Making*. New York: Cambridge University Press.

Ho, Samuel P. S. 1978. *Economic Development of Taiwan, 1860–1970*. New Haven, CT: Yale University Press.

———. 1979a. "Decentralized Industrialization and Rural Development: Evidence from Taiwan." *Economic Development and Cultural Change* 28 (1): 77–96.

———. 1979b. "Rural-Urban Imbalance in South Korea in the 1970s." *Asian Survey* 19 (7): 645–59.

Hollyer, James R., B. Peter Rosendorff, and James Raymond Vreeland. 2018. *Information, Democracy, and Autocracy: Economic Transparency and Political (In)Stability*. New York: Cambridge University Press.

Hong, Young-lim. 2008. "Saemaul Undong, 1988 Olympics, Five-Year Economic Development Plans Top the List: The People's Greatest Achievements." *Chosun Daily*, March 5.

Hough, Richard Lee. 1969. "Development and Security in Thailand: Lessons from Other Asian Countries." *Asian Survey* 9 (3): 178–87.

Hsiao, Hsin-huang Michael. 1981. *Government Agricultural Strategies in Taiwan and South Korea: A Macrosociological Assessment*. Taipei: Institute of Ethnology, Academia Sinica.

Hsing, You-Tien. 2010. *The Great Urban Transformation: Politics of Land and Property in China*. New York: Oxford University Press.

Hsiung Li-sheng (Xiong Lisheng). 1973. *Shequ fazhan yu minzhong canyu* [Community development and public participation]. Taipei: Republic of China Community Development Research and Training Center.

Hsueh, Roselyn. 2011. *China's Regulatory State: A New Strategy for Globalization*. Ithaca, NY: Cornell University Press.

Hsueh Wen-liang (Xue Wenliang). 1987. *Wo guo shequ fazhan de lilun yu shiji* [The theory and practice of community development in Taiwan]. Taipei: Xiaoyuan chubanshe [Hsiao Yuan Publication Co.].

Hu, Zhanping, Qian Forrest Zhang, and John A. Donaldson. 2017. "Farmers' Cooperatives in China: A Typology of Fraud and Failure." *China Journal* 78: 1–24.

Huang Chun-chieh (Huang Junjie). 1991. *Zhongguo nongcun fuxing lianhe weiyuanhui shiliao huibian* [Compilation of historical material on the Sino-American Joint Commission on Rural Reconstruction]. Taipei: Sanmin shuju [San Min Book Co.].

——. 1992. *Zhongguo nongcun fuxing lianhe weiyuanhui koushu lishi fangwen jilu* [The reminiscences of the staffs of the Sino-American Joint Commission on Rural Reconstruction]. Taipei: Institute of Modern History, Academia Sinica.

—— 2006. *Taiwan in Transformation, 1895–2005: The Challenge of a New Democracy to an Old Civilization*. New Brunswick, NJ: Transaction.

Huang, Philip C. C. 2011. "China's New-Age Small Farms and Their Vertical Integration: Agribusiness or Co-ops?" *Modern China* 37 (2): 107–34.

Huang, Sophia Wu. 1993. "Structural Change in Taiwan's Agricultural Economy." *Economic Development and Cultural Change* 42 (1): 43–65.

Huang Ta-chou (Huang Dazhou). 1978. *Lun shequ fazhan he xiangcun jiceng jianshe* [On community development and grassroots rural construction]. Taipei: Ministry of Education, Department of Social Education.

——. 1979. *Xiangcun jianshe wenji* [Rural construction anthology]. Taipei: Huanqiu shushe [Global Books].

——. 1981. *Taiwan jiceng nonghui jingying guanli zhi shizheng yanjiu* [An empirical study of the management of local farmers' associations in Taiwan]. Taipei: Yuanda wenhua chuban shiye gongsi [Great Culture Publishing Co.].

Huang, Yasheng. 2008. *Capitalism with Chinese Characteristics: Entrepreneurship and the State*. New York: Cambridge University Press.

Hui Liangyu and Liu Zhenwei. 1993. *Jianshe you Zhongguo tese shehuizhuyi de xin nongcun* [Building a New Socialist Countryside with Chinese characteristics]. Kunming: Yunnan renmin chubanshe [Yunnan People's Press].

Hung Yu-kun (Hong Yukun). 1978. *Guofu difang zizhi tizhi yu Taiwan shequ fazhan zhi yanjiu* [Research on Sun Yat-sen's local self-governance system and Taiwanese community development]. Taipei: Zhongyang wenwu gongyingshe [Central Supply Agency of Cultural Relics].

Huntington, Samuel P. 1968. *Political Order in Changing Societies*. New Haven, CT: Yale University Press.

Im, Hyug Baeg. 2011. "The Origins of the Yushin Regime: Machiavelli Unveiled." In *The Park Chung Hee Era: The Transformation of South Korea*, edited by Byung-Kook Kim and Ezra F. Vogel, 233–61. Cambridge, MA: Harvard University Press.

Jager, Sheila Miyoshi. 2003. *Narratives of Nation Building in Korea: A Genealogy of Patriotism*. Armonk, NY: M. E. Sharpe.

Jang, Seong-Jun. 1983. "Tradition and Development in Korean Rural Architecture: A Critical Review of the Modernization of Rural Housing in Korea in the 1970s." PhD diss., Catholic University of Leuven.

Jiang Yunzhang. 2011. "Liang buwei yancha tudi churang jin quxiang zhongdian zhengzhi 24 ge shidian" [Two ministries thoroughly investigate land transfer rent transactions, focus on 24 experimental sites]. *Jingji guancha bao* [Economic Observer], January 17.

Johnson, Chalmers. 1982. *MITI and the Japanese Miracle: The Growth of Industrial Policy, 1925–1975*. Stanford, CA: Stanford University Press.

Johnson, Ian. 2014. "In China, 'Once the Villages Are Gone, the Culture Is Gone.'" *New York Times*, February 1.

Joint Commission on Rural Reconstruction. 1960. *Intensive Village Improvement in Taiwan*. Taipei: Joint Commission on Rural Reconstruction.

——. 1978. *Nongfuhui sanshi nian jishi: Zhongguo nongcun fuxing lianhe weiyuanhui chengli sanshi zhou nian jinian tekan* [JCRR and agricultural development in Taiwan, 1948–1978: A thirtieth anniversary publication of the Joint Commission on Rural Reconstruction]. Taipei: Joint Commission on Rural Reconstruction.

Jowitt, Kenneth. 1975. "Inclusion and Mobilization in European Leninist Regimes." *World Politics* 28 (1): 69–96.

Kada, Ryohei. 1981. "Employment Creation in Rural Areas: The Achievement of Saemaul Undong and Further Development." In *Toward a New Community: Reports of International Research-Seminar on the Saemaul Movement*, edited by Man-Gap Lee, 245–72. Seoul: Institute of Saemaul Undong Studies, Seoul National University.

Kane, Penny. 1988. *Famine in China, 1959–1961: Demographic and Social Implications*. New York: St. Martin's Press.

Kasza, Gregory J. 1995. *The Conscription Society: Administered Mass Organizations*. New Haven, CT: Yale University Press.

Kay, Cristóbal. 2002. "Why East Asia Overtook Latin America: Agrarian Reform, Industrialisation and Development." *Third World Quarterly* 23 (6): 1073–102.

Keidel, Albert. 1981. *Korean Regional Farm Product and Income, 1910–1975*. Honolulu: University of Hawai'i Press.

Kelliher, Daniel R. 1992. *Peasant Power in China: The Era of Rural Reform, 1979–1989*. New Haven, CT: Yale University Press.

Kennedy, John James. 2007. "From the Tax-for-Fee Reform to the Abolition of Agricultural Taxes: The Impact on Township Governments in North-West China." *China Quarterly* 189: 43–59.

Kennedy, Scott. 2010. "The Myth of the Beijing Consensus." *Journal of Contemporary China* 19 (65): 461–77.

Kim, Byung-Kook, and Ezra Vogel, eds. 2011. *The Park Chung Hee Era: The Transformation of South Korea*. Cambridge, MA: Harvard University Press.

Kim, Chung-yum. 1994. *Policymaking on the Front Lines: Memoirs of a Korean Practitioner, 1945–1979*. Washington, DC: Economic Development Institute of the World Bank.

Kim, Ilpyong J. 1973. *The Politics of Chinese Communism: Kiangsi under the Soviets*. Berkeley: University of California Press.

Kim, Yoo-hyuk, ed. 1981. *Saemaul Undong: Determination and Capability of the Koreans.* Seoul: Institute of Saemaul Studies.

Kim Young-mi (Kim Yŏngmi). 2008. "Maŭl ŭi kŭndaehwa kyŏnghŏm kwa saemaŭl undong: ich'ŏn aori maŭl ŭi sarye rŭl chungsim ŭro" [The New Village Movement and modernization: The case of (a) village]. *Chŏngsin munhwa yŏn'gu* [Korean Studies Quarterly] 31 (1): 271–99.

Knapp, Ronald G. 1996. "Rural Housing and Village Transformation in Taiwan and Fujian." *China Quarterly* 147: 779–94.

Knight, John B. 2014. "China as a Developmental State." *World Economy* 37 (10): 1335–47.

Knight, John B., and Lina Song. 1999. *The Rural-Urban Divide: Economic Disparities and Interactions in China.* New York: Oxford University Press.

Kohli, Atul. 1987. *The State and Poverty in India: The Politics of Reform.* New York: Cambridge University Press.

——. 2004. *State-Directed Development: Political Power and Industrialization in the Global Periphery.* New York: Cambridge University Press.

Kroeber, Arthur R. 2011. "Developmental Dreams: Policy and Reality in China's Economic Reforms." In *Beyond the Middle Kingdom: Comparative Perspectives on China's Capitalist Transformation,* edited by Scott Kennedy, 44–65. Stanford, CA: Stanford University Press.

Kueh, Y. Y. 1985. "The Economics of the 'Second Land Reform' in China." *China Quarterly* 101: 122–31.

Kung, James Kaising. 1995. "Equal Entitlement versus Tenure Security under a Regime of Collective Property Rights: Peasants' Preference for Institutions in Post-reform Chinese Agriculture." *Journal of Comparative Economics* 21 (1): 82–111.

Kuo, Min-hsueh (Min-Hsioh). 1964. *Farmers' Associations and Their Contributions towards Agriculture and Rural Development in Taiwan.* Bangkok: Food and Agriculture Organization of the United Nations.

—— (Guo Minxue). 1984. *Taiwan nonghui fazhan guiji* [Development trajectory of Taiwan's farmers' associations]. Taipei: Taiwan shangwu yinshuguan [Commercial Press].

Kuznets, Paul W. 1988. "An East Asian Model of Economic Development: Japan, Taiwan, and South Korea." *Economic Development and Cultural Change* 36 (3): S11–43.

Ladejinsky, Wolf Isaac. 1977. *Agrarian Reform as Unfinished Business: The Selected Papers of Wolf Ladejinsky,* edited by Louis J. Walinksy. New York: Oxford University Press.

Lai, Tse-han, Ramon H. Myers, and Wei Wou. 1991. *A Tragic Beginning: The Taiwan Uprising of February 28, 1947.* Stanford, CA: Stanford University Press.

Landry, Pierre F. 2008. *Decentralized Authoritarianism in China: The Communist Party's Control of Local Elites in the Post-Mao Era.* New York: Cambridge University Press.

Lardy, Nicholas R. 1983. *Agriculture in China's Modern Economic Development.* New York: Cambridge University Press.

Lee Chung-yan (Li Zhongyuan). 1979. "Hanguo de Saemaul Undong xin shequ yundong" [The Saemaul New Community Movement in Korea]. *Shequ fazhan jikan* [Community Development Journal] 6: 107–12.

Lee, Man-Gap, ed. 1981. *Toward a New Community: Reports of International Research-Seminar on the Saemaul Movement.* Seoul: Institute of Saemaul Undong Studies, Seoul National University.

Lee Shou-lian (Li Shoulian). 1965. *Jiceng minsheng jianshe zai Taiwan* [People's livelihood construction in Taiwan]. Taipei: Provincial People's Livelihood Construction Steering Committee.

Lee, Teng-hui. 1971. *Intersectoral Capital Flows in the Economic Development of Taiwan, 1895–1960*. Ithaca, NY: Cornell University Press.

Lee, Young Jo. 2011. "The Countryside." In *The Park Chung Hee Era: The Transformation of South Korea*, edited by Byung-Kook Kim and Ezra Vogel, 345–72. Cambridge, MA: Harvard University Press.

Levitsky, Steven, and Lucan A. Way. 2002. "The Rise of Competitive Authoritarianism." *Journal of Democracy* 13 (2): 51–65.

Lewis, Michael. 1990. *Rioters and Citizens: Mass Protest in Imperial Japan*. Berkeley: University of California Press.

Lewis, W. Arthur. 1954. "Economic Development with Unlimited Supplies of Labor." *Manchester School* 22 (2): 139–91.

Li Changping. 2002. *Wo xiang zongli shuo shihua* [I tell the truth to the premier]. Beijing: Guangming ribao chubanshe [Guangming Daily Press].

———. 2012. *Zai xiang zongli shuo shihua* [Telling the truth to the premier again]. Beijing: Zhongguo caifu chubanshe [China Fortune Press].

Li, Cheng. 2003. "Poised to Take the Helm: Rising Stars and the Transition to the Fourth Generation." In *China's Leadership in the Twenty-First Century: The Rise of the Fourth Generation*, edited by David M. Finkelstein and Maryanne Kivlehan, 21–44. Armonk, NY: M. E. Sharpe.

———. 2009. "Hu Jintao's Land Reform: Ambition, Ambiguity, and Anxiety." *China Leadership Monitor* 27: 1–22.

Li Jiange. 2009. *Zhongguo xin nongcun jianshe diaocha* [Survey on China's building a new countryside]. Shanghai: Shanghai yuandong chubanshe [Shanghai Far East Publishers].

Li, Kwoh-ting. 1988. *Economic Transformation of Taiwan, ROC*. London: Shepheard-Walwyn.

Li, Linda Chelan. 2012. *Rural Tax Reform in China: Policy Processes and Institutional Change*. New York: Routledge.

Li, Lixing. 2012. "Land Titling in China: Chengdu Experiment and Its Consequences." *China Economic Journal* 5 (1): 47–64.

Li Ping, Yu Daguang, Fang Shichen, and Li Wen. 2006. "Yi xiang huiji yiwan nongmin de weida gongcheng—Jianshe shehuizhuyi xin nongcun quan jiedu" [The great project to benefit hundreds of millions of peasants—an interpretation of Building a New Socialist Countryside]. *Xin changzheng (dangjian ban)* [New Long March (party building edition)] 6: 10–30.

Li Ruifen. 2004. *Zhongguo nongmin zhuanye hezuo jingji zuzhi de shijian yu fazhan* [China's farmers' professional cooperative organizations, practices and development]. Beijing: Zhongguo nongye chubanshe [China Agriculture Press].

Li Shuishan. 2006. *Hanguo xincun yundong ji qishi* [The Korean New Village Movement and its lessons]. Nanning: Guangxi jiaoyu chubanshe [Guangxi Education Press].

Li Xiaoyun, Zuo Ting, and Ye Jingzhong, eds. 2009. *2008 Zhongguo nongcun qingkuang baogao* [2008 status of rural China report]. Beijing: Shehui kexue wenxian chubanshe [Social Sciences Academic Press].

Li Yun and Ling Buji, eds. 2006. *Gannan dangshi renwu zhi, 1949–2005* [Gannan Party history biographical gazetteer, 1949–2005]. Beijing: Zhongguo wenshi chubanshe [Chinese Literature and History Press].

Li Zuojun, ed. 2008. *Lingdao ganbu juece da cankao: Zhongguo xin nongcun jianshe baogao* [Decision-making reference book for leading cadres: Report on China's building a new countryside]. Beijing: Shehui kexue wenxian chubanshe [Social Sciences Academic Press].

Liao Cheng-hung, Huang Chun-chieh, and Hsiao Hsin-huang Michael. 1986. *Guang-fuhou Taiwan nongye zhengce de yanbian: Lishi yu shehui de fenxi* [The development of agricultural policies in postwar Taiwan: Historical and sociological perspectives]. Taipei: Institute of Ethnology, Academia Sinica.

Lin Hsin-yi (Lin Xinyi). 2004. *Sanxia nonghui zhi* [Sanxia Farmers' Association gazetteer]. Banqiao, Taiwan: Taipei County Department of Cultural Affairs.

Lin Justin Yifu. 2005. "Xin nongcun yundong yu qidong neixu" [A new village movement and stimulating domestic demand]. *Xiao chengzhen jianshe* [Development of Small Cities and Towns] 8: 13–5.

——. 2012. *Demystifying the Chinese Economy*. New York: Cambridge University Press.

Lin, Wanlong, and Christine Wong. 2012. "Are Beijing's Equalization Policies Reaching the Poor? An Analysis of Direct Subsidies under the 'Three Rurals' (Sannong)." *China Journal* 67: 23–45.

Linz, Juan J. 1975. "Totalitarian and Authoritarian Regimes." In *Handbook of Political Science*, vol. 3, *Macropolitical Theory*, edited by Fred I. Greenstein and Nelson W. Polsby, 175–411. Reading, MA: Addison-Wesley.

Lipton, Michael. 1976. *Why Poor People Stay Poor: Urban Bias in World Development*. Cambridge, MA: Harvard University Press.

Liu, Chengfang, Linxiu Zhang, Renfu Luo, and Scott Rozelle. 2009. "Infrastructure Investment in Rural China: Is Quality Being Compromised during Quantity Expansion?" *China Journal* 61: 105–29.

Liu Jui-chung (Liu Ruizhong). 1991. *Sanminzhuyi shehui jianshe de linian yu shijian: Taiwan diqu shequ fazhan zhi yanjiu* [Theory and practice of building a society based on the three principles of the people: Research on community development in the Taiwan region]. Taipei: Zhengzhong shuju [Cheng Chung Book Co.].

Liu Laoshi, ed. 2008. *Xin xiangcun jianshe jiangyi* [Lectures on new rural reconstruction]. Haikou: Hainan chubanshe [Hainan Press].

Liu, Mingxing, Juan Wang, Ran Tao, and Rachel Murphy. 2009. "The Political Economy of Earmarked Transfers in a State-Designated Poor County in Western China: Central Policies and Local Responses." *China Quarterly* 200: 973–94.

Liu Moyan. 2006. "Lun Ganzhou moshi dui wo guo xin nongcun jianshe de yingxiang" [Discussion of the Ganzhou model's influence on China's new rural construction]. In *Zhongguo nongye jingji xuehui 2006 nian nianhui ji shehuizhuyi xin nongcun jianshe xueshu yanjiu luntan wenji* [Proceedings of the China Agricultural Economics Association 2006 annual meeting and the Building a New Socialist Countryside Academic Research Forum], November 1, 160–71.

Liu Shian and Qiqiang Wu. 2013. "Ganzhou zhengce hongli puhui baixing jin 70 wan hu tupi fang jiakuai gaizao" [Ganzhou policy benefits the people, nearly 700,000 households to renovate mud-brick homes]. *Renmin ribao* [People's Daily], July 6.

Liu Tangyu. 2010. "Zhongbu qian fada diqu nongmingong hui xiang chuangye yingxiang yinsu yanjiu—yi Jiangxi Ganzhou diqu wei li" [Factor analysis of return migrant workers' entrepreneurship in central underdeveloped regions—case study of Jiangxi's Ganzhou Prefecture]. PhD diss., Fujian Agriculture and Forestry University.

Looney, Kristen E. 2015. "China's Campaign to Build a New Socialist Countryside: Village Modernization, Peasant Councils, and the Ganzhou Model of Rural Development." *China Quarterly* 224: 909–32.

Looney, Kristen, and Meg Rithmire. 2017. "China Gambles on Modernizing through Urbanization." *Current History* 791 (116): 203–9.

Lowenthal, Richard. 1970. "Development vs. Utopia in Communist Politics." In *Change in Communist Systems*, edited by Chalmers Johnson, 33–116. Stanford, CA: Stanford University Press.

Lü Tianling and Wen Xia. 2010. "Cu nongmin jianfang cheng Zhongguo jingji jin yaoshi" [Promote rural home construction as the golden key for the Chinese economy]. *Nanfang ribao* [Southern Daily], February 2.

Lü Xinye and Lu Xianghu. 2008. *Xin xingshi xia nongmin zhuanye hezuo zuzhi yanjiu* [Research on farmers' professional cooperatives in a new context]. Beijing: Zhongguo nongye chubanshe [China Agriculture Press].

Luo, Kevin, and Fang-Yu Chen. 2018. "Four Key Takeaways from Taiwan's Recent Election Surprises." *Washington Post* (*Monkey Cage*), December 17. https://www.washingtonpost.com/news/monkey-cage/wp/2018/12/17/four-key-takeaways-from-taiwans-recent-election-surprises/?utm_term=.807c7b4d934b.

Ma Guochuan. 2011. "Du Runsheng: Yao gei nongmin ziyou" [Du Runsheng: We must give farmers freedom]. *Caijing* [Finance and Economics], January 3.

Ma Xiaohe, ed. 2008. *Zhongguo de xin nongcun jianshe yu Hanguo de xincun yundong: 2006 nian Zhong Han jingji hezuo yanjiu hui wenji* [China's Building a New Countryside and Korea's New Village Movement: Papers from the 2006 Sino-Korean Economic Cooperation Symposium]. Beijing: Zhongguo jihua chubanshe [China Planning Press].

MacFarquhar, Roderick. 1983. *The Origins of the Cultural Revolution.* Vol. 2, *The Great Leap Forward, 1958–1960.* New York: Columbia University Press.

MacFarquhar, Roderick, and Michael Schoenhals. 2006. *Mao's Last Revolution.* Cambridge, MA: Belknap Press of Harvard University Press.

Madsen, Richard. 1984. *Morality and Power in a Chinese Village.* Berkeley: University of California Press.

Mahoney, James. 2003. "Knowledge Accumulation in Comparative Historical Research: The Case of Democracy and Authoritarianism." In *Comparative Historical Analysis in the Social Sciences*, edited by James Mahoney and Dietrich Rueschemeyer, 131–74. New York: Cambridge University Press.

Mahoney, James, and Dietrich Rueschemeyer, eds. 2003. *Comparative Historical Analysis in the Social Sciences.* New York: Cambridge University Press.

Mahoney, James, and Kathleen Thelen, eds. 2015. *Advances in Comparative-Historical Analysis.* New York: Cambridge University Press.

Major Statistics of the Korean Economy. 1982. Seoul: Economic Planning Board.

Manion, Melanie. 2004. *Corruption by Design: Building Clean Government in Mainland China and Hong Kong.* Cambridge, MA: Harvard University Press.

Mao Tse-tung. 1965. *The Selected Works of Mao Tse-tung.* Vol. 1. Beijing: Foreign Languages Press.

Marx, Karl. 1964. *The Eighteenth Brumaire of Louis Bonaparte.* New York: International.

Masao, Tsutsui. 2003. "The Impact of the Local Improvement Movement on Farmers and Rural Communities." In *Farmers and Village Life in Twentieth-Century Japan*, edited by Ann Waswo and Nishida Yoshiaki, 60–78. New York: RoutledgeCurzon.

Mason, Edward S., Mahn Je Kim, Dwight H. Perkins, Kwang Suk Kim, and David C. Cole. 1980. *The Economic and Social Modernization of the Republic of Korea.* Studies in the Modernization of the Republic of Korea: 1945–1975. Cambridge, MA: Harvard University Press.

Mattingly, Daniel. 2016. "Elite Capture: How Decentralization and Informal Institutions Weaken Property Rights in Rural China." *World Politics* 68 (3): 383–412.

McGregor, Richard. 2006. "China Launches 'New Deal' for Farmers." *Financial Times*, February 22.

Meier, Richard L. 1982. *Reconsideration of Regional Development Planning of Nonmetropolitan Areas: New Principles Derived from the Successes of the Korean New Community Movement.* Berkeley: University of California, Berkeley, Institute of Urban and Regional Development.

Merkel-Hess, Kate. 2016. *The Rural Modern: Reconstructing the Self and State in Republican China*. Chicago: University of Chicago Press.

Mertha, Andrew C. 2005. "China's 'Soft' Centralization: Shifting Tiao/Kuai Authority Relations." *China Quarterly* 184: 791–810.

——. 2017. "'Stressing Out': Cadre Calibration and Affective Proximity to the CCP in Reform-Era China." *China Quarterly* 229: 64–85.

Michelson, Ethan. 2012. "Public Goods and State-Society Relations: An Impact Study of China's Rural Stimulus." In *The Global Recession and China's Political Economy*, edited by Dali L. Yang, 131–57. New York: Palgrave Macmillan.

Minami, Ryoshin, and Xinxin Ma. 2010. "The Lewis Turning Point of Chinese Economy: Comparison with Japanese Experience." *China Economic Journal* 3 (2): 163–79.

Ministry of Construction, People's Republic of China. 2005. "Jianshe bu buzhang Wang Guangdao zai quanguo cunzhuang zhengzhi gongzuo huiyi de jianghua" [Minister of Construction Wang Guangdao's speech from the National Work Conference on Village Renovation]. http://www.gov.cn/gzdt/2005-12/01/content_114735.htm.

Ministry of Strategy and Finance, Republic of Korea. 2013. *New Research on Saemaul Undong: Lessons and Insights from Korea's Development Experience*. Seoul: Korea Development Institute and Korea Saemaul Undong Center.

Montinola, Gabriella, Yingyi Qian, and Barry R. Weingast. 1995. "Federalism, Chinese Style: The Political Basis for Economic Success in China." *World Politics* 48 (1): 50–81.

Moon, Chung-in, and Byung-joon Jun. 2011. "Modernization Strategy: Ideas and Influences." In *The Park Chung Hee Era: The Transformation of South Korea*, edited by Byung-Kook Kim and Ezra Vogel, 115–39. Cambridge, MA: Harvard University Press.

Moon, Pal Yong, and Kwang-Eon Sul. 1997. "Agricultural Policies and Development." In *The Korean Economy 1945–1995: Performance and Vision for the 21st Century*, edited by Dong-Se Cha, Kwang Suk Kim, and Dwight H. Perkins, 468–505. Seoul: Korea Development Institute.

Moore, Mick. 1984–1985. "Mobilization and Disillusion in Rural Korea: The Saemaul Movement in Retrospect." *Pacific Affairs* 57 (4): 577–98.

——. 1988. "Economic Growth and the Rise of Civil Society: Agriculture in Taiwan and South Korea." In *Developmental States in East Asia*, edited by Gordon White, 113–52. New York: St. Martin's Press.

——. 1993. "Economic Structure and the Politics of Sectoral Bias: East Asian and Other Cases." *Journal of Development Studies* 29 (4): 79–128.

Mulgan, Aurelia George. 2000. *The Politics of Agriculture in Japan*. New York: Routledge.

——. 2006. *Japan's Agricultural Policy Regime*. New York: Routledge.

National Council of Saemaul Undong. 1999. *Saemaul Undong in Korea*. Seoul: National Council of Saemaul Undong Movement in Korea.

National Income in Korea. 1975. Seoul: Bank of Korea.

Naughton, Barry. 1995. *Growing Out of the Plan: Chinese Economic Reform, 1978–1993*. New York: Cambridge University Press.

——. 2007. *The Chinese Economy: Transitions and Growth*. Cambridge, MA: MIT Press.

North, Douglass C. 1981. *Structure and Change in Economic History*. New York: Norton.

——. 1990. *Institutions, Institutional Change, and Economic Performance*. New York: Cambridge University Press.

O'Brien, Kevin J., and Lianjiang Li. 1999. "Selective Policy Implementation in Rural China." *Comparative Politics* 31 (2): 167–86.

——. 2006. *Rightful Resistance in Rural China*. New York: Cambridge University Press.

Oi, Jean C. 1985. "Communism and Clientelism: Rural Politics in China." *World Politics* 37 (2): 238–66.

——. 1993. "Reform and Urban Bias in China." *Journal of Development Studies* 29 (4): 129–48.

——. 1995. "The Role of the Local State in China's Transitional Economy." *China Quarterly* 144: 1132–49.

——. 1999a. *Rural China Takes Off: Institutional Foundations of Economic Reform*. Berkeley: University of California Press.

——. 1999b. "Two Decades of Rural Reform in China: An Overview and Assessment." *China Quarterly* 159: 616–28.

Oi, Jean C., Kim Singer Babiarz, Linxiu Zhang, Renfu Luo, and Scott Rozelle. 2012. "Shifting Fiscal Control to Limit Cadre Power in China's Townships and Villages." *China Quarterly* 211: 649–75.

Ong, Lynette H. 2012a. "Between Developmental and Clientelist States: Local State-Business Relationships in China." *Comparative Politics* 44 (2): 191–209.

——. 2012b. *Prosper or Perish: Credit and Fiscal Systems in Rural China*. Ithaca, NY: Cornell University Press.

——. 2014. "State-Led Urbanization in China: Skyscrapers, Land Revenue and 'Concentrated Villages.'" *China Quarterly* 217: 162–79.

Owen, Wyn F. 1966. "The Double Developmental Squeeze on Agriculture." *American Economic Review* 56 (1–2): 43–70.

Paige, Jeffery M. 1976. *Agrarian Revolution: Social Movements and Export Agriculture in the Underdeveloped World*. New York: Free Press.

Pak, Ki Hyuk. 1956. "Economic Analysis of Land Reform in the Republic of Korea with Special Reference to an Agricultural Economic Survey, 1954–1955." PhD diss., University of Illinois at Urbana-Champaign.

Pan Guojian and Yao Jiawei. 2010. "Nongmin jizhong juzhu deshi" [The gains and losses of farmers living in concentrated housing]. *Caijing* [Finance and Economics], October 25.

Pan Wei and He Xuefeng, eds. 2006. *Shehuizhuyi xin nongcun jianshe de lilun yu shijian* [Building a New Socialist Countryside in theory and practice]. Beijing: Zhongguo jingji chubanshe [China Economic Publishing House].

Pan Yiyang. 2002. *Nongmin zhutilun* [A peasant-centered theory]. Beijing: Renmin chubanshe [People's Press].

——. 2005a. "Jiakuai tuijin xin nongcun jianshe" [Accelerate new rural construction]. *Renmin ribao* [People's Daily], June 8.

——. 2005b. "Zhazha shishi di jianshe shehuizhuyi xin nongcun—xuexi shiliu jie wuzhong quanhui jingshen de tihui" [Solidly build a new socialist countryside—learning from the spirit of the 5th Plenary Session of the 16th Party Congress]. *Qiushi* [Seeking Truth] 24: 8–10.

Parish, William L., ed. 1985. *Chinese Rural Development: The Great Transformation*. Armonk, NY: M. E. Sharpe.

Park, Chung-hee. 1979. *Saemaul: Korea's New Community Movement*. Seoul: Korea Textbook Co.

Park, Jin-hwan. 1998. *The Saemaul Movement: Korea's Approach to Rural Modernization in the 1970s*. Seoul: Korea Rural Economic Institute.

—— (Piao Zhenhuan). 2005. *Hanguo xincun yundong: 20 shiji 70 niandai Hanguo nongcun xiandaihua zhi daolu* [The Saemaul movement: Korea's approach to rural modernization in the 1970s]. Beijing: Zhongguo nongye chubanshe [China Agriculture Press].

Park, Keun Hae (Geun-hye). 1979. *The New Spirit Movement*. Seoul: Naeway Business Journal and Korea Herald.

Park, Sooyoung. 2009. "Saemaul Undong: A Korean Rural Development Program in the 1970s." *Asia-Pacific Development Journal* 16 (2): 113–40.

Partner, Simon. 2001. "Taming the Wilderness: The Lifestyle Improvement Movement in Rural Japan, 1925–1965." *Monumenta Nipponica* 56 (4): 487–520.

Pei, Minxin. 2006. *China's Trapped Transition: The Limits of Developmental Autocracy*. Cambridge, MA: Harvard University Press.

Pempel, T. J., ed. 1999. *The Politics of the Asian Economic Crisis*. Ithaca, NY: Cornell University Press.

Perkins, Dwight, and Shahid Yusuf. 1984. *Rural Development in China*. Baltimore: Johns Hopkins University Press, published for the World Bank.

Perry, Elizabeth J. 2011. "From Mass Campaigns to Managed Campaigns: Constructing a 'New Socialist Countryside.'" In *Mao's Invisible Hand: The Political Foundations of Adaptive Governance in China*, edited by Sebastian Heilmann and Elizabeth J. Perry, 30–61. Cambridge, MA: Harvard University Press.

———. 2014. "Citizen Contention and Campus Calm: The Paradox of Chinese Civil Society." *Current History* 113 (764): 211–17.

Perry, Elizabeth J., Grzegorz Ekiert, and Yan Xiaojun, eds. 2020. *Ruling by Other Means: State-Mobilized Movements*. New York: Cambridge University Press.

Petras, James, and Henry Veltmeyer. 2001. "Are Latin American Peasant Movements Still a Force for Change? Some New Paradigms Revisited." *Journal of Peasant Studies* 28 (2): 83–118.

Phillips, Tom. 2018. "China to Move Millions of People from Homes in Anti-poverty Drive." *Guardian*, January 7.

Pierson, Paul. 2004. *Politics in Time: History, Institutions, and Social Analysis*. Princeton, NJ: Princeton University Press.

Pyle, Kenneth B. 1973. "The Technology of Japanese Nationalism: The Local Improvement Movement, 1900–1918." *Journal of Asian Studies* 33 (1): 51–65.

Quick, Stephen A. 1980. "The Paradox of Popularity: 'Ideological' Program Implementation in Zambia." In *Politics and Policy Implementation in the Third World*, edited by Merilee S. Grindle, 40–63. Princeton, NJ: Princeton University Press.

Ramo, Joshua Cooper. 2004. *The Beijing Consensus*. London: Foreign Policy Centre.

Ranis, Gustav. 1995. "Another Look at the East Asian Miracle." *World Bank Economic Review* 9 (3): 509–34.

———. 2004. "Arthur Lewis's Contribution to Development Thinking and Policy." *Manchester School* 72 (6): 712–23.

Rath, Eric C. 2007. "Rural Japan and Agriculture." In *A Companion to Japanese History*, edited by William M. Tsutsui, 477–92. Malden, MA: Blackwell.

Read, Benjamin L. 2012. *Roots of the State: Neighborhood Organization and Social Networks in Beijing and Taipei*. Stanford, CA: Stanford University Press.

Republic of China Community Development Research and Training Center. 1972. *Zhonghua minguo shequ fazhan gongzuo yantao hui zong baogao* [Republic of China Community Development Work Conference general report]. Taipei: Republic of China Community Development Research and Training Center.

Rithmire, Meg E. 2015. *Land Bargains and Chinese Capitalism: The Politics of Property Rights under Reform*. New York: Cambridge University Press.

Rosenberg, Lior. 2013. "Urbanising the Rural: Local Strategies for Creating 'New Style' Rural Communities in China." *China Perspectives* 3: 63–71.

Rossmiller, George E. 1972. *Korean Agricultural Sector Analysis and Recommended Development Strategies, 1971–1985*. East Lansing: Department of Agricultural Economics, Michigan State University.

Rowen, Henry S., ed. 1998. *Behind East Asian Growth: The Political and Social Foundations of Prosperity*. New York: Routledge.

Saemaul. 1975, 1976. Seoul: Office of the President.

Sargeson, Sally. 2002. "Subduing 'The Rural House Building Craze': Attitudes towards Housing Construction and Land Use Control in Four Zhejiang Villages." *China Quarterly* 172: 927–55.

——. 2012. "Villains, Victims, and Aspiring Proprietors: Framing 'Land-Losing Villagers' in China's Strategies of Accumulation." *Journal of Contemporary China* 21 (77): 757–77.

——. 2013. "Violence as Development: Land Expropriation and China's Urbanization." *Journal of Peasant Studies* 40 (6): 1063–85.

Schmitter, Philippe C., and Gerhard Lehmbruch, eds. 1979. *Trends towards Corporatist Intermediation*. London: Sage.

Schneider, Mindi. 2017. "Dragon Head Enterprises and the State of Agribusiness in China." *Journal of Agrarian Change* 17 (1): 3–21.

Schubert, Gunter, and Anna L. Ahlers. 2012. "County and Township Cadres as a Strategic Group: 'Building a New Socialist Countryside' in Three Provinces." *China Journal* 67: 67–86.

Schultz, Theodore W. 1964. *Transforming Traditional Agriculture*. New Haven, CT: Yale University Press.

——. 1978. *Distortions of Agricultural Incentives*. Bloomington: Indiana University Press.

Schurmann, Franz. 1966. *Ideology and Organization in Communist China*. Berkeley: University of California Press.

Scott, James C. 1985. *Weapons of the Weak: Everyday Forms of Peasant Resistance*. New Haven, CT: Yale University Press.

——. 1998. *Seeing Like a State: How Certain Schemes to Improve the Human Condition Have Failed*. New Haven, CT: Yale University Press.

Sharma, Rajnish. 2015. "NDA Warned as Rural Distress Worsens, Farmer Unrest Spurts." *Mint*, September 9.

Shih, Victor. 2004. "Development, the Second Time Around: The Political Logic of Developing Western China." *Journal of East Asian Studies* 4 (3): 427–51.

——. 2008. "'Nauseating' Displays of Loyalty: Monitoring the Factional Bargain through Ideological Campaigns in China." *Journal of Politics* 70 (4): 1177–92.

Shin, Gi-Wook. 1998. "Agrarian Conflict and the Origins of Korean Capitalism." *American Journal of Sociology* 103 (5): 1309–51.

Shin, Gi-Wook, and Do-hyun Han. 1999. "Colonial Corporatism: The Rural Revitalization Campaign, 1932–1940." In *Colonial Modernity in Korea*, edited by Gi-Wook Shin and Michael Robinson, 70–96. Cambridge, MA: Harvard University Press.

Shirk, Susan L. 1993. *The Political Logic of Economic Reform in China*. Berkeley: University of California Press.

Shue, Vivienne. 1988. *The Reach of the State: Sketches of the Chinese Body Politic*. Stanford, CA: Stanford University Press.

Sigurdson, Jon, and Young Chul Kim. 1981. "Relationship between Farm Mechanization, Rural Industrialization and Saemaul Movement in Korea." In *Toward a New Community: Reports of International Research-Seminar on the Saemaul Movement*, edited by Man-Gap Lee, 203–44. Seoul: Institute of Saemaul Undong Studies, Seoul National University.

Singh, Jewellord Nem, and Jesse Salah Ovadia. 2018. "The Theory and Practice of Building Developmental States in the Global South." *Third World Quarterly* 39 (6): 1033–55.

Skinner, G. William, and Edwin A. Winckler. 1969. "Compliance Succession in Rural China: A Cyclical Theory." In *A Sociological Reader on Complex Organizations*, 2nd ed., edited by Amitai Etzioni, 410–38. New York: Holt, Rinehart and Winston.

Smith, Graeme. 2009. "Political Machinations in a Rural County." *China Journal* 62: 29–59.
———. 2010. "The Hollow State: Rural Governance in China." *China Quarterly* 203: 601–18.
Smith, Kerry. 2001. *A Time of Crisis: Japan, the Great Depression, and Rural Revitaliza-tion*. Cambridge, MA: Harvard University Press.
———. 2003. "Building the Model Village: Rural Revitalization and the Great Depression." In *Farmers and Village Life in Twentieth-Century Japan*, edited by Ann Waswo and Nishida Yoshiaki, 126–55. New York: RoutledgeCurzon.
Solinger, Dorothy J. 1999. *Contesting Citizenship in Urban China: Peasant Migrants, the State, and the Logic of the Market*. Berkeley: University of California Press.
Sonn, Jung Won, and Dong-Wan Gimm. 2013. "South Korea's Saemaul (New Village) Movement: An Organizational Technology for the Production of Developmental-ist Subjects." *Canadian Journal of Development Studies* 34 (1): 22–36.
Sorace, Christian P. 2014. "China's Vision for Developing Sichuan's Post-earthquake Countryside: Turning Unruly Peasants into Grateful Urban Citizens." *China Quarterly* 218: 404–27.
———. 2017. *Shaken Authority: China's Communist Party and the 2008 Sichuan Earth-quake*. Ithaca, NY: Cornell University Press.
Sorensen, Clark W. 2011. "Rural Modernization under the Park Regime in the 1960s." In *Reassessing the Park Chung Hee Era, 1961–1979*, edited by Hyung-A Kim and Clark W. Sorensen, 145–65. Seattle: University of Washington Press.
Statistical Yearbook of the Republic of China. 1982. Taipei: Directorate-General of Budget, Accounting, and Statistics, Executive Yuan.
Stavis, Benedict. 1974. *Rural Local Governance and Agricultural Development in Taiwan*. Ithaca, NY: Rural Development Committee, Center for International Studies, Cornell University.
Steinberg, David. 1982. *The Economic Development of Korea, Sui Generis or Generic? Reflections on the Harvard University Press Studies of the Modernization of the Republic of Korea, 1974–75*. Washington, DC: US Agency for International Development.
Stiglitz, Joseph E., and Shahid Yusuf, eds. 2001. *Rethinking the East Asian Miracle*. Washington, DC: World Bank.
Strauss, Julia C. 2017. "Campaigns of Redistribution: Land Reform and State Build-ing in China and Taiwan, 1950–1953." In *States in the Developing World*, edited by Miguel A. Centeno, Atul Kohli, and Deborah J. Yashar, with Dinsha Mistree, 339–62. New York: Cambridge University Press.
Stubbs, Richard. 2005. *Rethinking Asia's Economic Miracle: The Political Economy of War, Prosperity, and Crisis*. New York: Palgrave Macmillan.
Su, Minzi. 2009. *China's Rural Development Policy: Exploring the "New Socialist Country-side."* Boulder, CO: First Forum.
Sun Zhengcai, ed. 2008. *Nongcun gaige lilun yu shijian: 1978–2008* [Rural reform in theory and practice: 1978–2008]. Beijing: Zhongguo nongye chubanshe [China Agriculture Press].
Taiwan Agricultural Statistics (1901–1965). 1966. Taipei: Joint Commission on Rural Reconstruction, Rural Economics Division.
Taiwan Agricultural Statistics (1961–1975). 1977. Taipei: Joint Commission on Rural Reconstruction, Rural Economics Division.
Taiwan Provincial Government. 1970. *A Brief Account of Community Development in Taiwan, Republic of China*. Taipei: Taiwan Provincial Government, Department of Social Affairs.
Taiwan Statistical Data Book. 1982. Taipei: Council for International Economic Coop-eration and Development.

Takeuchi, Hiroki. 2014. *Tax Reform in Rural China: Revenue, Resistance, and Authoritarian Rule.* New York: Cambridge University Press.

Tan Chin-hsi (Tan Zhenxi). 1972. *Shequ fazhan de yanjiu* [A study of community development]. Taipei: Republic of China Community Development Research and Training Center.

Tan, Qingshan. 2007. *Hu-Wen's Efforts to Strengthen Governance: Regulating Central-Local Relations.* Singapore: East Asian Institute, National University of Singapore.

Tan Yi-min (Tan Yimin). 1969. *Shequ fazhan gailun* [Introduction to community development]. Yangmingshan, Taiwan: Guofang yanjiuyuan [Institute for National Defense Research].

Tang, Wenfang. 2016. *Populist Authoritarianism: Chinese Political Culture and Regime Sustainability.* New York: Oxford University Press.

Teets, Jessica C. 2014. *Civil Society under Authoritarianism: The China Model.* New York: Cambridge University Press.

Teiwes, Frederick C., and Warren Sun. 1999. *China's Road to Disaster: Mao, Central Politicians, and Provincial Leaders in the Unfolding of the Great Leap Forward.* Armonk, NY: M. E. Sharpe.

Thaxton, Ralph A. 2008. *Catastrophe and Contention in Rural China: Mao's Great Leap Forward Famine and the Origins of Righteous Resistance in Da Fo Village.* New York: Cambridge University Press.

Thøgersen, Stig. 2009. "Revisiting a Dramatic Triangle: The State, Villagers, and Social Activists in Chinese Rural Reconstruction Projects." *Journal of Current Chinese Affairs* 38 (4): 9–33.

Thornton, Patricia M. 2009. "Crisis and Governance: SARS and the Resilience of the Chinese Body Politic." *China Journal* 61: 23–48.

Tong, James W. 2009. *Revenge of the Forbidden City: The Suppression of the Falungong in China, 1999–2005.* New York: Oxford University Press.

Townsend, James R. 1967. *Political Participation in Communist China.* Berkeley: University of California Press.

Trappel, René. 2016. *China's Agrarian Transition: Peasants, Property, and Politics.* New York: Lexington Books.

Tsai Hung-chin (Cai Hongjin). 2006. *Taiwan nonghui gaige yu xiangcun chongjian* [Reform of the Taiwan's Farmers' Associations and the reconstruction of rural areas]. Taipei: Tangshan chubanshe [Tangshan Press].

Tsai, Lily L. 2007. *Accountability without Democracy: Solidary Groups and Public Goods Provision in Rural China.* New York: Cambridge University Press.

Tsang, Steve. 2009. "Consultative Leninism: China's New Political Framework." *Journal of Contemporary China* 18 (62): 865–80.

Tucker, Robert C. 1961. "Towards a Comparative Politics of Movement-Regimes." *American Political Science Review* 55 (2): 281–89.

US Mutual Security Agency Mission to China. 1952a. *Chinese-American Economic Cooperation* 1 (2).

——. 1952b. *Chinese-American Economic Cooperation* 1 (12).

——. 1953. *Chinese-American Economic Cooperation* 2 (1).

Unger, Jonathan. 2002. *The Transformation of Rural China.* Armonk, NY: M. E. Sharpe.

Uphoff, Norman, and Milton J. Esman. 1974. *Local Organization for Rural Development in Asia.* Ithaca, NY: Rural Development Committee, Center for International Studies, Cornell University.

van Gevelt, Terry. 2014. "Rural Electrification and Development in South Korea." *Energy for Sustainable Development* 23: 179–87.

van Rooij, Benjamin. 2006. "Implementation of Chinese Environmental Law: Regular Enforcement and Political Campaigns." *Development and Change* 37 (1): 57–74.

Wade, Robert H. 1982. *Irrigation and Agricultural Politics in South Korea*. Boulder, CO: Westview.

——. 1990. *Governing the Market: Economic Theory and the Role of Government in East Asian Industrialization*. Princeton, NJ: Princeton University Press.

——. 2018. "The Developmental State: Dead or Alive?" *Development and Change* 49 (2): 518–46.

Waldner, David. 1999. *State Building and Late Development*. Ithaca, NY: Cornell University Press.

Wallace, Jeremy. 2014. *Cities and Stability: Urbanization, Redistribution, and Regime Survival in China*. New York: Oxford University Press.

Wang Pei-hsun (Wang Peixun), ed. 1974. *Shequ fazhan wenda* [Community development questions and answers]. Taipei: Republic of China Community Development Research and Training Center.

Wang Shiguan, ed. 2009. *Xin nongcun jiceng zuzhi jianshe yu guanli* [Building and managing new rural grassroots organizations]. Shanghai: Fudan daxue chubanshe [Fudan University Press].

Wang Yan. 2014. "P'ungdŏk maŭl saemaŭl undong ŭi ch'ujin chuch'e wa chojik kiban" [The Promoting Body and Organization Foundation of Saemaul Undong in the Pungdeok village]. *Han'guk kŭnhyŏndaesa yŏn'gu* [Journal of Korean Modern and Contemporary History] 69: 168–97.

Wang, Zheng. 2012. *Never Forget National Humiliation: Historical Memory in Chinese Politics and Foreign Relations*. New York: Columbia University Press.

Waswo, Ann. 1988. "The Transformation of Rural Society, 1900–1950." In *The Cambridge History of Japan*, vol. 6, *The Twentieth Century*, edited by Peter Duus, 541–605. New York: Cambridge University Press.

——. 2003. Introduction to *Farmers and Village Life in Twentieth-Century Japan*, edited by Ann Waswo and Nishida Yoshiaki, 1–6. New York: RoutledgeCurzon.

Weber, Max. 1930. *The Protestant Ethic and the Spirit of Capitalism*. Translated by Talcott Parsons. London: Allen & Unwin.

——. 1958. "The Three Types of Legitimate Rule." Translated by Hans H. Gerth. *Berkeley Publications in Society and Institutions* 4 (1): 1–11.

Wedeman, Andrew. 2012. *Double Paradox: Rapid Growth and Rising Corruption in China*. Ithaca, NY: Cornell University Press.

Weiss, Jessica Chen. 2014. *Powerful Patriots: Nationalist Protest in China's Foreign Relations*. New York: Oxford University Press.

Weller, Robert P. 2008. "Responsive Authoritarianism." In *Political Change in China: Lessons from Taiwan*, edited by Bruce Gilley and Larry Diamond, 117–33. Boulder, CO: Lynne Reiner.

Wen, Jiabao. 2012. "Report on the Work of the Government." http://en.people.cn/90785/7759779.html.

Wen Rui and Chen Shengxiang. 2007. "Zhengfu zhudao yu nongmin zhuti de hudong—Yi Jiangxi xin nongcun jianshe diaocha fenxi wei li" [Interaction of the government leads and peasants are the main actors—survey and analysis of Jiangxi's Building a New Countryside]. *Zhongguo nongcun jingji* [China Rural Economy] 1: 4–11.

Wen Tiejun. 2006. *Xin nongcun jianshe lilun tansuo* [Theoretical explanation of rural reconstruction]. Beijing: Wenjin chubanshe [Wenjin Press].

——. 2011. *Zhongguo xin nongcun jianshe baogao* [Report on China's Building a New Countryside]. Fuzhou: Fujian renmin chubanshe [Fujian People's Press].

White, Gordon, ed. 1988. *Developmental States in East Asia.* New York: St. Martin's Press.

White, Tyrene. 2006. *China's Longest Campaign: Birth Planning in the People's Republic, 1949–2005.* Ithaca, NY: Cornell University Press.

Whiting, Susan. 2001. *Power and Wealth in Rural China: The Political Economy of Institutional Change.* New York: Cambridge University Press.

——. 2011. "Values in Land: Fiscal Pressures, Land Disputes and Justice Claims in Rural and Peri-Urban China." *Urban Studies* 48 (3): 569–87.

Whyte, Martin K., ed. 2010. *One Country, Two Societies: Rural-Urban Inequality in Contemporary China.* Cambridge, MA: Harvard University Press.

Wik, Mette, Prabhu Pingali, and Sumiter Broca. 2008. "Global Agricultural Performance: Past Trends and Future Prospects." Background paper for the World Development Report 2008. Washington, DC: World Bank.

Woo, Jung-en. 1991. *Race to the Swift: State and Finance in Korean Industrialization.* New York: Columbia University Press.

Woo Sang-ryul (U Sangnyŏl). 2013. "Chosŏn ŭi 'ch'ŏllima undong' kwa Han'guk ŭi 'saemaŭl undong' pigyo yŏn'gu siron—Chungguk ŭi 'taeyakchin undong' ŭl kyŏttŭryŏ" [A comparative study of North Korea's Chollima movement, South Korea's Saemaul movement, and China's Great Leap Forward]. *T'ongil inmunhak nonch'ong* [Journal of Unification Humanities] 55: 247–88.

Woo-Cumings, Meredith, ed. 1999. *The Developmental State.* Ithaca, NY: Cornell University Press.

World Bank. 2015. "Agriculture Overview." http://www.worldbank.org/en/topic/agriculture/overview#1.

——. 2017. World Development Indicators. *Agriculture, value added (% of GDP)* [data file]. Retrieved from https://data.worldbank.org/indicator/NV.AGR.TOTL.ZS.

Wu Po-hsiung (Wu Boxing). 1986. *Shequ fazhan de huigu yu zhanwang* [Community development reflections and future prospects]. Taipei: Republic of China Community Development Research and Training Center.

Xie Xuren. 2008. *Zhongguo caizheng yu gaige kaifang sanshi nian* [China's Ministry of Finance and 30 years of reform and opening]. Beijing: Jingji kexue chubanshe [Economic Science Press].

——. 2009. *Zhongguo caizheng 60 nian* [China's Ministry of Finance after 60 years]. Beijing: Jingji kexue chubanshe [Economic Science Press].

Xinhua News. 2017. "Quanguo nongmin zhuanye hezuoshe shuliang da 193 wan duo jia" [The number of farmers' professional cooperatives in China exceeds 1.93 million]. *Xinhua she* [Xinhua News Agency], September 4.

Xue, Longyi, Mark Y. Wang, and Tao Xue. 2013. "'Voluntary' Poverty Alleviation Resettlement in China." *Development and Change* 44 (5): 1159–80.

Yager, Joseph A. 1988. *Transforming Agriculture in Taiwan: The Experience of the Joint Commission on Rural Reconstruction.* Ithaca, NY: Cornell University Press.

Yan, Hairong, and Yiyuan Chen. 2013. "Debating the Rural Cooperative Movement in China, the Past and Present." *Journal of Peasant Studies* 40 (6): 955–81.

Yang, Dali. 1996. *Calamity and Reform in China: State, Rural Society, and Institutional Change since the Great Leap Famine.* Stanford, CA: Stanford University Press.

Yang, Jisheng. 2012. *Tombstone: The Great Chinese Famine, 1958–1962.* Translated by Stacy Mosher and Jian Guo. Edited by Edward Friedman, Jian Guo, and Stacy Mosher. New York: Farrar, Straus and Giroux.

Yang, Martin M. C. 1970. *Socio-economic Results of Land Reform in Taiwan.* Honolulu: East-West Center.

Yang Tuan and Sun Bingyao. 2013. *Zonghe nongxie: Zhongguo "sannong" gaige tupokou* [Comprehensive farmers' associations: Breakthrough reform for China's "three rural problems"]. Beijing: Shehui kexue wenxian chubanshe [Social Sciences Academic Press].

Yang, Yunjeong. 2017. "*Saemaul Undong* Revisited: A Case of State-Society Dynamics in Social Capital Mobilisation, Focusing on the Role of Local Leaders in South Korea of the 1970s." *Journal of International Development* 29 (7): 993–1010.

Ye Jingzhong. 2006. *Nongmin shijiao de xin nongcun jianshe* [Construction of the New Countryside: Farmers' perspectives]. Beijing: Shehui kexue wenxian chubanshe [Social Sciences Academic Press].

Yeh, Emily. 2013. *Taming Tibet: Landscape Transformation and the Gift of Chinese Development*. Ithaca, NY: Cornell University Press.

Yim Song-ja (Im Songja). 2010. "1970 nyŏndae Han'guk noch'ong ŭi kongjang saemaŭl undong chŏn'gae yangsang kwa tŭkching" [A study on the development phase and characteristics of factory Saemaul movement performed by the Federation of Korean Trade Unions in 1970s]. *Han'guk kŭnhyŏndaesa yŏn'gu* [Journal of Korean Modern and Contemporary History] 52: 181–218.

Yoon Chung-ro (Yun Ch'ungno). 2011. "Kusul ŭl t'onghae pon 1970 nyŏndae saemaŭl undong—Saemaŭl chido ka 'mandŭlgi' wa 'toegi' sai esŏ" [The Saemaul movement in the 1970s seen by oral testimonies: In between the building and becoming its leaders]. *Sahoe wa yŏksa* [Society and History] 90: 79–109.

You, Tae-Yeung. 1986. *The Patterns of Rural Development in Korea, 1970's*. Seoul: Institute of Saemaul, Kon-Kuk University.

Yu, Frederick T. C. 1967. "Campaigns, Communications, and Development in Communist China." In *Communication and Change in Developing Countries*, edited by David Lerner and Wilbur L. Schramm, 195–215. Honolulu: East-West Center.

Yu Jianrong. 2007. *Dangdai Zhongguo nongmin de weiquan kangzheng: Hunan Hengyang kaocha* [Organized peasant resistance in contemporary China: An investigation of Hengyang County, Hunan Province]. Beijing: Zhongguo wenhua chubanshe [China Culture Publishing House].

Yu Jianrong, He Jianhua, and Yuan Feng, eds. 2007. *Zhongguo nongmin wenti yanjiu ziliao huibian* [Collection of research materials related to China's peasant problem]. Beijing: Zhongguo nongye chubanshe [China Agriculture Press].

Yu Jianrong, Weng Ming, and Lu Lei, eds. 2007. *Nongmin zuzhi yu xin nongcun jianshe: Lilun yu shijian* [Farmers' organizations and new countryside construction: Theory and practice]. Beijing: Zhongguo nongye chubanshe [China Agriculture Press].

Zhang Deyuan. 2011. "'Pibao hezuoshe' zheshe chu de jiceng guanmin guanxi: Dui nongmin hezuoshe de suojian suosi de diaocha ganyu" [Government relations with the people as reflected in "briefcase cooperatives": Reflections on a survey of farmers' professional cooperatives]. *Renmin luntan* [People's Tribune] 25: 58–9.

Zhang Huimin, ed. 2007. *Shehuizhuyi xin nongcun jianshe jianming duben* [Building a New Socialist Countryside, concise reader]. Yangling District (Shaanxi Province): Xibei nonglin keji daxue chubanshe [Northwest Agriculture and Forestry University Press].

Zhang Kaihua and Zhang Qinglian. 2007. "Nongmin zhuanye hezuoshe chengzhang de kunhuo yu sikao" [Reflections on the growth of Farmers' Professional Cooperatives]. *Nongye jingji wenti* [Issues in Agricultural Economy] 5: 62–6.

Zhang Luxiong. 2009. "Wo guo gengdi zhidu cunzai de wenti ji zhengce xuanze" [China's farmland system, problems and policy choices]. *Hongqi wengao* [Red Flag Manuscript] 6: 9–12.

Zhang Ping. 2009. *Zhongguo gaige kaifang: 1978–2008* [China's reform and opening: 1978–2008]. Beijing: Renmin chubanshe [People's Press].

Zhang, Qian Forrest, and John A. Donaldson. 2008. "The Rise of Agrarian Capitalism with Chinese Characteristics: Agricultural Modernization, Agribusiness and Collective Land Rights." *China Journal* 60: 25–47.

Zhong, Sheng. 2011. "Towards China's Urban-Rural Integration: Issues and Options." *International Journal of China Studies* 2 (2): 345–67.

Zhongguo liangshi nianjian [China Grain Yearbook]. 2013. Beijing: Jingji guanli chubanshe [Economy and Management Publishing House].

Zhongguo nongcun tongji nianjian [China Rural Statistical Yearbook]. 2013. Beijing: Zhongguo tongji chubanshe [China Statistics Press].

Zhongguo nongye fazhan baogao [China Agricultural Development Report]. 2013. Beijing: Zhongguo nongye chubanshe [China Agriculture Press].

Zhongguo tongji nianjian [China Statistical Yearbook]. 2013. Beijing: Zhongguo tongji chubanshe [China Statistics Press].

Zhou, Kate Xiao. 1996. *How the Farmers Changed China: Power of the People*. Boulder, CO: Westview.

Zhou, Kate Xiao, and Lynn T. White III. 1995. "Quiet Politics and Rural Enterprise in Reform China." *Journal of Developing Areas* 29 (4): 461–90.

Zweig, David. 1989. *Agrarian Radicalism in China, 1968–1981*. Cambridge, MA: Harvard University Press.

———. 1997. *Freeing China's Farmers: Rural Restructuring in the Reform Era*. Armonk, NY: M. E. Sharpe.

Index

Page numbers appended by the letters t or f indicate tables and figures.

Lightning Source UK Ltd.
Milton Keynes UK
UKHW041000110121
376727UK00009BA/177/J